American Map

Road Atlas

United States
Canada
Mexico

U.S. STATES

CANADIAN PROVINCES

U.S. CITIES

CANADIAN CITIES

MEXICO & MEXICAN CITIES

PUERTO RICO

NATIONAL PARKS & RECREATION AREAS

*Also has downtown city map

Cover Photo: Monterey County, California
Photo by Owaki-Kulla / CORBIS
Index Photos: PhotoDisc™

Tourism Information

WHERE TO CALL OR WRITE

UNITED STATES

Alabama
Alabama Bureau of Tourism & Travel
401 Adams Ave, P.O. Box 4927
Montgomery, AL 36103
800.252.2262, 334.242.4169
www.touralabama.org

Alaska
Alaska Div. of Tourism
P.O. Box 110801
Juneau, AK 99811-0801
907.929.2200
www.dced.state.ak.us/tourism

Arizona
Arizona Office of Tourism
2702 N. Third St., Ste. 4015
Phoenix, AZ 85004
800.842.8257, 602.230.7733
www.arizonaguide.com

Arkansas
Arkansas Dept. of Parks & Tourism
One Capitol Mall
Little Rock, AR 72201
800.628.8725, 501.682.7777
www.1800natural.com

California
California Div. of Tourism
P.O. Box 1499, Dept. TIA
Sacramento, CA 95814
800.862.2543, 916.322.2881
www.gocalif.ca.gov

Colorado
Colorado Tourism Office
1625 Broadway
Ste. 1700
Denver, CO 80202
800.265.6723
www.colorado.com

Connecticut
Connecticut Office of Tourism
505 Hudson St.
Hartford, CT 06106
800.282.6863, 860.270.8080
www.ctbound.org

Delaware
Delaware Tourism Office
99 Kings Highway
Dover, DE 19901
800.441.8846, 302.739.4271
www.visitdelaware.net

Florida
Visit Florida
P.O. Box 1100
Tallahassee, FL 32302
888.735.2872, 850.488.5607
www.flausa.com

Georgia
Georgia Dept. of Industry, Trade & Tourism
P.O. Box 1776
Atlanta, GA 30301-1776
800.847.4842, 404.656.3590
www.georgia.org

Hawaii
Hawaii Visitors & Conv. Bureau
2270 Kalakaua Ave., Ste. 801
Honolulu, HI 96815
800.464.2924, 808.923.1811
www.gohawaii.com

Idaho
Idaho Dept. of Commerce
P.O. Box 83720
Boise, ID 83720-0093
800.635.7820
www.visitid.org

Illinois
Illinois Bureau of Tourism
100 W. Randolph St., Ste. 3-400
Chicago, IL 60601
800.226.6632
www.enjoyillinois.com

Indiana
Indiana Tourism
1 N. Capitol Ave. Suite 700
Indianapolis, IN 46204
800.759.9191, 317.232.4685
www.enjoyindiana.com

Iowa
Iowa Div. of Tourism
200 E. Grand Ave.
Des Moines, IA 50309
800.345.4692, 515.242.4705
www.traveliowa.com

Kansas
Kansas Travel & Tourism Development Div.
700 S.W. Harrison, Ste. 1300
Topeka, KS 66603
800.252.6727, 785.296.2009
www.travelks.com

Kentucky
Kentucky Dept. of Travel
Capital Plaza Tower
500 Mero St., Ste. 22
Frankfort, KY 40601
800.225.8747
www.kentuckytourism.com

Louisiana
Louisiana Office of Tourism
P.O. Box 94291
Baton Rouge, LA 70804
800.334.8626, 225.342.8100
www.louisianatravel.com

Maine
Maine Publicity Bureau
P.O. Box 2300
Hallowell, ME 04347-2300
888.624.6345, 207.287.8070
www.visitmaine.com

Maryland
Maryland Office of Tourism Development
217 E. Redwood St.
Baltimore, MD 21202
800.445.4558
www.mdisfun.org

Massachusetts
Massachusetts Office of Travel & Tourism
10 Park Plaza, Suite 4510
Boston, MA 02116
800.447.6277, 617.973.8500
www.massvacation.com

Michigan
Michigan Travel Bureau
P.O. Box 30226
Lansing, MI 48909-7726
888.784.7328, 517.373.0670
www.michigan.org

Minnesota
Minnesota Office of Tourism
100 Metro Square
121 Seventh Place East
St. Paul, MN 55101
800.657.3700, 651.296.5029
www.exploreminnesota.com

Mississippi
Mississippi Development Authority/Tourism
P.O. Box 849
Jackson, MS 39205
800.927.6378, 601.359.3297
www.visitmississippi.org

Missouri
Missouri Div. of Tourism
301 W. High St., P.O. Box 1055
Jefferson City, MO 65102
800.519.2300, 573.751.4133
www.visitmo.com

Montana
Travel Montana
1424 Ninth Ave.
P.O. Box 200533
Helena, MT 59620
800.847.4868, 406.444.2654
www.visitmt.com

Nebraska
Nebraska Travel & Tourism
P.O. Box 94666
Lincoln, NE 68509-4666
800.228.4307, 402.471.3796
www.visitnebraska.org

Nevada
Nevada Commission on Tourism
401 N. Carson St.
Carson City, NV 89701
800.638.2328, 775.687.4322
www.travelnevada.com

New Hampshire
New Hampshire Office of Travel & Tourism Development
172 Pembroke Rd., P.O. Box 1856
Concord, NH 03302-1856
800.386.4664 (seasonal), 603.271.2666
www.visitnh.gov

New Jersey
New Jersey Office of Travel & Tourism
20 W. State St., P.O. Box 820
Trenton, NJ 08625-0820
609.292.2470, 800.537.7397
www.visitnj.org

New Mexico
New Mexico Dept. of Tourism
491 Old Santa Fe Trail
Santa Fe, NM 87503
800.733.6396
www.newmexico.org

New York
New York State Div. of Tourism
P.O. Box 2603
Albany, NY 12220-0603
800.225.5697, 518.474.4116
www.iloveny.com

North Carolina
North Carolina Div. of Tourism, Film & Sports Development
301 N. Wilmington St.
Raleigh, NC 27601
800.847.4862, 919.733.4171
www.visitnc.com

North Dakota
North Dakota Tourism
604 E. Boulevard Ave.
Bismarck, ND 58505-0825
800.435.5663, 701.328.2525
www.ndtourism.com

Ohio
Ohio Div. of Travel & Tourism
77 S. High St., 29th Fl.
P.O. Box 1001
Columbus, OH 43216
800.282.5393
www.ohiotourism.com

Oklahoma
Oklahoma Dept. of Tourism & Recreation
P.O. Box 60789
Oklahoma City, OK 73146
800.652.6552, 405.521.2406
www.travelok.com

Oregon
Oregon Tourism Commission
775 Summer St. NE
Salem, OR 97301-1282
800.547.7842, 503.986.0000
www.traveloregon.com

Pennsylvania
Pennsylvania Office of Travel, Tourism & Film Promotion
Rm. 404, Forum Building
Harrisburg, PA 17120
800.847.4872, 717.787.5453
www.experiencepa.com

Rhode Island
Rhode Island Tourism Div.
1 W. Exchange St.
Providence, RI 02903
800.556.2484
www.visitrhodeisland.com

South Carolina
South Carolina Dept. of Parks, Recreation & Tourism
P.O. Box 71
Columbia, SC 29201
888.727.6453
www.travelsc.com

South Dakota
South Dakota Dept. of Tourism
711 E. Wells Ave.
Pierre, SD 57501-3369
800.732.5682
www.travelsd.com

Tennessee
Tennessee Dept. of Tourist Development
320 Sixth Ave. N
Rachel Jackson Building
Nashville, TN 37243
800.468.6836, 615.741.2159
www.tnvacation.com

Texas
Texas Dept. of Economic Development, Tourism Div.
P.O. Box 12728
Austin, TX 78711-2728
800.888.8839, 512.462.9191
www.traveltex.com

Utah
Utah Travel Council
Council Hall/Capitol Hill
Salt Lake City, UT 84114
800.200.1160, 801.538.1030
www.utah.com

Vermont
Vermont Dept. of Tourism & Marketing
6 Baldwin St., Drawer 33
Montpelier, VT 05633-1301
800.837.6668, 802.828.3237
www.1-800-vermont.com

Virginia
Virginia Tourism Corporation
901 E. Byrd St.
Richmond, VA 23219
800.847.4882, 804.786.4484
www.virginia.org

Washington
Dept. of Community Trade & Economic Development,
Washington State Tourism Div.
P.O. Box 42500
Olympia, WA 98504-2500
800.544.1800
www.experiencewashington.com

Washington, DC
WCVA Visitors Services
1212 New York Ave. NW, Ste. 600
Washington, DC 20005
800.422.8644, 202.789.7000
www.washington.org

West Virginia
West Virginia Div. of Tourism
2101 Washington St. E
Charleston, WV 25305
800.225.5982, 304.558.2286
www.callwva.com

Wisconsin
Wisconsin Dept. of Tourism
P.O. Box 7976
Madison, WI 53707-7976
800.432.8747
www.travelwisconsin.com

Wyoming
Wyoming Div. of Tourism
I-25 at College Dr.
Cheyenne, WY 82002
800.225.5996, 307.777.7777
www.wyomingtourism.org

UNITED STATES TERRITORIES

Puerto Rico
Puerto Rico Convention Bureau
255 Recinto Sur
San Juan, PR 00901
787.725.2110
www.meetpuertorico.com

Virgin Islands
U.S. Virgin Islands Dept. of Tourism
P.O. Box 6400
St. Thomas, VI 00804
800.372.8784, 340.774.8784
www.usvi.org/tourism

CANADA

Alberta
Travel Alberta
17811 116 Ave.
Edmonton, AB, Canada T5S 2J2
800.661.8888
www.travelalberta.com

British Columbia
Super, Natural British Columbia
Box 9830
Stn. Prov. Govt.
1803 Douglas St., Third Floor
Victoria, BC, Canada V8W 9W5
800.663.6000, 250.387.1642
www.hellobc.com

Manitoba
Travel Manitoba
155 Carlton St., Seventh Floor
Winnipeg, MB, Canada R3C 3H8
800.665.0040
www.travelmanitoba.com

New Brunswick
Tourism New Brunswick
P.O. Box 12345
Campbellton, NB, Canada E3N 3T6
800.561.0123
www.tourismnewbrunswick.ca

Newfoundland
Newfoundland & Labrador Tourism Marketing
P.O. Box 8730
St. John's, NF, Canada A1B 4K2
800.563.6353, 709.729.2830
www.gov.nf.ca/tourism

Nova Scotia
Tourism Nova Scotia
2695 Dutch Village Rd.
Halifax, NS, Canada B3L 4V2
800.565.0000, 902.453.8400
www.explorens.com

Ontario
Ontario Tourism
Eighth Floor, Hearst Block
Toronto, ON, Canada M7A 2E1
800.668.2746, 416.314.0944
www.ontariotravel.net

Prince Edward Island
Dept. of Economical Development & Tourism
P.O. Box 940
Charlottetown, PE, Canada C1A 7M5
800.463.4734, 902.368.7795
www.peiplay.com

Québec
Tourisme Québec
P.O. Box 979
Montréal, QC, Canada H3C 2W3
877.266.5687
www.bonjourquebec.com

Saskatchewan
Tourism Saskatchewan
1922 Park St.
Regina, SK, Canada S4P 3V7
877.237.2273
www.sasktourism.com

MEXICO

Mexico Ministry of Tourism
Mariano Escobedo, No. 726
Col. Nueva Anzures
11590 México, D.F. Mexico
800.446.3942
www.visitmexico.com

CROSSING BORDERS

CANADA

U.S. citizens entering Canada from the U.S. are required to present passports or proof of U.S. citizenship accompanied by photo identification. U.S. citizens entering from a third country must have a valid passport. Visas are not required for U.S. citizens entering from the U.S. for stays of up to 180 days. Naturalized citizens should travel with their naturalization certificates. Alien permanent residents of the U.S. must present their Alien Registration Cards. Individuals under the age of 18 and travelling alone should carry a letter from a parent or legal guardian authorizing their travel in Canada.

U.S. driver's licenses are valid in Canada, and U.S. citizens do not need to obtain an international driver's license. Proof of auto insurance, however, is required.

For additional information, consult http://travel.state.gov/tips_canada.html before you travel.

UNITED STATES (FROM CANADA)

Canadian citizens entering the U.S. are required to demonstrate proof of their citizenship, normally with a photo identification accompanied by a valid birth certificate or citizenship card. Passports or visas are not required for visits lasting less than six months; for visits exceeding six months, they are mandatory. Individuals under the age of 18 and travelling alone should carry notarized documentation, signed by both parents, authorizing their travel.

Canadian driver's licenses are valid in the U.S. for one year, and automobiles may enter free of payment or duty fees. Drivers need only provide customs officials with proof of vehicle registration, ownership, and insurance.

MEXICO

U.S. citizens entering Mexico are required to present passports or proof of U.S. citizenship accompanied by photo identification. Visas are not required for stays of up to 180 days. Naturalized citizens should travel with their naturalization certificates, and alien permanent residents must present their Alien Registration Cards. Individuals under the age of 18 travelling alone, with one parent, or with other adults must carry notarized parental authorization or valid custodial documents.

In addition, all U.S. citizens visiting for up to 180 days must procure a tourist card, obtainable from Mexican consulates, tourism offices, and border crossing points, which must be surrendered upon departure. However, tourist cards are not needed for visits shorter than 72 hours to cities along the Mexico/U.S. border.

U.S. driver's licenses are valid in Mexico.

Visitors who wish to drive beyond the Baja California Peninsula or the Border Zone (extending approximately 25 km into Mexico) must obtain a temporary import permit for their vehicles. Permits may be obtained from a Mexican Customs Office at border crossing points as long as the original and two copies of the following documents bearing the driver's name are provided: passport/proof of U.S. citizenship, tourist card, vehicle registration, driver's license, and a major international credit card for use in paying the prevailing fee. Permits are valid for 180 days, and they must be surrendered upon final departure from Mexico.

All visitors driving in Mexico should be aware that U.S. auto insurance policies are not valid and that buying short-term tourist insurance is virtually mandatory. Many U.S. insurance companies sell Mexican auto insurance. American Automobile Association (for members only) and Sanborn's Mexico Insurance (800.638.9423) are popular companies with offices at most U.S. border crossings.

Fabulous Drives & Adventures

NORTHWEST

- Lewis and Clark Trail
- Yellowstone National Park, Wyoming
- Kenai Peninsula, Alaska
- Olympic National Park, Washington
- Sequoia and Kings Canyon, California

Lewis and Clark Trail

Find on: page 66, D-9

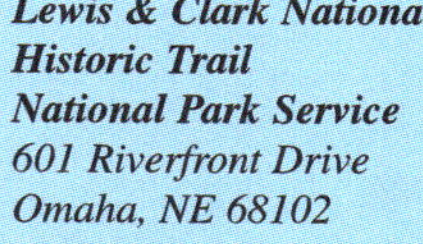

Lewis & Clark National Historic Trail National Park Service
601 Riverfront Drive
Omaha, NE 68102

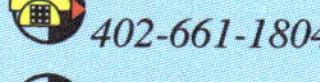

402-661-1804

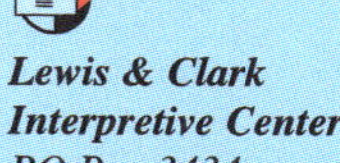

Lewis & Clark Interpretive Center
PO Box 3434
Great Falls, MT 59401

888-701-3434

www.lewisandclark.org
www.nps.gov/lecl

Northwest of Bozeman, Montana, along I-90 sits the town of Three Forks. It was named for the Missouri Headwaters – the Gallatin, Madison, and Jefferson rivers – all named by Lewis and Clark. Captains Meriwether Lewis and William Clark led their historic expedition through here in July 1805, having accepted the challenge of exploring the recently acquired Louisiana Purchase. They hoped that by tracing the Missouri river and its tributaries, they would find the long-sought Northwest Passage to the Pacific. The abundant wildlife they found at the headwaters is now gone, but a state park commemorates the site. Here, you can have a picnic at the very spot where the expedition stopped for breakfast on July 27, 1805, and climb up to Lewis Rock where Lewis sketched a map of the countryside.

Today many people retrace Lewis and Clark's trail through the Northwest, where many landmarks commemorate their journey. At Great Falls, Montana, they discovered a "sublimely grand spectacle," but also one of their greatest challenges. The expedition was delayed for nearly a month while canoes and supplies were portaged 18 miles around the falls. The town is home to the Lewis and Clark Interpretive Center and hosts the Lewis and Clark Festival each year in late June, with a re-creation of the expedition camp.

Near Helena, you can take a boat trip through gates of the Mountains, a stunning Missouri River canyon whose 1,200-foot cliffs seemed to close in on the explorers' party. Heading west, they followed the Lolo Trail, an old Nez Perce Indian trade and hunting route across the Bitterroot Mountains. It is now a National Historic Landmark and hiking trail. In Idaho, Lewis and Clark received food and help from the Nez Perce before continuing their journey along the Columbia River which led, at last, to the Pacific. Many Lewis and Clark landmarks along this Oregon-Washington border are located in state parks.

Photo: Umatilla Indian Reservation by Bob Woodward, The Oregon Tourism Commission.

Yellowstone National Park

Find on: page 120, B-2

Yellowstone National Park
P.O. Box 168
Yellowstone National Park, WY 82190-0168

307-344-7381

www.nps.gov/yell/home.htm

It is possibly the world's most famous natural preserve. And yet, despite its renown as the first national park ever created, Yellowstone is capable of surprising even those who know it well, let alone first-time visitors. Congress established the park in 1872 because of its amazing collection of geysers and hot springs, unmatched anywhere else. For years, mountain men had told tales of strange doings in the area – lakes of boiling mud, gushers of hot water shooting 200 feet or more into the air – and were largely disbelieved. But these stories turned out to be true, and Yellowstone's thermal features are no less wonderful today than they were then. Old Faithful Geyser may be the most famous, but there are more than 10,000 other thermal features, including even bigger geysers and several that erupt at more regular intervals than their celebrated cousin.

Most of Yellowstone occupies a high plateau which averages 7,000-8,000 feet in elevation, ringed by mountains that rise several thousand feet higher. It contains snow-covered peaks, several magnificent high-altitude lakes, numerous rivers and streams renowned for trout fishing, a brightly colored canyon that nearly dwarfs two major waterfalls, one of the most significant volcanic calderas in the world, and layer upon layer of buried petrified forest. None of this came easy. Yellowstone has a history of staggering geologic violence, and it remains one of the most geologically active places in the world.

In 1872, millions of bison still darkened the Great Plains. Who would have guessed that within 30 years, Yellowstone would become a refuge for the last surviving wild bison in America? Today the park's 2.2 million acres support approximately 20,000 elk, 3,500 bison, and hundreds of deer, along with moose, bighorn sheep, mountain goats, pronghorn antelope, black bears, grizzly bears, coyotes, trumpeter swans, Canada geese, sandhill cranes, white pelicans, cutthroat trout, and other species. After the long anticipated reintroduction of wolves, the park represents the entire panoply of Rocky Mountain wildlife.

Photo: Old Faithful Geyser, Wyoming.

IV Fabulous Drives and Adventures

Kenai Peninsula

This is Alaska in a nutshell: glaciers, salmon fishing, hiking trails, stunning scenery and friendly towns, all within easy reach of Anchorage. It is often said that Alaska is too big to see in a single lifetime, let alone a single vacation. But the Kenai Peninsula is one place where you can see the best of the state within a few weeks. It looks deceptively small on the map, but it covers 9,050 square miles – larger than the states of Rhode Island, Connecticut and Delaware combined. It is bordered by the Gulf of Alaska and Prince William Sound on the east, and the Cook Inlet on the west.

The Seward Highway is America's northernmost Scenic Byway. It runs for 127 miles from Anchorage south to Seward. After the stunning vistas of the Turnagain Arm, the road climbs into the Kenai Mountains, running through the Chugach National Forest with several hiking trails and scenic viewpoints, where you can often spot wildlife. Beyond the Turnagain Pass, the first of the peninsula's famous glaciers come into view. The road ends at Seward, at the head of Resurrection Bay. From here you can take sightseeing cruises into the Kenai Fjords National Park for close-up views of the mighty glaciers, as well as seals, dolphins, whales, and other sea life.

Another option is to turn west onto the Sterling Highway (Alaska Route 1). It runs through the Kenai National Wildlife Refuge on its way to Sterling, a popular salmon-fishing area. The road turns south along the Cook Inlet, passing through Anchor Point, the most westerly point in North America that is accessible by a continuous road system. Homer, the road's southern terminus, is a picturesque town and a lively local arts center. From here, there are trips to glaciers and park land on the other side of the bay.

Photo: Bear Glacier, originating in the Harding Icefield in the Kenai Peninsula, is a Piedmont Glacier that ends in Resurrection Bay.

Find on: page 6, F-6

Kenai Peninsula Visitor Information
35477 Kenai Spur Hwy, Ste 205
Soldotna, Alaska 99669

907-283-3850

www.kenaipeninsula.org
www.travelalaska.com

Olympic National Park

Snuggled deep within the Olympic Peninsula in northwest Washington, Olympic National Park is often referred to as "three parks in one." It encompasses three distinct ecosystems, all within a day's drive of each other. These include magnificent stands of old-growth and temperate rain forest, rugged glacier-capped mountains, and 60 miles of wild Pacific coastline – the last wilderness ocean beaches in mainland United States. Eight kinds of plants and five kinds of animals found in this park live nowhere else in the world. Highway 101 wraps around three sides of the park, and spoke roads give limited access to the interior.

The Hoh Rainforest is the area's most-visited spot. It is the world's largest temperate rain forest, one of only three in the entire world. The mild coastal climate and perpetual mist and showers, together with a deep layer of decaying organic matter, produce trees of truly gargantuan size. In the moss-draped rain forest, colonnades of virgin spruce and hemlock rise to form an evergreen lattice; under them, vine maples spiral from pillowy forest-floor coverings of club moss. There are easy walking trails and longer hiking routes. Another beautiful area is the Quinault Rainforest in the southwest corner of the park.

The Olympic Mountains are a cluster of lofty canyons, flower-covered ridges, and glaciated peaks. The highest is Mount Olympus, which stands at 7,980 feet. Seven glaciers hang from Olympus; its massive shoulders have been draped in ice for thousands of years. Hurricane Ridge is the highest point you can reach by car. Olympic's wild ocean beaches are memorable. Wildlife includes bald eagles, harbor seals, shorebirds, and migrating whales. Highway 101 runs along the southern-most region near Kalaloch, with a number of beaches just a few hundred yards from the car.

Photo: Through the Mist to Royal Basin, Olympic National Park, Washington.

Find on: page 114, E-7

Olympic National Park
600 East Park Avenue
Port Angeles, WA 98362

360-565-3130 (visitor information)
360-565-3131 (recorded message)

www.nps.gov/olym

Sequoia and Kings Canyon

Sequoia National Park and Kings Canyon National Park are the twin jewels of California's towering Sierra Nevada. Here, under the gaze of the Golden State's highest peaks, a tiara of snowcapped mountains stands guard over alpine lakes. Sparkling streams flow through canyons rimmed with dense forests. Foothills and meadows sustain wildflowers and wildlife. John Muir described the canyon of the Kings River as "a rival to Yosemite." The scenery is spectacular, but these twin parks are even better known for their trees – the largest in the world – some more than 3,000 years old.

Two major roads link the parks together, affording spectacular views of the big trees, deep canyons, and other scenic wonders. Start at the Ash Mountain entrance, where Highway 198 from Visalia becomes the Generals Highway, a 47-mile-long scenic road that winds through some of the parks' most stunning landscapes. About 16 miles beyond, the Giant Forest is the centerpiece of Sequoia National park. Here, standing at an elevation of 6,500 feet, are the largest organisms in the world, the giant sequoias. Hundreds of these huge trees dominate the landscape, their massive, rust-colored trunks rising in solemn majesty. This is a relict species, whose ancesters once grew throughout western North America before climatic and geologic changes left them stranded in the southern Sierra. Further on is the General Sherman Tree, the world's largest living thing, rising 274 feet high with a diameter of 30 feet.

Beyond the rugged canyon of Tokopah Valley, the road exits the park at Lost Grove and enters Kings Canyon National Park at Grant Grove. The 30 miles from here to Cedar Grove across Sequoia National Forest is a National Scenic Byway, and one of the most spectacular drives in the West. The road plummets nearly 4,500 feet to the depths of the majestic, glacially shaped Kings Canyon. From Cedar Grove and Road's End, there are walking trails to Roaring River Falls and other scenic spots.

Photo: Sequoia and Kings Canyon – At the Top of Muir's Pulpit in the Kings River.

Find on: page 13, J-19

Sequoia and Kings Canyon National Parks
47050 Generals Highway
Three Rivers, CA 93271-9700

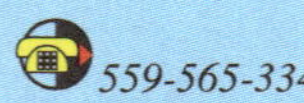
559-565-3341

http://www.nps.gov/seki

SOUTHWEST

- Santa Fe and Taos, New Mexico
- The Grand Canyon, Arizona
- Trail Ridge Road, Colorado
- Arches National Park, Utah
- Death Valley and the Mojave Desert, California
- San Juan Skyway

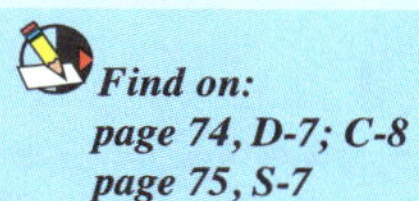
Find on:
page 74, D-7; C-8
page 75, S-7

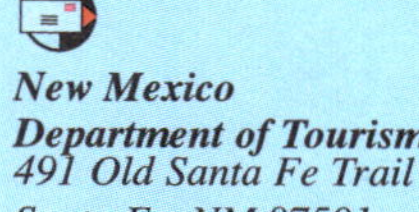
New Mexico Department of Tourism
491 Old Santa Fe Trail
Santa Fe, NM 87501

505-827-7400

Taos Chamber of Commerce
1139 Paseo del Pueblo Sur
Taos, NM 87571

800-732-8267

www.newmexico.org
www.taoschamber.com

Santa Fe and Taos

Of all the towns and cities in the American Southwest, Santa Fe and Taos have become prime destinations – Santa Fe for its historic colonial plaza, fine museums, and art galleries, Taos for its ancient pueblo. The roads between them are rich in the region's Hispanic and Native American heritage. SR 68, the main road northward from Santa Fe to Taos, is peppered with a number of pueblos that are active communities today. Tesuque, San Ildefonso, and Santa Clara are known for their outstanding potters. Many pueblos hold festivals of Native dancing which visitors may attend. If stopping at a pueblo, remember that there may be restrictions on photography. The Bandelier National Monument and the Puye Cliff Dwellings both lie a few miles to the east, where ancient ruins and cliff dwellings give a fascinating glimpse of ancestral pueblo life.

The heartbeat of traditional Hispanic culture resonates as strongly as ever in the tiny mountain villages of the Upper Rio Grande Valley. The studios of weavers, tinsmiths, potters, and woodcarvers can be found along the winding "high road" to Taos, SR 76. El Santuario, a charming old mission church in Chimayo, is called the Lourdes of America for the many miracles attributed to its healing powers. The altar, screen, and artworks are fine examples of religious folk art. To the left of the altar is a room hung with crutches and offerings from the devout, and a room where pilgrims can take a pinch of the holy earth of Chimayo from the dirt floor. The town is also famous for its hand-woven, brightly colored blankets. On the southern edge of Taos, the San Francisco de Asis Church at Ranchos de Taos is one of the best known and most photographed churches in New Mexico because of its classic Pueblo architecture.

Photo: Taos, Old Town Plaza Park.

Find on:
page 9, U-10

Grand Canyon National Park
P.O. Box 129
Grand Canyon, AZ 86023

928-638-7888

http://www.nps.gov/grca

The Grand Canyon

Humbling, exalting, beautiful beyond words. The Grand Canyon in northern Arizona is undeniably one of the world's great sights. The ancients spoke of the four basic elements of earth, water, wind, and fire. But here another element must be added – light. It is light that brings the canyon to life, bathing the buttes and highlighting the spires, infusing color and adding dimension, creating beauty that takes your breath away. Where else are sunrise and sunset the two biggest events of the day? In early morning and late afternoon, the oblique rays of sunlight, sometimes filtered through clouds, set red rock cliffs on fire and cast abysses into purple shadow.

The approach to the canyon gives no hint of what awaits. The highway passes a sweeping land of sagebrush and grass, through dwarf pinyon and juniper woodland, and into a forest of tall ponderosa pines. Then, suddenly, the earth falls away at your feet. Before you stretches an immensity that is almost incomprehensible. From the canyon rim, some 7,000 feet above sea level, the mighty Colorado River below looks like a tiny stream. This river is the chisel that has carved the Grand Canyon, rushing through it for 277 miles. Over several million years it has eroded the canyon to its present depth of one mile. The surrounding Grand Canyon National Park encompasses more than a million acres.

The South Rim, open year-round, is the most heavily visited. For most of the year the road beyond Grand Canyon Village is closed to private vehicles, and a shuttle bus takes you to viewpoints along the West Rim Drive. There are more viewpoints along the East Rim Drive, which is accessible all year. The North Rim may not look far away, but it is 215 miles by road. Less crowded but equally spectacular, it is closed from last October until mid-May because of snow.

Find on:
page 19, G-12

Rocky Mountain National Park
1000 Highway 36
Estes Park, CO 80517-8397

970-586-1206
(Recorded Message)
970-586-1333

http://www.nps.gov/romo

Trail Ridge Road

Straddling the Continental Divide, Rocky Mountain National Park contains sky-scraping peaks, 150 lakes, rushing mountain streams, alpine tundra, pristine forests, and an amazing array of wildlife. Running through the park is Trail Ridge Road, the highest paved road in America and one of the country's most scenic drives. Open seasonally from mid-may until the first heavy snowstorms blanket the interior in October, it features well over a dozen spectacular overlooks and exposes visitors to a large expanse of alpine tundra, one of the rarest ecosystems in the lower 48 states. It runs for 53 miles, from the resort town of Estes Park on the eastern side to Grand Lake on the west. Many of the peaks within the park's 414 square miles soar well over 14,000 feet.

Photo: Colorado River District, Beaver Ponds.

Beyond the stunning overlook at Forest Canyon, the road enters alpine tundra and stays above the treeline for 11 miles, cresting at 12,183 feet near Lava Cliffs. For a closer look at this treeless, windblown realm with its delicate wildflowers, walk the Tundra Nature Trail near Rock Cut, or stop at the Alpine Visitor Center. At Milner Pass, Trail Ridge Road crosses the Continental Divide, known as the "backbone of America." The road zigzags several dizzying miles and then heads south toward the Colorado River Trailhead. Nearby are the headwaters of the mighty river that flows through the Grand Canyon, several hundred miles away. The final stretch of the road descends into Kawuneeche Valley, with coniferous forests and aspen trees that explode with autumn color.

Photo: Sprague Lake.

VI Fabulous Drives and Adventures

Arches National Park

The sandstone arches that give this park its name are only part of the story. Spires, pinnacles, pedestals, and balanced rocks are among its other extraordinary geological features. This 120-square-mile desert park, 5 miles north of Moab, Utah, is home to more than 1,700 natural arches and other strangely eroded rock giants. Unlike neighboring Canyonlands, which requires many visits to appreciate, Arches is small enough to experience in a day by way of its paved scenic drive, pullouts where you can take in the view, and many short trails.

Arches has the largest number of natural sandstone arches in the world, with many more being formed all the time – the fortuitous result of location, geology, and water erosion. Some 300 million years ago, the region was covered by a large, shallow inland sea whose salt deposits helped to sculpt the reddish-brown monuments. For a look at the many different types of carved phenomena in the park, such as single and double arches, buttes and windows, take the 18-mile scenic drive from the visitor center to Devils Garden, stopping to hike along the short trails that wind through this oversized Zen garden of standing stones. Many have whimsical names such as Fiery Furnace, the Tower of Babel, and the Three Gossips. Balanced Rock and Delicate Arch – the world-famous symbol of Utah's red rock country – are among the most dramatic.

The nearby Dead Horse Point State Park, which lies between Arches and Canyonlands, is also recommended for its dramatic, sweeping views over the Colorado River.

Photo: Delicate Arch.

Find on:
page 109, K-8

Arches National Park
PO Box 907
Moab, UT 84532-0907

435-719-2299

http://www.nps.gov/arch

Death Valley and the Mojave Desert

The name says it all. Most people who travel to California's Mojave Desert do so in order to experience some of the most desolate, challenging landscapes in the Americas. It covers much of the southeastern corner of the state, adjoining the Nevada border. The first settlers who had the misfortune to wander into Death Valley in 1849 on their way to the Gold Rush found the name to be unfortunately true, but travel these days is infinitely easier and safer. The climate between November and April is ideal for outdoor travel, while May through October burn with heat like the North African Sahara.

State Route 190 is the main artery through Death Valley National Park. This 120-mile-long valley is the result of a geological phenomenon. At least five million years ago, the deep gap between the Panamint and Funeral mountains was formed by earthquakes and the folding of the earth's crust. Badwater, 282 feet below sea level, is the lowest spot on earth. Despite the harshness of Death Valley's environment, about 900 different species of plants grow in the national park and there is an amazing variety of wildlife, mostly nocturnal. You can scramble up the sand dunes near Stovepipe Wells, marvel at the view from Zabriskie Point, and see ancient craters, old mines and ghost towns. Furnace Creek is the hub for visitor activities.

East of Palm Springs, Joshua Tree National Park is filled with strange rocks, fascinating flora and fauna, and the tall, fibrous plants after which it is named. Mormon explorers journeying to Utah in 1851 thought the tree's outstretched tufted branches resembled arms beckoning them across the desert, and named it after the Biblical patriarch. Two paved roads and several dirt roads provide access to some of the most scenic areas. The western part of the park contains whole forests of Joshua trees and some of the most interesting geological displays in California's deserts.

Photo: Joshua Tree National Park.

Find on:
page 15, P-17

Death Valley National Park
Hwy 190 Visitors' Center
P.O. Box 579
Death Valley, CA 92328

(760) 786-3200

Joshua Tree National Park
74485 National Park Dr.
Twentynine Palms, CA 92277-3597

760-367-5500

http://www.nps.gov/deva
http://www.nps.gov/jotr

San Juan Skyway

The San Juan Mountains in southwestern Colorado have more 13,000 and 14,000-foot peaks than anywhere else in the Rocky Mountains. The vast majority of this country is public land, and you're never far from a designated wilderness area in the San Juans. The 236-mile San Juan Skyway is a scenic byway that forms a loop through five million acres of national forest, from Ridgeway in the north to Cortez and Durango in the south, taking in some of western Colorado's most picturesque towns. The section between Silverton and Ouray is dubbed the Million Dollar Highway. It may have received its name because it cost a million dollars to build. Others say it's because gold ore was used in the roadbed. But more likely, it's because, as you climb the highest point, Red Mountain Pass, the views make you feel like a million bucks, even if you don't have a penny.

The old mining towns of Silverton and Ouray are Victorian gems set against stunning mountain backdrops. Telluride has transformed itself from a rustic mining camp into a hip ski resort, with top jazz, bluegrass, and film festivals. But the real jewel in the San Juans' crown is Mesa Verde, in the state's southwestern corner. This national park preserves thousands of archeological sites, including 600 cliff dwellings built by the ancestors of today's Pueblo tribes. Cliff Palace, Balcony House and other ruins give a fascinating glimpse of ancient life in the Southwest. In few places do the works of man blend with a natural landscape of such beauty and rich resources.

Find on:
Page 20. The San Juan Skyway is formed by US 550, Highway 62, Highway 145 and US 160. See Durango (M-7) for the beginning and end of the skyway.

San Juan National Forest
15 Burnett Court
Durango, CO 81301

970-247-4874

NORTHEAST

- The Adirondacks, New York
- Cape Cod and the Islands, Massachusetts
- The Green Mountains, Vermont
- Gulf of Maine, Maine
- Chesapeake Bay, Maryland

The Adirondacks

The mountain landscape of the Adirondacks has been the setting for many notable events, from fierce Revolutionary War battles to the international stage of two Winter Olympics. The mountains range across the largest park preserve in the northeastern United States, an area of nearly six million acres, occupying most of New York State north of the Mohawk River. Rugged and densely forested, the Adirondacks were the last part of the state to be explored and settled. Among the range's High Peaks, clustered roughly 25 miles west of Lake Champlain, are 42 summits exceeding 4,000 feet. The highest is Mount Marcy, at 5,344 feet, where the waters that form the Hudson River first gather at Lake Tear of the Clouds. The best Adirondack views, however, are from free-standing Whiteface Mountain, which offers 85-mile vistas that take in much of Lake Champlain and Vermont's Green Mountains to the east, the St Lawrence River valley and the city of Montreal to the north.

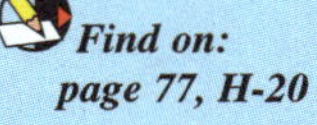
Find on:
page 77, H-20

Adirondack Regional Tourism Council
PO Box 2149
Plattsburgh, NY 12901

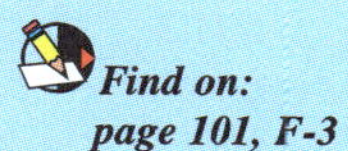

Find on: page 101, F-3

Badlands National Park
P.O. Box 6
Interior, SD 57750

605-433-5361

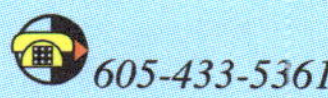

www.nps.gov/badl

The Badlands

The Badlands are an immensely rugged country of furrowed cliffs, gnarled spires, and deep, branching ravines that were torn from the plains of South Dakota by a half-million years of soil erosion. In the early 19th century, French fur traders called the area "the bad lands to cross" because of the maze of twisting canyons that blocked their passage to the White River basin.

Visitors to Badlands National Park may find they are as stark and barren as any ancient ruin. The effect is especially chilling in the light of the midday sun, when short shadows exaggerate the landscape's fractured lines and give the Badlands an almost sinister look. Ridges twist like crooked spines; grass-capped buttes or "tables" rise to dizzying heights; turkey vultures hang on the wind. But in the evenings, when the light softens, the Badlands become warmer, more inviting. Delicate shadows creep along broken ridges, softening folds and crevices. The long rays bring out the deep bruise-colors that stripe the cliffs in shades of red, umber and burning violet.

Entering the park from the northeast, Highway 240 passes the Big Badlands Overlook, your first grand view of the country's ravaged landscape, and then descends through the Badlands Wall, a 100-mile-long barrier between the upper prairie and the jumbled landscape below. Beyond the Ben Reifel Visitor Center, the road continues along the base of the Badlands Wall before making a winding ascent toward the Journey to Wounded Knee Overlook. Here the cliffs face north-west over Bigfoot Pass with nothing but broken land between you and the horizon. From Bigfoot Pass the road climbs to the upper prairie over arid grasslands where homesteaders worked "starvation claims" during the land boom after 1910. This final stretch of paved road is particularly spectacular, with wide-open views of jagged peaks, sheer-sided buttes and chromatic, low-lying humps laid bare by more than a half-million years of wind and water. The Rainbow, Pinnacles and Seabed Jungle overlooks are especially stunning.

SOUTHEAST

- The Everglades, Florida
- The Outer Banks, North Carolina
- Natchez Trace Parkway, Mississippi & Tennessee
- Cajun Country, Louisiana
- The Blue Ridge Parkway, Virginia & North Carolina

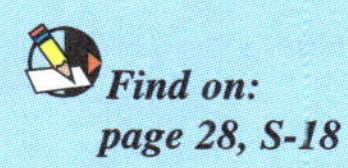

Find on: page 28, S-18

Ten Thousand Islands Everglades National Park
40001 State Road 9336
Homestead, FL 33034

305-242-7700

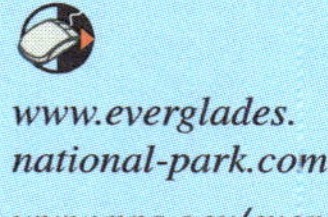

www.everglades. national-park.com
www.nps.gov/ever

The Everglades

A drive of just an hour or two from Miami takes you into the heart of the wildest part of the state – a great, wildlife-rich swamp that gives a taste of how inhospitable Florida was not so very long ago. Everglades National Park, second in size only to Yellowstone, encompasses Florida's southern tip. But the park makes up only a fraction of the slow-flowing "river of grass" that forms this fascinating blend of earthy and watery environments, with tropical and temperate plant and animal life. The Everglades flow for about 200 miles, bulging up to 70 miles in width and at a mean depth of only six inches. The seas of sawgrass stretch in all directions, embellished only by island hammocks of hardwood trees and clumps of mangrove. Around 350 varieties of birds, 500 kinds of fish, 55 species of reptile, and 40 mammal species call the Everglades home. It even has 45 indigenous species of plants that are found nowhere else on earth. There is nothing quite like the Everglades anywhere else in the world.

The park's main entrance is on SR 9336 west of Homestead, and the road continues through the Everglades for 38 miles to its dead end at Flamingo. There are nature trails with boardwalks at several stops which allow you to get a close-up view. Tour boats will take you to the white sand shores of Cape Sable, the southernmost point in the continental United States. The other way to penetrate the Everglades on four wheels is to take the Tamiami Trail (US 41) west from Miami to Tampa. Popular stops along this route include Shark Valley with its alligator observation tower, the swamplands of Big Cypress National Preserve, and the labyrinth of mangroves known as the Ten Thousand Islands.

Photo: Everglades National Park, Florida, aerial view. .

Find on: page 83, G-19

Outer Banks Visitors Bureau
One Visitors Center Circle
Manteo, NC 27954

877-629-4386

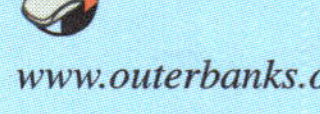

www.outerbanks.org

The Outer Banks

A string of narrow islands and peninsulas along the far eastern shore of North Carolina, the Outer Banks emerge like the head of a whale breaching into the Atlantic. With wide, water-thrashed beaches and sea oats and beach grasses along low sand dunes, they retain a certain wildness despite encroaching development. Two coastlines, Cape Hatteras National Seashore and Cape Lookout National Seashore, preserve 120 miles of these beaches on Bodie, Hatteras, and Ocracoke islands, and Core and Shackleford banks. While most coastal islands lie within 10 miles of shore, the Outer Banks belong to the realm of the sea. In places, 30 miles of water separate Hatteras Island from the mainland. The Outer Banks are perfect for peace, watersports, fishing, and getting away from it all.

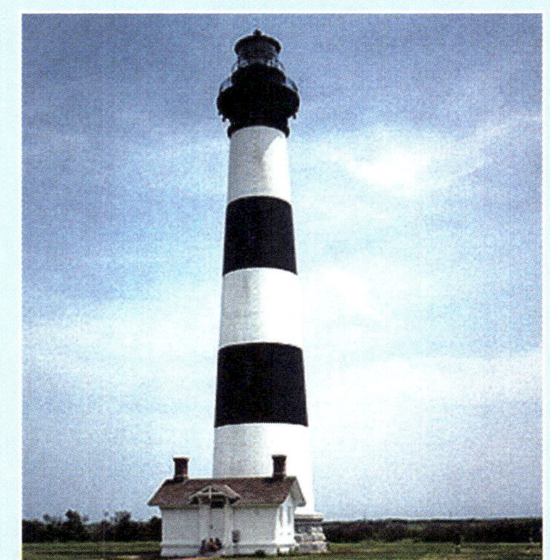

Cape Hatteras's islands are linked by Route 12. The Bodie Island and Hatteras Island sections of the seashore surround Pea Island National Wildlife Refuge. Observation platforms and several short trails lead from the highway to excellent viewpoints for watching migratory waterfowl. Pull-offs along Route 12 offer access to the beach, and there are several long piers for fishing. Strong currents and low-lying islands and sandbars made navigation tricky along the Outer Banks, and the construction of lighthouses was a high priority. The present Cape Hatteras Lighthouse, built in 1870, is the tallest in the United States at 208 feet. Many other lighthouses stand along these shores, all with distinctive exterior patterns such as stripes or diamonds.

Near Kitty Hawk is Kill Devil Hills and the granite Wright Brothers National Memorial, which commemorates the first powered airplane flight in 1903. At Nags Head, you can walk on Jockeys Ridge, a towering sand dune that migrates with the prevailing winds. Access to Ocracoke Island, at the southern end of Cape Hatteras, is via ferry. From here you can visit the historic village of Portsmouth, at the north end of Cape Lookout.

Photo: Bodie Island Lighthouse, part of the Cape Hatteras National Seashore.

Fabulous Drives and Adventures

Natchez Trace Parkway

The Natchez Trace Parkway runs for 444 miles from Natchez, Mississippi to Nashville, Tennessee. It commemorates an ancient trail that was "traced out" along animal paths thousands of years ago. Native American tribes such as the Choctaw and Chickasaw used the trail, followed by trappers and traders in the frontier days. Boatmen floated their goods down the Mississippi River to Natchez and New Orleans, sold their cargo and flatboats, and returned north on foot along the Trace to Nashville and beyond. Now a federal scenic byway, the parkway makes a leisurely, scenic drive across the Deep South. Billboards are banned, the speed limit is 50 miles per hour, and there are historic markers at places of interest along the way.

The Trace begins at Natchez, a beautiful city of antebellum mansions and historic homes set on a bluff overlooking the Mississippi River. The paddlewheelers and old saloons alongside the waterfront at Natchez-under-the Hill recall the riverboat days. The parkway runs northeast through a wooded, rural landscape, passing swampland, pastures and vine-covered hillsides. Scattered along the Trace are ancient burial mounds built by the Natchez Indians, including Emerald Mound, the second-largest in the country. Short detours off the parkway bring you to the historic towns of Port Gibson and Vicksburg with their Civil War battlefields. There is a break in the Trace at Jackson, Mississippi's capital, but it picks up again on the north side of the city. It continues for 170 miles to Tupelo, birthplace of Elvis Presley, where you'll also find the Natchez Trace Visitor Center. The parkway continues on through the northwest corner of Alabama, near Florence, and into Tennessee, where it ends at the great country music capital, Nashville.

Photo: Double Arch Bridge (Natchez Trace Parkway)

Find on:
Natchez, page 62, J-3
Nashville, page 103, C-11

Natchez Trace Parkway
2680 Natchez Trace Parkway
Tupelo, MS 38804-9715

662-680-4025
800-305-7417

www.nps.gov/natr

Cajun Country

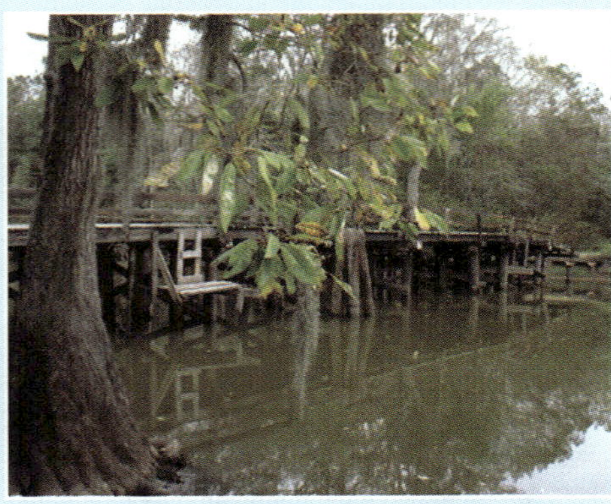

Foot-stompin' music and down-home cooking are two of the attractions in what might be America's most distinctive region. But there are also gardens, good yarns, and grand houses in Louisiana's Cajun country, named for the French Canadian settlers from Acadia. The capital of the region is Lafayette, which lies 128 miles west of New Orleans. For the scenic route, drive south on US 90 to Houma, a lazy little town snuggled in among marshlands and bayous, and a good place for swamp tours. Continue on US 90 to Morgan City, whose Amazon-like environs served as the set for the first Tarzan movie. Just past Patterson, detour to LA 182 to follow Bayou Teche, the state's largest bayou. Its name is an Indian word meaning "snake." Rejoin US 90 at the pretty little town of Franklin, approached from the east beneath an arch of handsome oak trees. Settled by the English, it has a wealth of beautiful white mansions and a historic district.

New Iberia is another handsome town, with the magnificent Shadows on the Teche plantation house museum. Take a detour to Avery Island, where Tabasco sauce was created, and tour the spectacular Jungle Gardens. St Martinville, ten miles north of New Iberia, is a center of Cajun music and legends. Further north on US 31 is Breaux Bridge, famous for its Crawfish Festival and Cajun dance halls. Nearby is the awesome Atchafalaya Basin, a huge swampland replete with bald cypresses standing in murky waters, dripping with Spanish moss. West of Breaux Bridge on LA 94 is Lafayette, regional capital and home of the Cajun Mardi Gras. You can soak up Cajun culture at the Acadian Cultural Center, Vermilionville, and the Acadian Village. North of Lafayette, two small-town hotspots for Cajun music and storytelling are Eunice and Mamou. You can return to New Orleans on I-10 via the state capital, Baton Rouge.

Photo: Lorrain Bridge, Louisiana's Cajun Country.

Find on:
Page 46, L-14

Lafayette Convention & Visitors Bureau
PO Box 52066
Lafayette, LA 70505

337-232-3737
800-346-1958

www.lafayettetravel.com

The Blue Ridge Parkway

The Blue Ridge Parkway has often been described as "the most graceful road in America." It stretches 469 miles along the backbone of the Appalachian Mountains between Shenandoah and Great Smoky Mountain national parks, crossing Virginia and North Carolina. Along the way are countless overlooks, historic sites, wayside exhibits, hiking trails, and museums. Virginia's Shenandoah National Park is a long, narrow corridor of ridges and valleys clothed in dense forest and laced with streams and waterfalls. Running along the top of the Blue Ridge Mountains is Skyline Drive, a 105-mile scenic highway that serves as the park's main thoroughfare. Both roads are marked by mileposts, with a speed limit that means a leisurely pace is strictly enforced. Together, these two roads form the longest and one of the most stunning drives in the United States.

The Blue Ridge Parkway then continues southwest across the state into North Carolina. Here the two-lane roadway is winding and often narrow, with steep grades. Fabulous overlooks encourage frequent stops to savor the stupendous views. Wildflowers bloom along the parkway throughout the summer. The Southern Highlands Craft Guild displays traditional mountain handicrafts at a number of stops. Highlights in North Carolina include the Boone/Blowing Rock area, Asheville, and Chimney Rock Park.

The parkway's final milepost is just outside Cherokee, home of the eastern branch of the Cherokee Nation. Behind the reservation rise the Great Smokies, the largest untamed wilderness remaining in the eastern United States, with wild streams and waterfalls, excellent trails, and wildlife from black bears to red wolves. It is also the most visited of all the national parks. The main route through the park, which straddles the North Carolina/Tennessee border, is the 33-mile road over Newfound Gap to Gatlinburg. The highest peak in the Smokies is Clingmans Dome, at 6,643 feet. Cades Cove has one of the country's best collections of pioneer homes and farmsteads.

Photo: Mabry Mill, Blue Ridge Parkway.

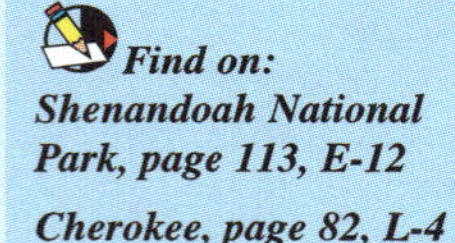

Find on:
Shenandoah National Park, page 113, E-12
Cherokee, page 82, L-4

Blue Ridge Parkway
199 Hemphill Knob Road
Asheville, NC 28803-8686

828-271-4779
828-298-0398
(recorded information)

www.nps.gov/blri

US National Parks Locator

The National Parks of the United States

The national parks are a promise that we Americans have made to ourselves. As a people, we have resolved to protect a small portion of our precious wildlands from the ravages of "progress," to leave room for the bears and butterflies, wildflowers and ancient forests, to preserve as a "vignette of primitive America" the crown jewels of America's natural and cultural heritage.

But the parks are more than islands of nature. They are sanctuaries of the human heart. More than just pretty places where one can snap a few pictures, they are an

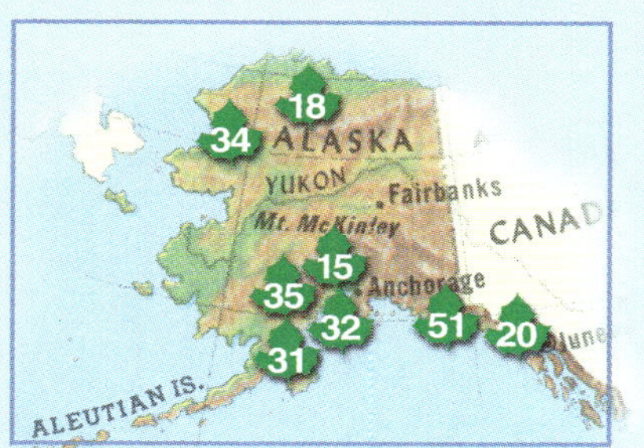

acknowledgment of the human need for wilderness. These are places, as Colin Fletcher wrote of the Grand Canyon, where people can move "closer to rock and sky, to light and shadow, to space and silence." Where there's room for lone hikers to lose, or find, themselves: for mountaineers to test their mettle against the elements; for scientists to study the natural world in a nearly pristine environment; for ordinary visitors to gape at something greater than themselves and let their dreams run wild.

Best Time to Visit

The parks - particularly the popular mountain parks - tend to be crowded in summer. Traffic jams, inadequate parking and crowded facilities are common at Grand Canyon, Yellowstone, Yosemite, Mount Rainier and many other parks during the peak of the season. To avoid the rush, consider visiting in late spring or early fall. In the northern parks the weather may not be quite as balmy, there may even be some snow on the ground, but it's worthwhile to see the parks without the crowds. Weekends are the busiest times, so try to visit on weekdays. Some park roads and most trails may be closed in winter, but snowshoeing, cross-country skiing and other winter activities are often permitted and give visitors a unique perspective on the parks.

In desert parks such as Death Valley, Joshua Tree, Organ Pipe Cactus, Saguaro, Carlsbad Caverns, Guadalupe Mountains and Big Bend, fall, spring and winter are the busy seasons. With summer temperatures in excess of 100°F (38°C), it is too hot then to do much sightseeing or hiking.

#	PARK NAME	STATE	INFORMATION ADDRESS	TELEPHONE	AREA SQ.MI.	ATLAS LOCATION	
						PAGE	GRID
1	Acadia	Maine	P.O. Box 177, Bar Harbor, ME 04609.	(207) 288-3338	71	49	P - 9
2	Arches	Utah	P.O. Box 907, Moab, UT 84532.	(435) 259-8161	120	109	K - 8
3	Badlands	South Dakota	P.O. Box 6, Interior, SD 57750.	(605) 433-5361	364	101	F - 3
4	Big Bend	Texas	P.O. Box 129, Big Bend NP, TX 79834.	(915) 477-2251	1,252	105	Q - 7
5	Biscayne	Florida	9700 SW 328 St., Homestead, FL 33033.	(305) 230-7275	270	28	T - 20
6	Black Canyon of the Gunnison	Colorado	102 Elk Creek, Gunnison, CO 81230.	(970) 641-2337	43	20	H - 8
7	Bryce Canyon	Utah	P.O. Box 170001, Bryce Canyon, UT 84717.	(435) 834-5322	55	109	M - 4
8	Canyonlands	Utah	125 West 2nd St., Moab, UT 84532.	(435) 259-7164	527	109	L - 7
9	Capitol Reef	Utah	HC 70, Box 15, Torrey, UT 84775.	(435) 425-3791	378	109	L - 5
10	Carlsbad Caverns	New Mexico	3225 National Parks Hwy., Carlsbad, NM 88220.	(505) 785-2232	73	75	N - 10
11	Channel Islands	California	1901 Spinnaker Dr., Ventura, CA 93001.	(805) 658-5700	390	14	V - 12
12	Crater Lake	Oregon	P.O. Box 7, Crater Lake, OR 97604.	(541) 594-2211	286	92	K - 5
13	Cuyahoga Valley	Ohio	15610 Vaughn Rd., Brecksville, OH 44141.	(216) 524-1497	51	87	F - 15
14	Death Valley	California	P.O. Box 579, Death Valley, CA 92328.	(760) 786-2331	5,262	15	N - 17
15	Denali	Alaska	P.O. Box 9, Denali Park, AK 99755.	(907) 683-2294	9,375	6	E - 6
16	Dry Tortugas	Florida	P.O. Box 6208, Key West, FL 33041.	(305) 242-7700	101	※	
17	Everglades	Florida	40001 State Rd. 9336, Homestead, FL 33034.	(305) 242-7700	2,356	28	S - 18
18	Gates of the Arctic	Alaska	201 First Ave., Fairbanks, AK 99707.	(907) 456-0281	13,281	6	C - 6
19	Glacier	Montana	West Glacier, MT 59936.	(406) 888-7800	1,584	66	A - 4
20	Glacier Bay	Alaska	P.O. Box 140, Gustavus, AK 99826.	(907) 697-2230	5,040	6	G - 10
21	Grand Canyon	Arizona	P.O. Box 129, Grand Canyon, AZ 86023.	(520) 638-7888	1,902	8	C - 6
22	Grand Teton	Wyoming	P.O. Drawer 170, Moose, WY 83012.	(307) 739-3399	484	120	C - 5
23	Great Basin	Nevada	Highway 488, Baker, NV 89311.	(775) 234-7331	121	70	F - 10
24	Great Smoky Mountains	Tennessee	107 Park Headquarters Rd., Gatlinburg, TN 37738.	(865) 436-1200	814	103	E - 19
25	Guadalupe Mountains	Texas	HC 60, Box 400, Salt Flat, TX 79847.	(915) 828-3251	135	105	K - 4
26	Haleakala	Hawaii	P.O. Box 369, Makawao, HI 96768.	(808) 572-4400	47	32	E - 9
27	Hawaii Volcanoes	Hawaii	P.O.Box 52, Hawaii NP, HI 96718.	(808) 985-6000	328	32	M - 9
28	Hot Springs	Arkansas	P.O.Box 1860, Hot Springs, AR 71902.	(501) 624-3383	8	10	H - 7
29	Isle Royale	Michigan	800 East Lakeshore Dr., Houghton, MI 49931.	(906) 482-0984	893	56	B - 2
30	Joshua Tree	California	74485 National Park Dr., Twentynine Palms, CA 92277.	(760) 367-5500	1,590	15	V - 20
31	Katmai	Alaska	P.O.Box 7, King Salmon, AK 99613.	(907) 246-3305	5,741	6	G - 5
32	Kenai Fjords	Alaska	P.O.Box 1727, Seward, AK 99664.	(907) 224-3175	1,048	6	G - 6
33	Kings Canyon	California	47050 Generals Highway, Three Rivers, CA 93271.	(559) 565-3341	722	15	N - 14
34	Kobuk Valley	Alaska	P.O. Box 1029, Kotzebue, AK 99752.	(907) 442-3890	2,735	6	C - 5
35	Lake Clark	Alaska	4230 University Dr., Ste. 311, Anchorage, AK 99508.	(907) 781-2218	4,120	6	F - 6
36	Lassen Volcanic	California	P.O. Box 100, Mineral, CA 96080.	(530) 595-4444	167	12	D - 9
37	Mammoth Cave	Kentuky	P.O. Box 7, Mammoth Cave, KY 42259.	(270) 758-2328	83	44	L - 7
38	Mesa Verde	Colorado	P.O. Box 8, Mesa Verde NP, CO 81330.	(970) 529-5036	81	20	M - 6
39	Mount Rainier	Washington	Tahoma Woods, Star Route, Ashford, WA 98304.	(360) 569-2211	368	114	H - 10
40	North Cascades	Washington	2105 Hwy. 20, Sedro Woolley, WA 98284.	(360) 856-5700	789	115	B - 11
41	Olympic	Washington	600 East Park Ave., Port Angeles, WA 98362.	(360) 565-3130	1,442	114	E - 6
42	Petrified Forest	Arizona	P.O. Box 2217, Petrified Forest NP, AZ 86028.	(928) 524-6228	146	8	F - 11
43	Redwood	California	1111 Second St., Crescent City, CA 95531.	(707) 464-6101	172	12	B - 3
44	Rocky Mountain	Colorado	1000 Highway 36, Estes Park, CO 80517.	(970) 586-1206	415	21	C - 12
45	Saguaro	Arizona	3693 Old Spanish Trail, Tucson, AZ 85730.	(520) 733-5153	143	9	N - 10
46	Sequoia	California	47050 Generals Highway, Three Rivers, CA 93271.	(559) 565-3341	629	15	P - 14
47	Shenandoah	Virginia	Route 4, Box 348, Luray, VA 22835.	(540) 999-2243	307	113	E - 11
48	Theodore Roosevelt	North Dakota	P.O. Box 7, Medora, ND 58645.	(701) 623-4466	110	85	D - 2
49	Voyageurs	Minnesota	3131 Hwy. 53 South, International Falls, MN 56649.	(218) 283-9821	341	60	E - 9
50	Wind Cave	South Dakota	R.R. 1, Box 190, Hot Springs, SD 57747.	(605) 745-4600	44	101	F - 2
51	Wrangell-St. Elias	Alaska	P.O. Box 439, Copper Center, AK 99573.	(907) 822-5234	20,588	6	F - 8
52	Yellowstone	Wyoming	P.O. Box 168, Yellowstone NP, WY 82190.	(307) 344-7381	3,468	120	A - 4
53	Yosemite	California	P.O. Box 577, Yosemite NP, CA 95389.	(209) 372-0200	1,189	13	K - 12
54	Zion	Utah	SR 9, Springdale, UT 84767.	(435) 772-3256	229	109	N - 3

※ #16 not shown on state map. Located approx. 70 miles west of Key West, in the Gulf of Mexico.

BRITISH COLUMBIA
ALBERTA
SASKATCHEWAN
MANITOBA
WASHINGTON
OREGON
IDAHO
MONTANA
WYOMING
NORTH DAKOTA
SOUTH DAKOTA
NEBRASKA
KANSAS
OKLAHOMA
TEXAS
NEVADA
UTAH
COLORADO
CALIFORNIA
ARIZONA
NEW MEXICO
BAJA CALIFORNIA
SONORA
CHIHUAHUA
COAHUILA
NUEVO LEON
TAMAULIPAS
MEXICO
PACIFIC OCEAN
GREAT BASIN
COLORADO PLATEAU
GREAT PLAINS
LLANO ESTACADO
EDWARDS PLATEAU
SIERRA MADRE
Vancouver
Calgary
Regina
Winnipeg
Seattle
Spokane
Portland
Salem
Eugene
Boise
Helena
Billings
Bismarck
Pierre
Cheyenne
Denver
Salt Lake City
Reno
Sacramento
San Francisco
San Jose
Fresno
Las Vegas
Los Angeles
San Diego
Tijuana
Phoenix
Tucson
Albuquerque
Santa Fe
El Paso
Ciudad Juárez
Chihuahua
Lincoln
Wichita
Oklahoma City
Amarillo
Lubbock
Dallas
Fort Worth
Austin
San Antonio
Monterrey
Laredo
Brownsville
Matamoros
ALASKA
ARCTIC OCEAN
BROOKS RANGE
ALASKA RANGE
CANADA
RUSSIA
YUKON TERRITORY
NORTHWEST TERRITORIES
Barrow
Fairbanks
Anchorage
Juneau
Gulf of Alaska
HAWAII
Honolulu
Hilo
© MapQuest.com, Inc.

One inch equals approx. 145 MI or 234 KM

MI 125 250

KM 125 250 375

United States

"In God We Trust"

Alabama

Index page 134

	ANNISTON	AUBURN	BIRMINGHAM	CHATTANOOGA, TN	COLUMBUS, GA	DECATUR	DEMOPOLIS	DOTHAN	FLORENCE	GADSDEN	HAMILTON	HUNTSVILLE	MERIDIAN, MS	MOBILE	MONTGOMERY	OPP	SELMA	TUSCALOOSA
BIRMINGHAM	66	141		149	167	83	120	191	121	63	92	101	149	258	88	166	94	61
DOTHAN	207	125	191	311	97	273	198		310	251	282	291	246	199	103	66	147	237
HUNTSVILLE	100	241	101	109	266	25	215	291	65	74	104		245	357	187	265	194	156
MOBILE	279	227	258	403	252	340	144	199	377	317	286	357	132		173	146	194	205
MONTGOMERY	106	54	88	234	79	170	100	103	207	148	179	187	153	173		81	51	134

DRIVING DISTANCES IN MILES

SEE ALSO MILEAGE AND DRIVING TIME MAP ON PAGE 144

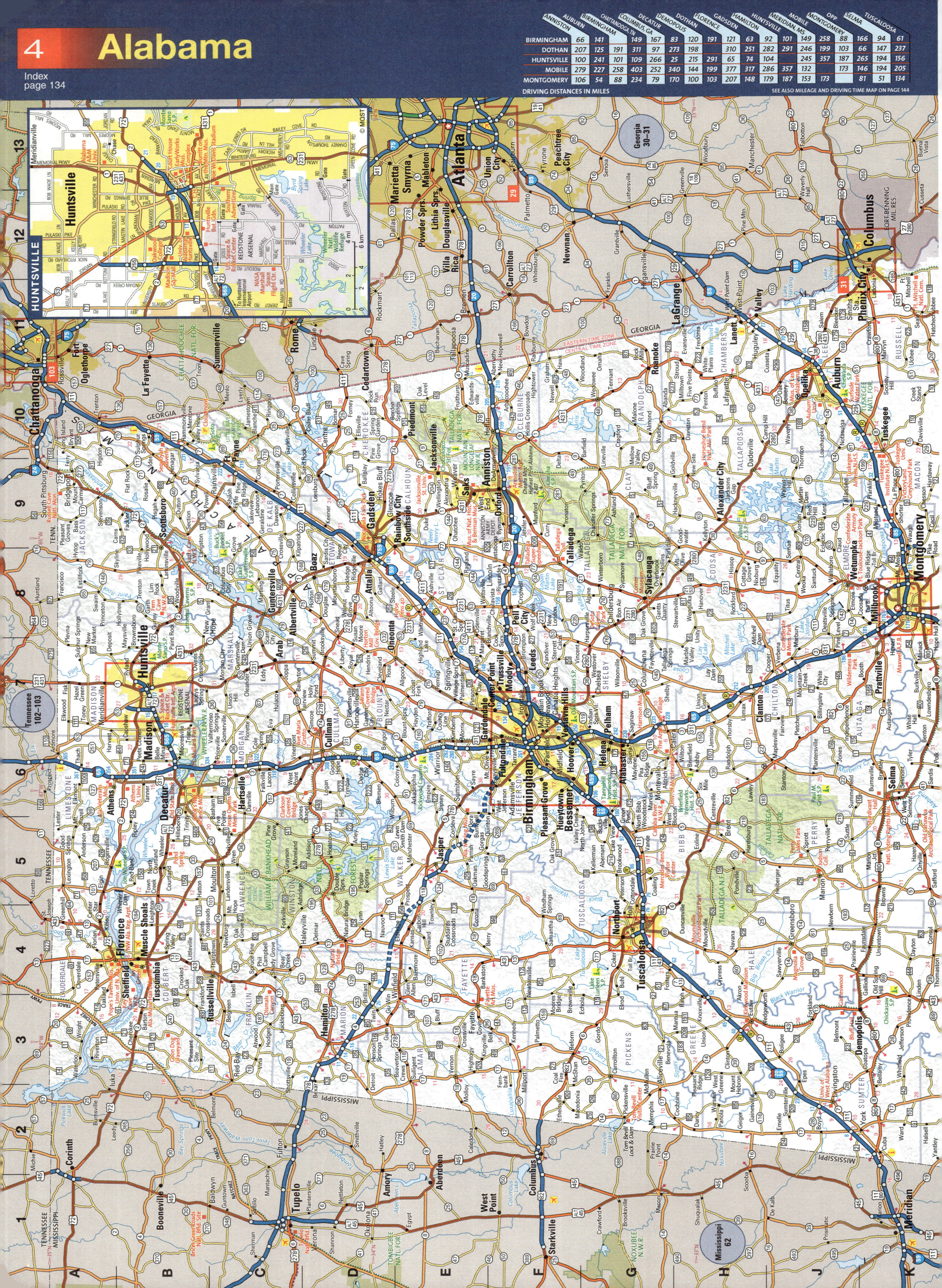

One inch equals approx. 19 MI or 31 KM

MI 10 20 30

KM 10 20 30 40

BIRMINGHAM

MOBILE

MONTGOMERY

TUSCALOOSA

Georgia 30–31

Florida 26–28

Mississippi 62

GULF OF MEXICO

Alaska

"North to the Future"

	ANCHORAGE	FAIRBANKS	GLENNALLEN	HAINES	HOMER	JUNEAU	KENAI	KETCHIKAN	SEWARD	SKAGWAY	TOK	VALDEZ
ANCHORAGE		378	184	760	225	841*	161	1608*	129	807	323	301
FAIRBANKS	378		249	645	603	726*	539	1493*	507	691	207	366
HOMER	225	603	408	985		1066*	87	1833*	172	1031	547	525
SKAGWAY	807	691	623	27	1031	101*	968	954*	935		484	740
TOK	323	207	139	438	547	518*	484	1258*	451	484		256

DRIVING DISTANCES IN MILES

* DISTANCE INCLUDES FERRY TRAVEL

One inch equals approx. 143.5 MI or 233 KM

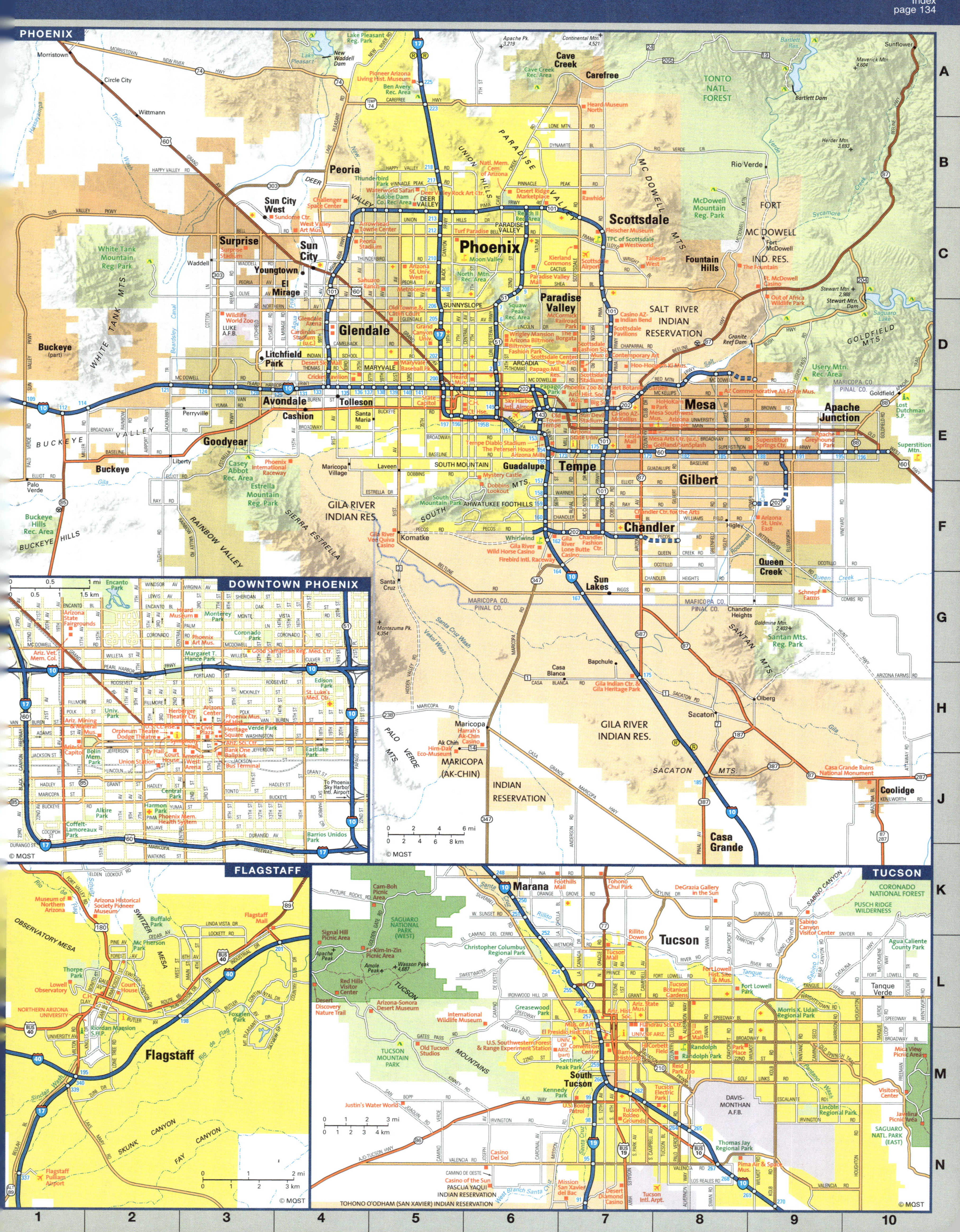
PHOENIX
DOWNTOWN PHOENIX
FLAGSTAFF
TUCSON
Phoenix
Scottsdale
Glendale
Peoria
Mesa
Tempe
Chandler
Gilbert
Paradise Valley
Sun City
Sun City West
Surprise
Youngtown
El Mirage
Litchfield Park
Avondale
Tolleson
Goodyear
Buckeye
Cave Creek
Carefree
Fountain Hills
Apache Junction
Guadalupe
Sun Lakes
Queen Creek
Coolidge
Casa Grande
Maricopa
Flagstaff
Tucson
South Tucson
Marana
TONTO NATL. FOREST
SALT RIVER INDIAN RESERVATION
GILA RIVER INDIAN RES.
SAGUARO NATIONAL PARK (WEST)
TUCSON MOUNTAIN PARK
© MQST

Index page 134

	BULLHEAD CITY	CASA GRANDE	CHINLE	DOUGLAS	FLAGSTAFF	GRAND CANYON	HOLBROOK	KINGMAN	LAKE HAVASU CITY	NOGALES	PAGE	PHOENIX	PRESCOTT	SAFFORD	SHOW LOW	TUCSON	WICKENBURG	YUMA
FLAGSTAFF	180	188	216	374		89	93	148	209	318	135	137	89	271	140	255	147	320
KINGMAN	34	235	364	421	148	175	240		60	365	281	184	150	353	288	302	134	215
PHOENIX	217	50	353	237	137	226	230	184	193	181	272		96	169	178	118	51	183
TUCSON	335	68	366	120	255	345	240	302	311	65	390	118	214	128	193		169	241
YUMA	222	179	536	360	320	409	413	215	155	304	455	183	213	368	352	241	170	

DRIVING DISTANCES IN MILES

SEE ALSO MILEAGE AND DRIVING TIME MAP ON PAGE 144

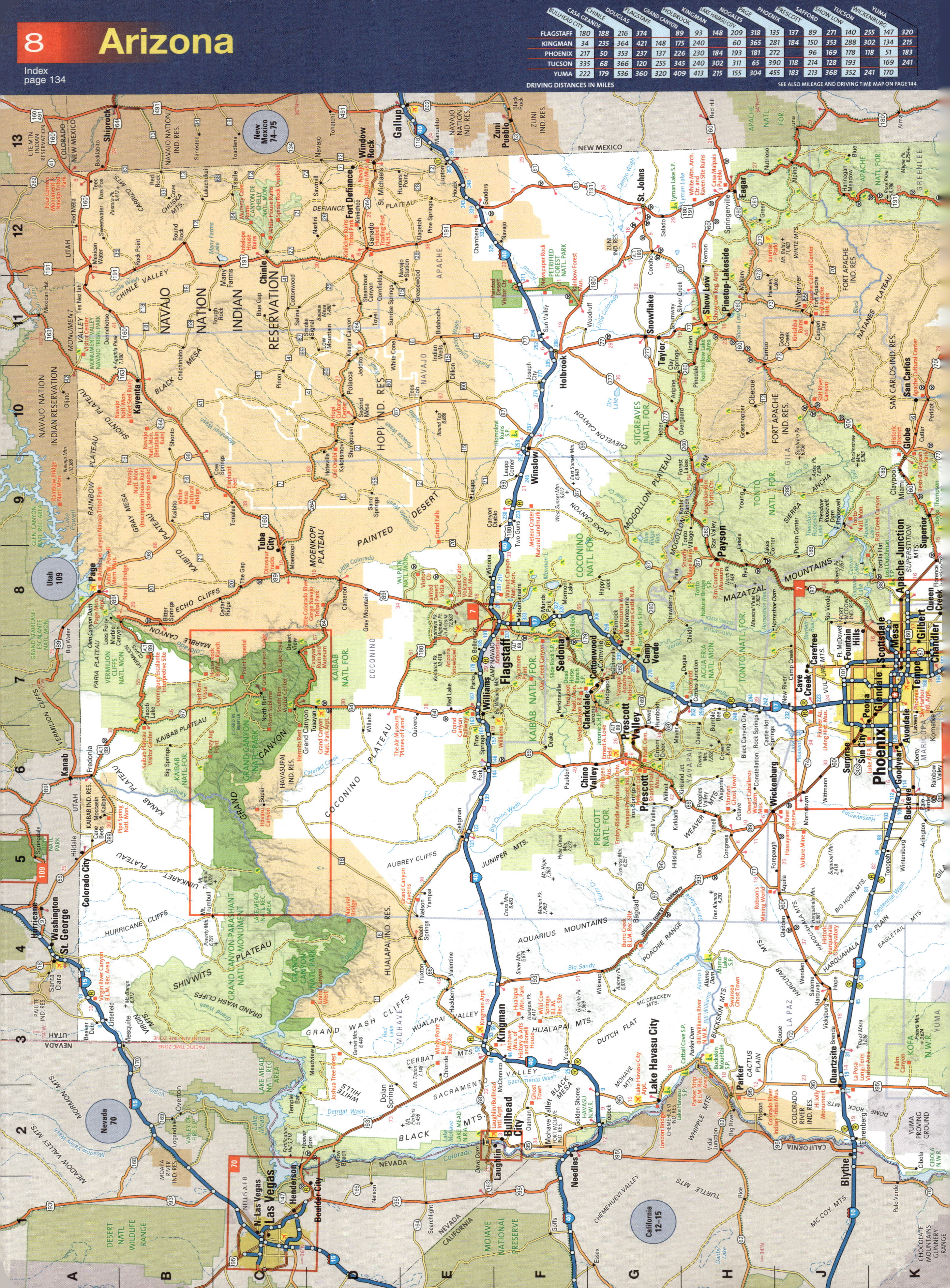

Arizona

"God Enriches"

Index page 134

One inch equals approx. 27 MI or 43 KM

MI 25 50

KM 25 50 75

Index page 134

	BLYTHEVILLE	CAMDEN	CONWAY	DUMAS	EL DORADO	FAYETTEVILLE	FORT SMITH	HARRISON	HELENA	HOT SPRINGS	JONESBORO	LITTLE ROCK	MEMPHIS, TN	MENA	NEWPORT	PINE BLUFF	RUSSELLVILLE	TEXARKANA
FORT SMITH	353	201	134	255	232	64		141	280	126	266	165	298	81	220	210	87	180
JONESBORO	53	236	133	185	253	287	266	178	111	200		135	70	276	46	180	182	49
LITTLE ROCK	195	101	31	90	118	186	165	136	122	65	135		140	141	89	45	81	110
PINE BLUFF	213	76	76	45	93	231	210	181	106	76	180	45	157	151	134		126	128
TEXARKANA	99	210	104	129	227	259	238	193	62	174	49	110	49	250	53	128	154	

DRIVING DISTANCES IN MILES

SEE ALSO MILEAGE AND DRIVING TIME MAP ON PAGE 144

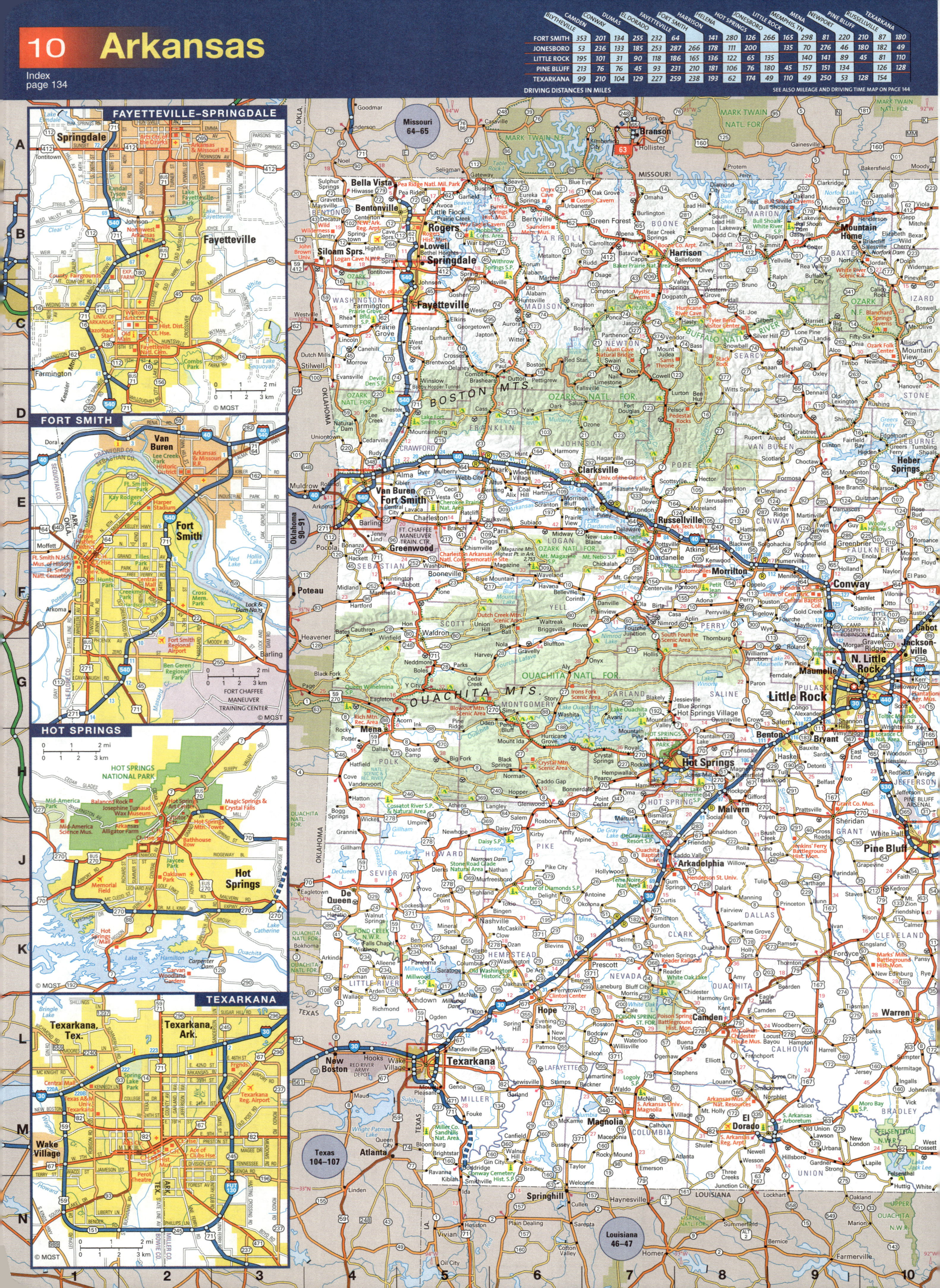

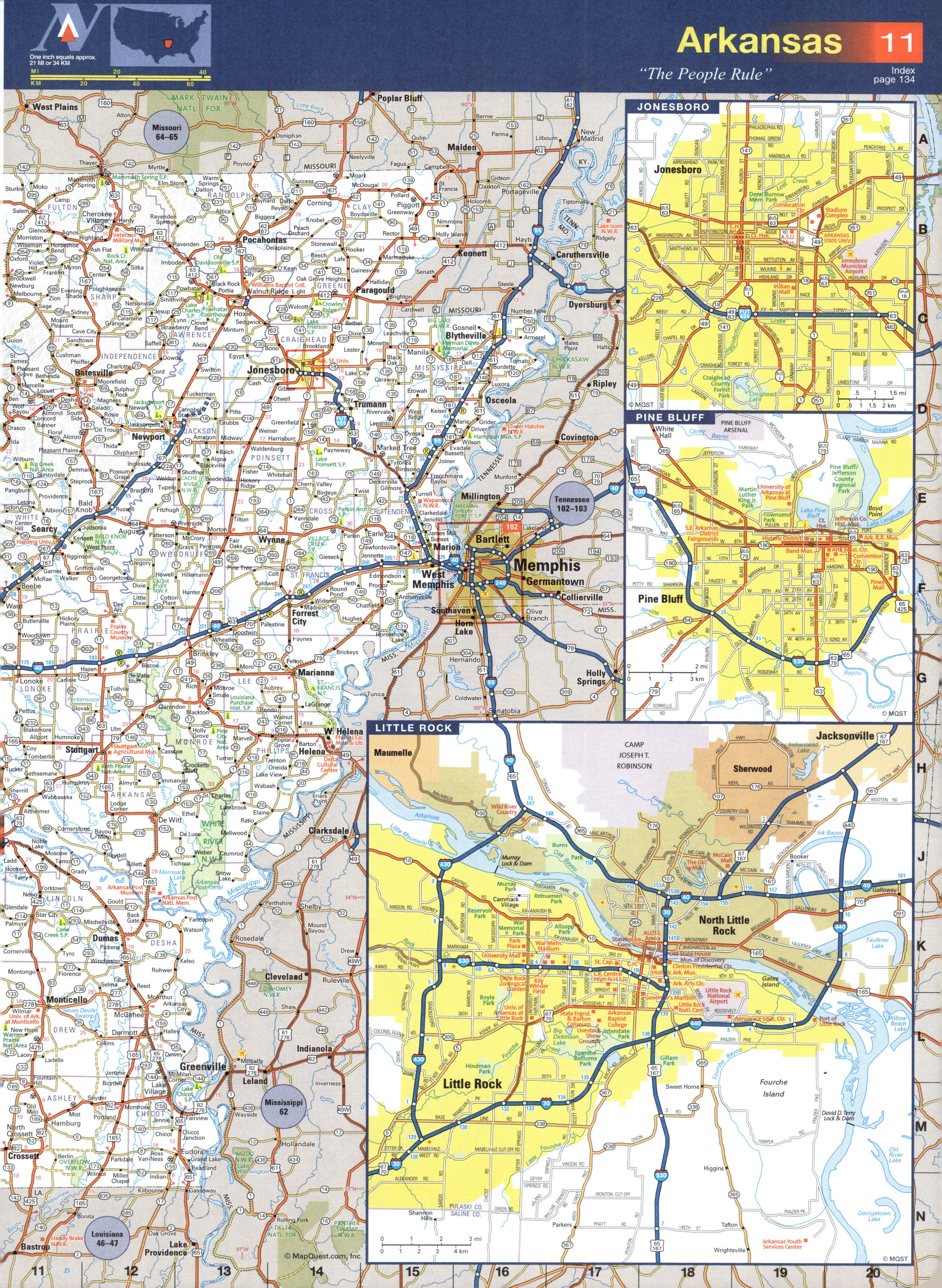

One inch equals approx. 21 MI or 34 KM
MI 20 40
KM 20 40 60
Missouri 64-65
Tennessee 102-103
Mississippi 62
Louisiana 46-47
JONESBORO
PINE BLUFF
LITTLE ROCK
Jonesboro
Pine Bluff
Little Rock
North Little Rock
Jacksonville
Sherwood
Maumelle
CAMP JOSEPH T. ROBINSON
Memphis
West Memphis
Germantown
Collierville
Bartlett
Southaven
Horn Lake
Olive Branch
Hernando
Holly Springs
Tunica
Senatobia
Coldwater
Clarksdale
Cleveland
Greenville
Leland
Indianola
Helena
W. Helena
Marianna
Forrest City
Wynne
Blytheville
Osceola
Dyersburg
Caruthersville
Kennett
Malden
Poplar Bluff
Paragould
Pocahontas
Walnut Ridge
Batesville
Newport
Searcy
Stuttgart
Dumas
Monticello
Crossett
Hamburg
Lake Village
Lake Providence
Bastrop
West Plains
Covington
Millington
Ripley
© MapQuest.com, Inc.
© MQST

California (north)

Index page 134

	Bishop	Chico	Eureka	Fresno	Merced	Monterey	Napa	Oakland	Redding	Sacramento	San Francisco	San Jose	Santa Rosa	South Lake Tahoe	Stockton	Susanville	Ukiah	Yosemite Village
EUREKA	537	186		444	385	380	235	262	133	278	263	306	208	379	336	247	148	436
REDDING	426	74	133	344	284	323	193	213		166	222	250	228	266	214	114	193	336
SACRAMENTO	260	88	278	178	118	188	58	78	166		87	115	93	100	48	183	153	170
SAN FRANCISCO	283	182	263	190	131	114	47	9	222	87		43	56	185	82	277	116	183
SOUTH LAKE TAHOE	179	165	379	267	208	286	156	176	266	100	185	213	191		142	146	251	180

DRIVING DISTANCES IN MILES

SEE ALSO MILEAGE AND DRIVING TIME MAP ON PAGE 144

TRAVEL NOTE: Beginning January 2002, California started numbering freeway exits using a mileage-based numbering system. Full implementation is expected to take three years. For more details, including a complete listing of California's exit numbers, go to *www.dot.ca.gov/hq/traffops/signtech/calnexus/index.htm.*

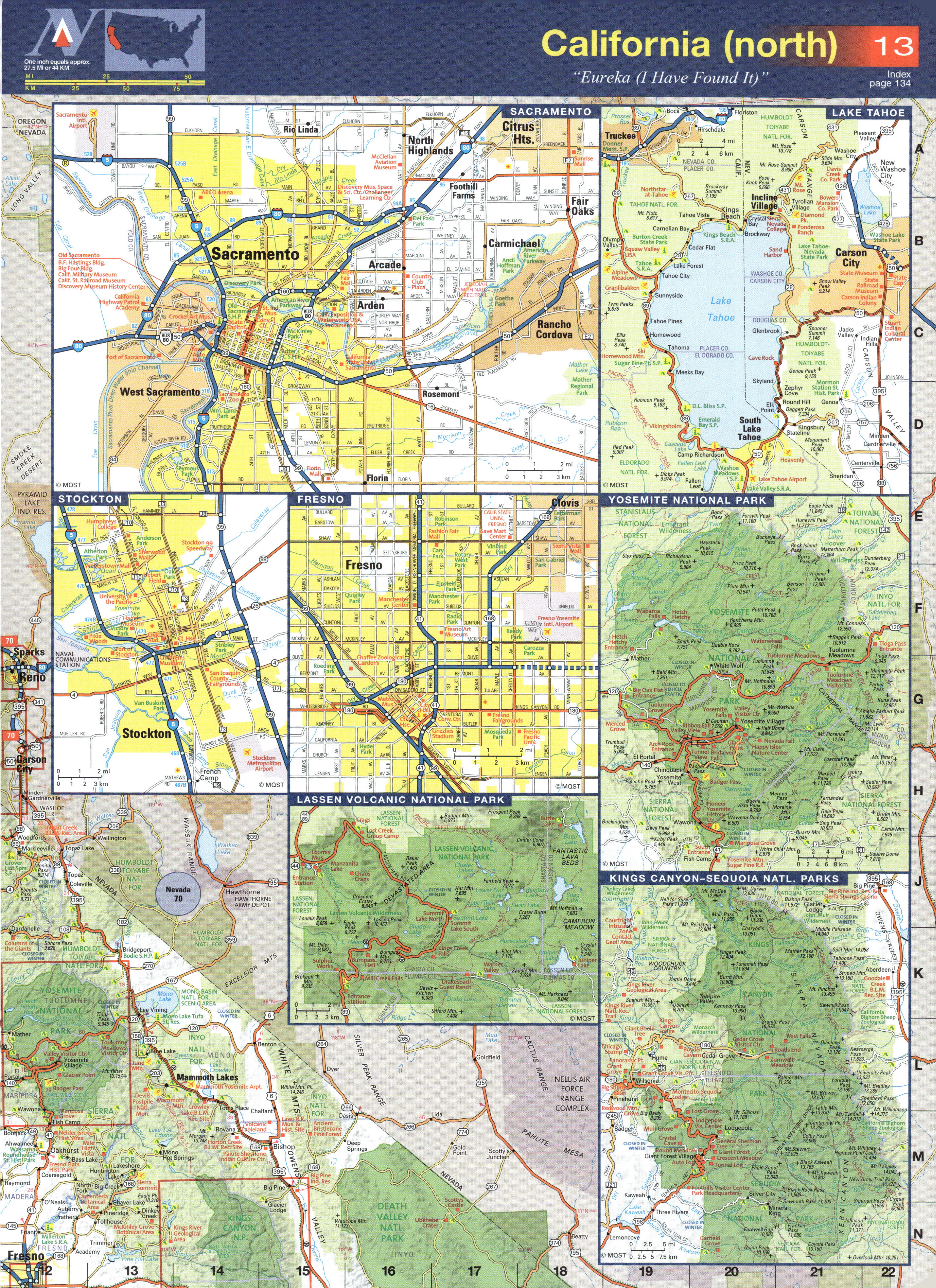

California (north)
13
"Eureka (I Have Found It)"
Index page 134
One inch equals approx. 27.5 MI or 44 KM
SACRAMENTO
LAKE TAHOE
STOCKTON
FRESNO
YOSEMITE NATIONAL PARK
LASSEN VOLCANIC NATIONAL PARK
KINGS CANYON–SEQUOIA NATL. PARKS
Sacramento
West Sacramento
North Highlands
Citrus Hts.
Rio Linda
Foothill Farms
Fair Oaks
Carmichael
Arcade
Arden
Rancho Cordova
Rosemont
Florin
Truckee
Incline Village
Carson City
Lake Tahoe
South Lake Tahoe
Stockton
Fresno
Clovis
Sparks
Reno
Mammoth Lakes
Nevada 70
NELLIS AIR FORCE RANGE COMPLEX
DEATH VALLEY NATL. PARK
KINGS CANYON N.P.
© MQST

Index page 134

	Bakersfield	Barstow	Bishop	El Centro	Fresno	Las Vegas, NV	Los Angeles	Merced	Monterey	Palm Springs	San Bernardino	San Diego	San Francisco	San Jose	San Luis Obispo	Santa Barbara	Visalia	Yosemite Village
FRESNO	111	246	219	451		399	219	59	158	324	277	342	190	153	134	258	43	90
LOS ANGELES	111	118	270	234	219	274		278	327	110	62	124	385	342	190	97	183	308
MONTEREY	229	365	315	559	158	517	327	122		432	385	450	114	74	149	242	204	201
SAN DIEGO	234	181	366	117	342	337	124	401	450	143	111		508	465	314	221	306	431
SAN FRANCISCO	287	423	283	617	190	575	385	131	114	490	443	508		43	234	327	233	183

DRIVING DISTANCES IN MILES

SEE ALSO MILEAGE AND DRIVING TIME MAP ON PAGE 144

TRAVEL NOTE: Beginning January 2002, California started numbering freeway exits using a mileage-based numbering system. Full implementation is expected to take three years. For more details, including a complete listing of California's exit numbers, go to *www.dot.ca.gov/hq/traffops/signtech/calnexus/index.htm.*

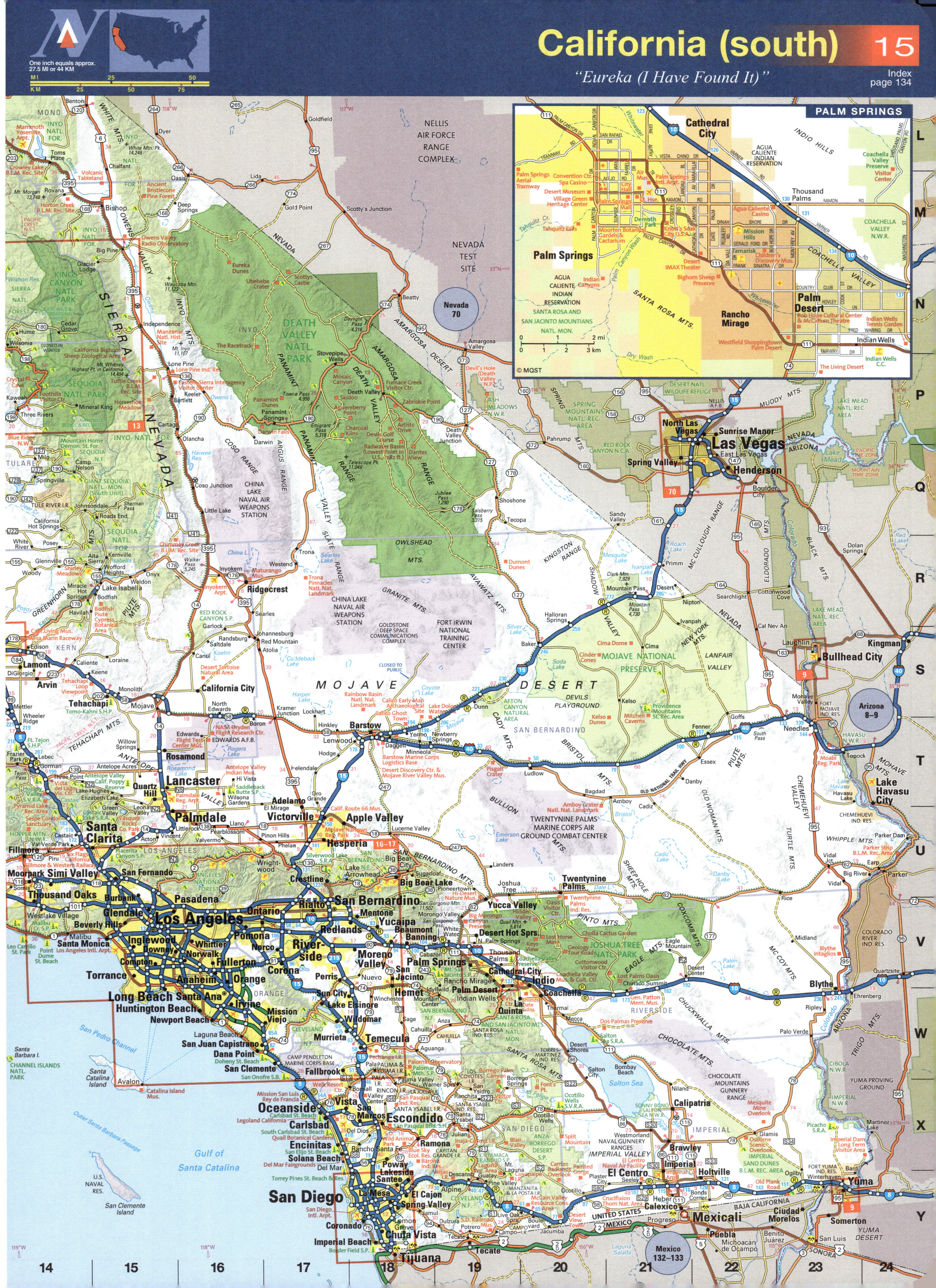

California (south)
15
"Eureka (I Have Found It)"
Index page 134
One inch equals approx. 27.5 MI or 44 KM
MI 25 50
KM 25 50 75
PALM SPRINGS
Cathedral City
Palm Springs
Palm Desert
Rancho Mirage
Thousand Palms
Indian Wells
AGUA CALIENTE INDIAN RESERVATION
SANTA ROSA AND SAN JACINTO MOUNTAINS NATL. MON.
INDIO HILLS
Coachella Valley Preserve Visitor Center
COACHELLA VALLEY N.W.R.
SANTA ROSA MTS.
Palm Springs Aerial Tramway
The Living Desert
© MQST
NELLIS AIR FORCE RANGE COMPLEX
NEVADA TEST SITE
Nevada 70
DEATH VALLEY NATL PARK
SEQUOIA NATL PARK
KINGS CANYON NATL PARK
SIERRA NEVADA
MOJAVE DESERT
MOJAVE NATIONAL PRESERVE
JOSHUA TREE NATL PARK
CHINA LAKE NAVAL AIR WEAPONS STATION
FORT IRWIN NATIONAL TRAINING CENTER
TWENTYNINE PALMS MARINE CORPS AIR GROUND COMBAT CENTER
EDWARDS A.F.B.
OWLSHEAD MTS.
Las Vegas
North Las Vegas
Henderson
Spring Valley
Sunrise Manor
Bullhead City
Kingman
Laughlin
Lake Havasu City
Needles
Barstow
Victorville
Apple Valley
Hesperia
Lancaster
Palmdale
Santa Clarita
Los Angeles
Pasadena
Glendale
Burbank
San Fernando
Simi Valley
Thousand Oaks
Moorpark
Ventura
Oxnard
Santa Monica
Inglewood
Torrance
Long Beach
Huntington Beach
Newport Beach
Santa Ana
Anaheim
Fullerton
Orange
Irvine
Pomona
Ontario
Rialto
San Bernardino
Redlands
Yucaipa
Riverside
Corona
Moreno Valley
Perris
Hemet
San Jacinto
Temecula
Murrieta
Mission Viejo
Laguna Beach
San Juan Capistrano
Dana Point
San Clemente
Oceanside
Vista
Carlsbad
San Marcos
Escondido
Encinitas
Solana Beach
Del Mar
Poway
Santee
El Cajon
Spring Valley
Chula Vista
La Mesa
San Diego
Coronado
Imperial Beach
Tijuana
Tecate
Mexicali
El Centro
Calexico
Imperial
Brawley
Holtville
Calipatria
Yuma
Blythe
Indio
Coachella
Twentynine Palms
Yucca Valley
Joshua Tree
Big Bear Lake
Ridgecrest
California City
Tehachapi
Mojave
Bishop
Lone Pine
Independence
Baker
Beatty
Pahrump
Salton Sea
Gulf of Santa Catalina
San Pedro Channel
Santa Catalina Island
San Clemente Island
UNITED STATES
MEXICO
Mexico 132–133
Arizona 8–9
13
70
9
16–17
L M N O P Q R S T U V W X Y
14 15 16 17 18 19 20 21 22 23 24

Index page 134

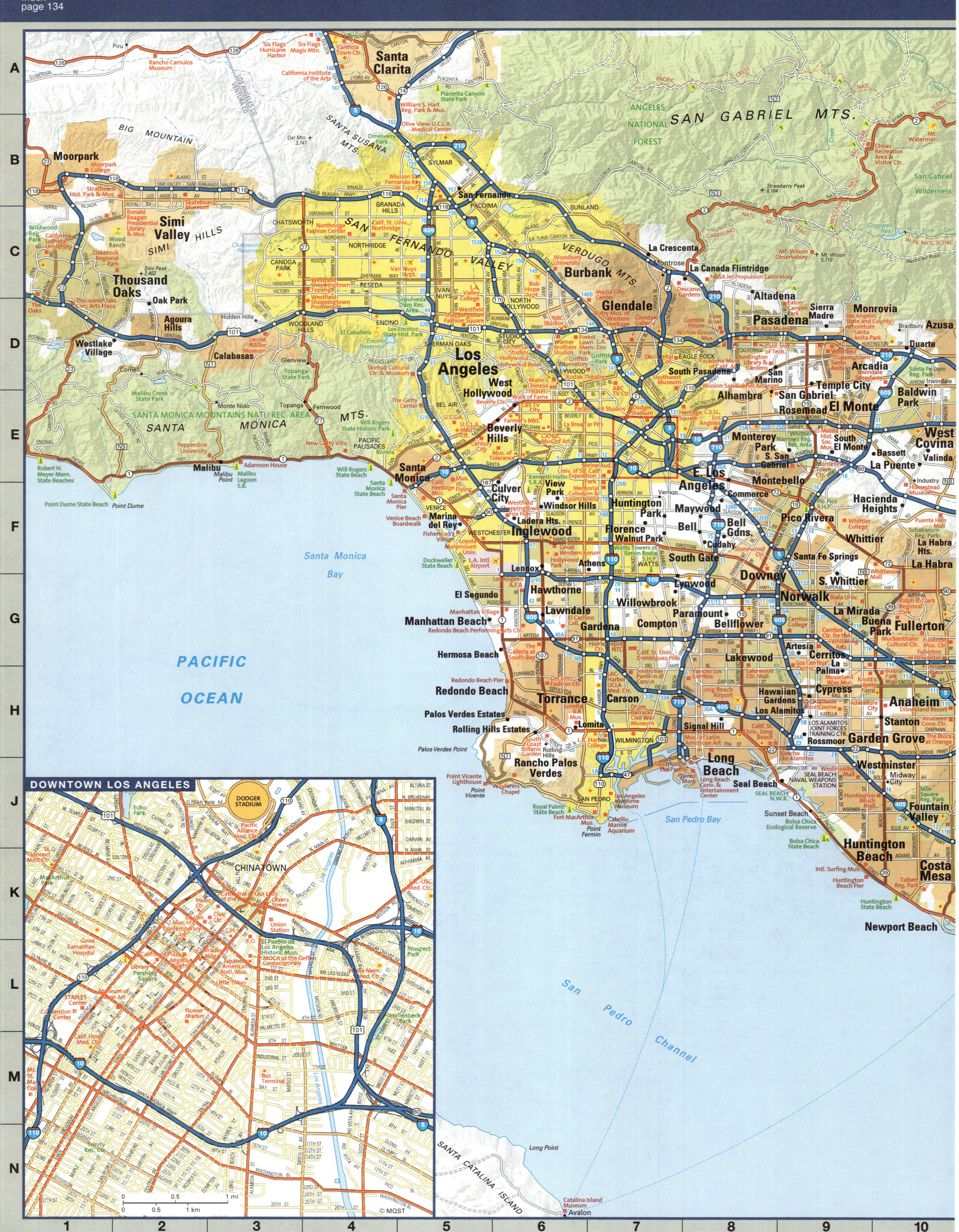

A
B
C
D
E
F
G
H
J
K
L
M
N
11
12
13
14
15
16
17
18
19
20
Hesperia
San Bernardino
Highland
Fontana
Rialto
Rancho Cucamonga
Upland
Claremont
La Verne
San Dimas
Glendora
Covina
Pomona
Montclair
Ontario
Chino
Chino Hills
Diamond Bar
Walnut
Rowland Heights
Colton
Grand Terrace
Loma Linda
Redlands
Yucaipa
Calimesa
Cherry Valley
Banning
Beaumont
Moreno Valley
Riverside
Rubidoux
Norco
Corona
Home Gardens
Woodcrest
Perris
Hemet
San Jacinto
Sun City
Canyon Lake
Lake Elsinore
Lakeland Village
Wildomar
Murrieta
Temecula
Brea
Yorba Linda
Placentia
Orange
Villa Park
Tustin
Santa Ana
Irvine
Lake Forest
Mission Viejo
Laguna Woods
Laguna Hills
Aliso Viejo
Laguna Niguel
Laguna Beach
Dana Point
San Juan Capistrano
San Clemente
Rancho Santa Margarita
Mentone
Muscoy
Bloomington
Crestline
Lake Arrowhead
Running Springs
ANGELES NATIONAL FOREST
SAN BERNARDINO NATIONAL FOREST
CLEVELAND NATIONAL FOREST
CHINO HILLS
SANTA ANA MTS.
ELSINORE MTS.
SAN JACINTO VALLEY
LAKEVIEW MTS.
SAN TIMOTEO CANYON
CAJON CANYON
SAN MATEO CANYON
SANTA MARGARITA MTS.
CAMP PENDLETON MARINE CORPS BASE
FALLBROOK NAVAL WEAPONS DETACHMENT
MARCH AIR RESERVE BASE
PECHANGA INDIAN RESERVATION
PALA INDIAN RESERVATION
Fallbrook
Rainbow
Pala
TRAVEL NOTE: Beginning January 2002, California started numbering freeway exits using a mileage-based numbering system. Full implementation is expected to take three years. For more details, including a complete listing of California's exit numbers, go to www.dot.ca.gov/hq/traffops/signtech/calnexus/index.htm.
© MQST

San Francisco Bay area (CA)

Index page 134

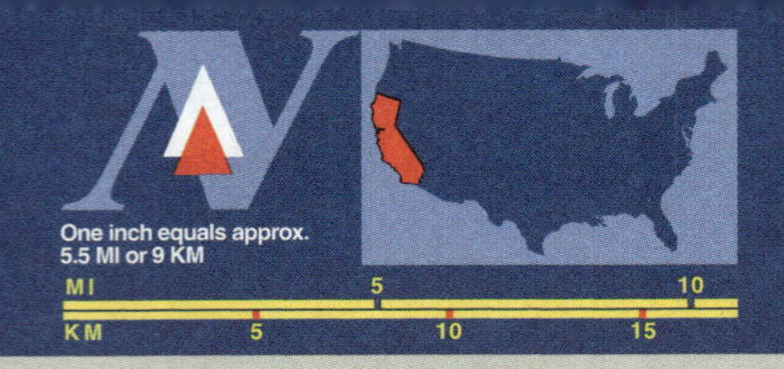

TRAVEL NOTE: Beginning January 2002, California started numbering freeway exits using a mileage-based numbering system. Full implementation is expected to take three years. For more details, including a complete listing of California's exit numbers, go to *www.dot.ca.gov/hq/traffops/signtech/calnexus/index.htm.*

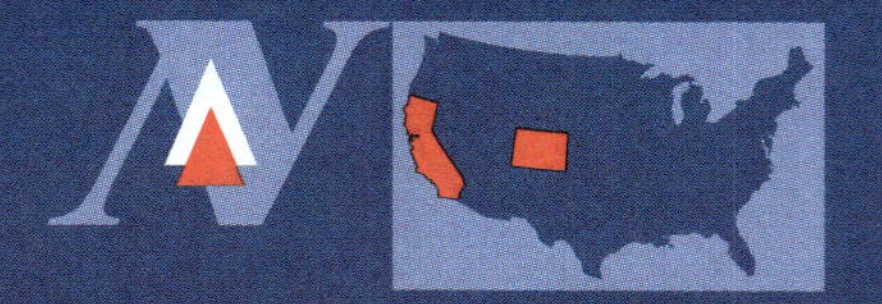

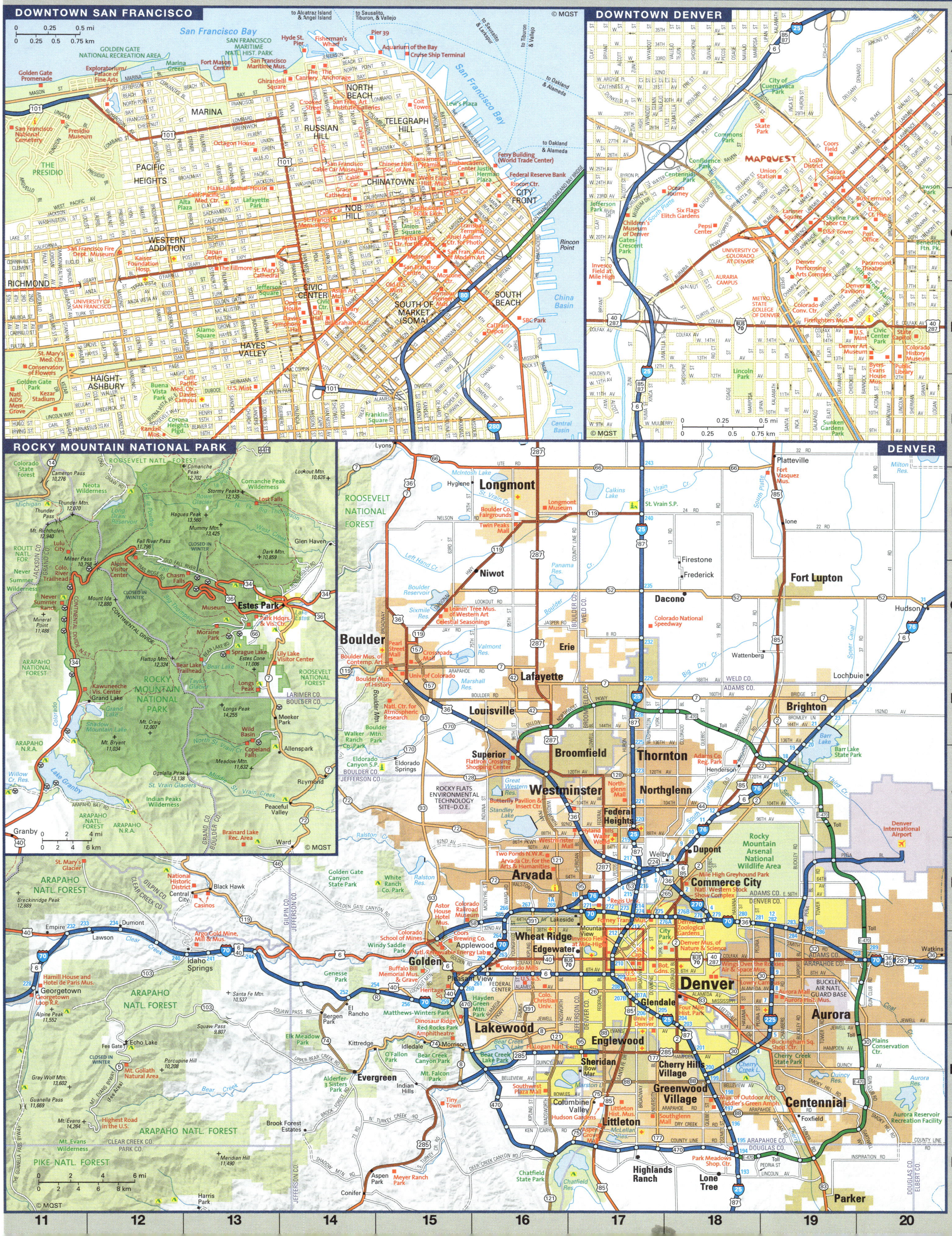

DOWNTOWN SAN FRANCISCO

0 0.25 0.5 mi
0 0.25 0.5 0.75 km

© MQST

DOWNTOWN DENVER

0 0.25 0.5 mi
0 0.25 0.5 0.75 km

© MQST

ROCKY MOUNTAIN NATIONAL PARK

0 2 4 mi
0 2 4 6 km

© MQST

DENVER

0 2 4 6 mi
0 2 4 6 8 km

© MQST

	ALAMOSA	ASPEN	BOULDER	BURLINGTON	COLORADO SPRINGS	CRAIG	DENVER	DURANGO	ESTES PARK	FORT COLLINS	GLENWOOD SPRINGS	GRAND JUNCTION	GREELEY	LAMAR	MONTROSE	PUEBLO	STERLING	TRINIDAD
COLORADO SPRINGS	162	157	97	152		270	70	314	134	133	226	318	133	161	236	43	194	127
DENVER	230	164	27	168	70	203		337	64	64	158	250	64	208	277	111	130	196
DURANGO	152	244	366	461	314	321	337		402	399	226	169	399	354	107	271	465	260
GRAND JUNCTION	261	135	254	418	318	152	250	169	291	311	92		311	458	62	360	377	444
PUEBLO	119	185	139	191	43	312	111	271	175	175	268	360	175	119	229		236	84

DRIVING DISTANCES IN MILES

SEE ALSO MILEAGE AND DRIVING TIME MAP ON PAGE 144

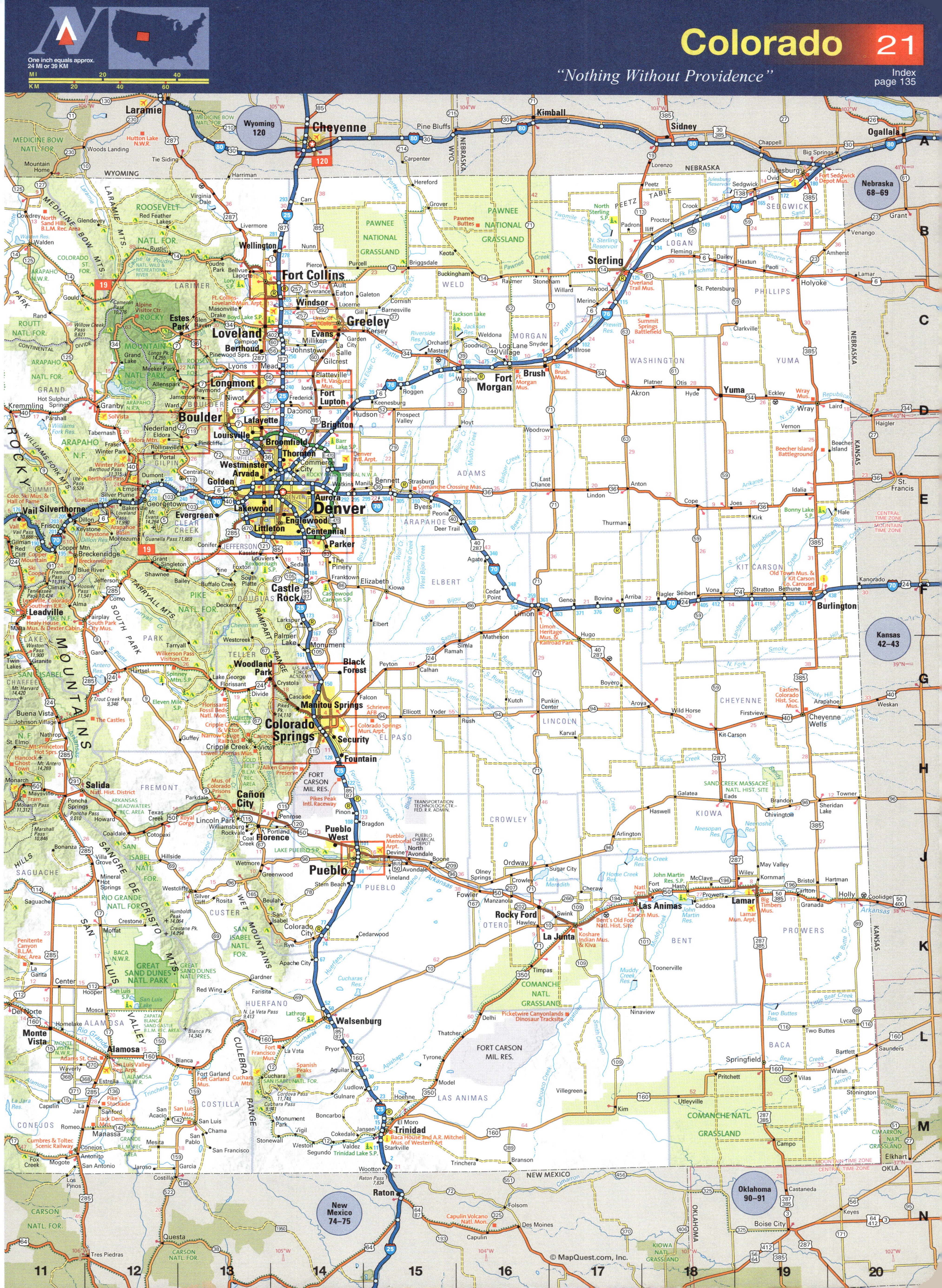

Colorado
21
"Nothing Without Providence"
Index page 135
One inch equals approx. 24 MI or 39 KM
MI 20 40
KM 20 40 60
Wyoming 120
Nebraska 68–69
Kansas 42–43
Oklahoma 90–91
New Mexico 74–75
Laramie
Cheyenne
Kimball
Sidney
Ogallala
Julesburg
Sterling
Fort Collins
Loveland
Greeley
Longmont
Boulder
Fort Morgan
Brush
Yuma
Wray
Denver
Aurora
Lakewood
Littleton
Englewood
Centennial
Parker
Golden
Arvada
Westminster
Thornton
Broomfield
Louisville
Lafayette
Brighton
Evergreen
Castle Rock
Limon
Burlington
Colorado Springs
Manitou Springs
Security
Fountain
Pueblo
Pueblo West
Cañon City
Florence
Salida
Leadville
Breckenridge
Frisco
Silverthorne
Vail
Estes Park
Granby
Kremmling
Walden
Alamosa
Monte Vista
Walsenburg
Trinidad
Raton
La Junta
Rocky Ford
Las Animas
Lamar
Springfield
Holyoke
Cheyenne Wells
Kit Carson
Eads
Ordway
Black Forest
Woodland Park
WELD
LARIMER
MORGAN
LOGAN
SEDGWICK
PHILLIPS
WASHINGTON
YUMA
ADAMS
ARAPAHOE
ELBERT
KIT CARSON
LINCOLN
CHEYENNE
EL PASO
CROWLEY
KIOWA
PUEBLO
OTERO
BENT
PROWERS
BACA
LAS ANIMAS
HUERFANO
CUSTER
FREMONT
TELLER
PARK
DOUGLAS
JEFFERSON
CLEAR CREEK
GILPIN
BOULDER
GRAND
SUMMIT
LAKE
CHAFFEE
SAGUACHE
ALAMOSA
CONEJOS
COSTILLA
ROCKY MOUNTAINS
PAWNEE NATIONAL GRASSLAND
COMANCHE NATL. GRASSLAND
ROOSEVELT NATL. FOR.
ARAPAHO N.F.
PIKE NATL. FOR.
SAN ISABEL NATL. FOR.
RIO GRANDE NATL. FOR.
GREAT SAND DUNES NATL. PARK
ROCKY MOUNTAIN NATL. PARK
FORT CARSON MIL. RES.
SANGRE DE CRISTO MTS.
WYOMING
NEBRASKA
KANSAS
OKLAHOMA
NEW MEXICO
CENTRAL TIME ZONE
MOUNTAIN TIME ZONE
A B C D E F G H J K L M N
11 12 13 14 15 16 17 18 19 20
© MapQuest.com, Inc.

Index page 135

	BRIDGEPORT	DANBURY	HARTFORD	MERIDEN	MIDDLETOWN	NEW HAVEN	NEW LONDON	NEW YORK, NY	NORWICH	PROVIDENCE, RI	PUTNAM	SPRINGFIELD, MA	STAMFORD	STORRS	TORRINGTON	WATERBURY	WILLIMANTIC	WINDSOR LOCKS
BRIDGEPORT		31	56	37	44	19	64	60	72	118	100	81	21	75	54	33	79	68
HARTFORD	56	57		21	16	39	46	115	38	73	46	25	77	21	25	30	25	13
NEW LONDON	64	81	46	50	40	46		124	15	58	51	71	85	41	72	65	29	59
TORRINGTON	54	40	25	40	40	50	72	107	64	98	71	50	74	46		21	51	38
WATERBURY	33	31	30	20	25	30	65	99	60	118	76	55	53	51	21		56	43

DRIVING DISTANCES IN MILES

SEE ALSO MILEAGE AND DRIVING TIME MAP ON PAGE 144

Connecticut
23
"He Who Transplanted Still Sustains"
Index page 135
One inch equals approx. 7 MI or 11.5 KM
Massachusetts 54–55
Rhode Island 99
NEW LONDON
HARTFORD
Hartford
West Hartford
Wethersfield
Glastonbury
Newington
New Britain
East Hartford
Bloomfield
New London
Groton
Norwich
Manchester
Vernon
Storrs
Willimantic
Putnam
Providence
Pawtucket
Cranston
Warwick
West Warwick
East Providence
Fall River
Woonsocket
Attleboro
New Haven
West Haven
East Haven
Hamden
North Haven
Milford
Shelton
Derby
Ansonia
Woodbridge
Orange
Branford
Westerly
Pawcatuck
Long Island Sound
Block Island Sound
Kensington
Rocky Hill
© MQST

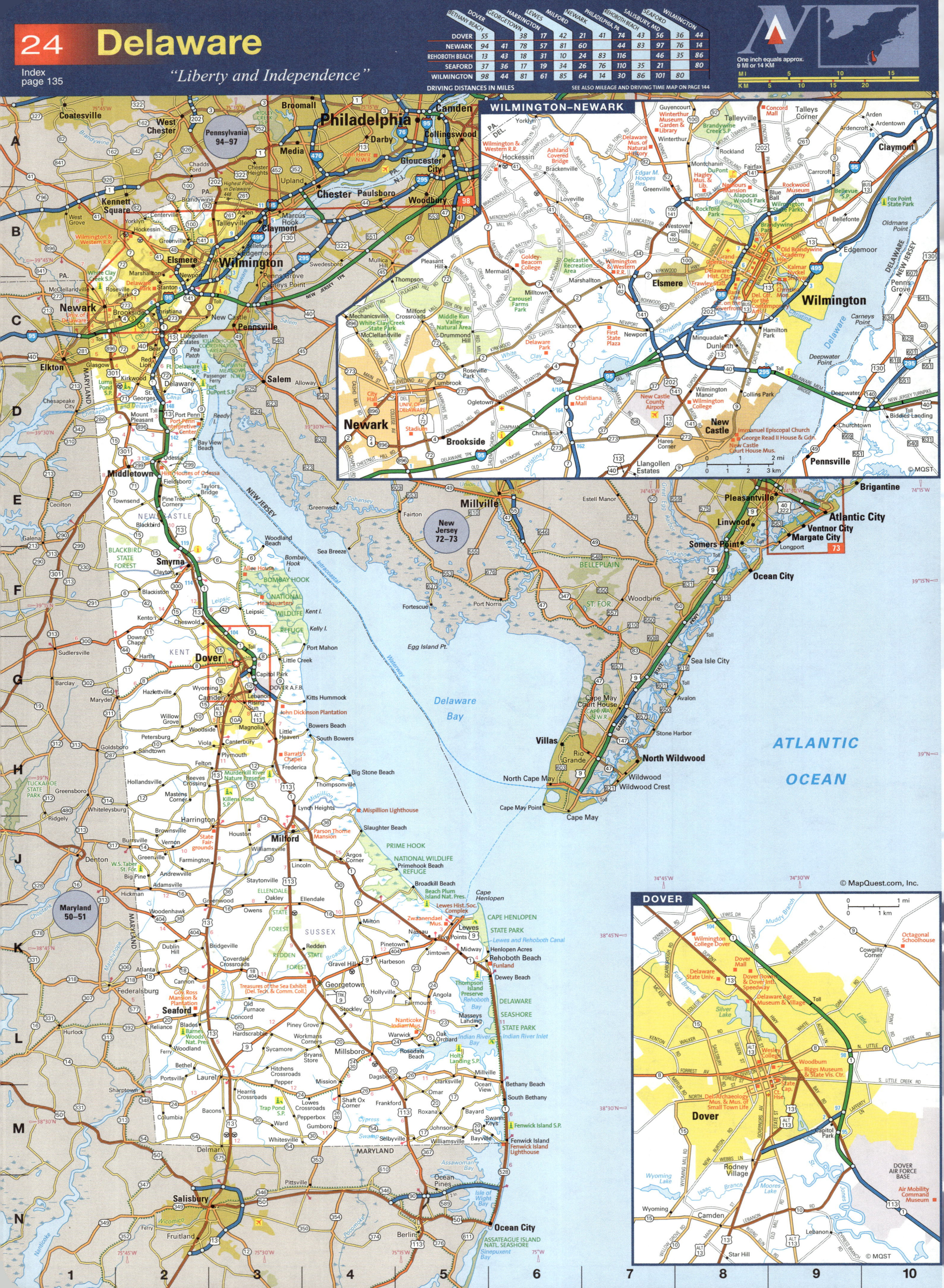

	BETHANY BEACH	DOVER	GEORGETOWN	HARRINGTON	LEWES	MILFORD	NEWARK	PHILADELPHIA, PA	REHOBOTH BEACH	SALISBURY, MD	SEAFORD	WILMINGTON
DOVER	55		38	17	42	21	41	74	43	56	36	44
NEWARK	94	41	78	57	81	60		44	83	97	76	14
REHOBOTH BEACH	13	43	18	31	10	24	83	116		46	35	86
SEAFORD	37	36	17	19	34	26	76	110	35	21		80
WILMINGTON	98	44	81	61	85	64	14	30	86	101	80	

DRIVING DISTANCES IN MILES

SEE ALSO MILEAGE AND DRIVING TIME MAP ON PAGE 144

TAMPA-ST. PETERSBURG AREA
MIAMI AREA
DOWNTOWN MIAMI
Tarpon Springs
Palm Harbor
Dunedin
Oldsmar
Safety Harbor
Clearwater
Largo
Pinellas Park
Seminole
St. Petersburg
Gulfport
St. Pete Beach
Treasure Island
South Pasadena
Tampa
Town 'n Country
Carrollwood
Lutz
Temple Terrace
Brandon
Plant City
Lakeland
Winter Haven
Apollo Beach
Ruskin
Sun City Center
Tampa Bay
Palmetto
Bradenton
Memphis
Longboat Key
Sarasota
Siesta Key
Venice
North Port
GULF OF MEXICO
Jupiter
Palm Beach Gardens
North Palm Beach
Riviera Bch.
West Palm Beach
Royal Palm Beach
Wellington
Greenacres
Lake Worth
Lantana
Boynton Beach
Delray Beach
Boca Raton
Deerfield Beach
Pompano Beach
Coral Springs
Coconut Creek
Margate
Tamarac
North Lauderdale
Lauderhill
Sunrise
Plantation
Fort Lauderdale
Davie
Weston
Cooper City
Pembroke Pines
Hollywood
Hallandale Beach
Miramar
Miami Gardens
Opa-locka
Hialeah
North Miami Beach
North Miami
Miami Beach
Miami
Coral Gables
South Miami
Kendall
Key Biscayne
ATLANTIC OCEAN
ARTHUR R. MARSHALL LOXAHATCHEE NATIONAL WILDLIFE REFUGE
BISCAYNE NATIONAL PARK
LITTLE HAVANA
OVERTOWN
© MQST

Index page 135

	Daytona Beach	Fort Myers	Fort Pierce	Fort Walton Beach	Gainesville	Jacksonville	Lake City	Lakeland	Melbourne	Miami	Ocala	Orlando	Panama City	Pensacola	St. Augustine	Tallahassee	Tampa	Titusville
JACKSONVILLE	91	295	223	328	70		62	197	175	345	101	141	267	363	41	166	196	133
ORLANDO	56	155	120	425	117	141	157	56	72	232	80		364	460	103	262	82	40
PENSACOLA	455	589	567	39	349	363	306	471	526	681	383	460	102		405	200	474	497
TALLAHASSEE	258	392	369	166	152	166	109	274	329	483	186	262	104	200	207		277	300
TAMPA	138	123	172	440	132	196	172	37	142	274	95	82	378	474	185	277		121

DRIVING DISTANCES IN MILES

SEE ALSO MILEAGE AND DRIVING TIME MAP ON PAGE 144

Florida (north) 27

"In God We Trust"

Index page 135

One inch equals approx. 23 MI or 37.5 KM

GAINESVILLE
DAYTONA BEACH
MELBOURNE–KENNEDY SPACE CENTER
Gainesville
Ormond Beach
Holly Hill
Daytona Beach
South Daytona
Port Orange
Daytona Beach Shores
ATLANTIC OCEAN
Mims
Titusville
Port St. John
Cocoa
Merritt Island
Cocoa Beach
Cape Canaveral
Rockledge
South Patrick Shores
Satellite Beach
Indian Harbour Beach
Melbourne
W. Melbourne
Palm Bay
Georgia 30–31
Thomasville
Valdosta
Quitman
OKEFENOKEE N.W.R.
St. Marys
Fernandina Beach
Jacksonville
Atlantic Beach
Neptune Beach
Jacksonville Beach
Palm Valley
Orange Park
Middleburg
Green Cove Springs
St. Augustine
Palatka
Palm Coast
Ormond-by-the-Sea
Daytona Beach
Port Orange
New Smyrna Beach
Edgewater
Live Oak
Lake City
Madison
Monticello
Perry
Starke
Alachua
Gainesville
Ocala
Silver Springs
Deltona
DeLand
Orange City
Sanford
Winter Springs
Oviedo
Apopka
Orlando
Kissimmee
St. Cloud
Leesburg
Eustis
Mt. Dora
Tavares
Lady Lake
Inverness
Beverly Hills
Brooksville
Spring Hill
Dade City
Zephyrhills
Land O' Lakes
Lakeland
Plant City
Winter Haven
Haines City
Lake Wales
Bartow
Brandon
Tampa
Clearwater
Dunedin
Largo
Pinellas Park
St. Petersburg
Treasure Island
St. Pete Beach
New Port Richey
Tarpon Springs
Palm Harbor
Holiday
Bayonet Point
Hudson
GULF OF MEXICO
Vero Bch.
Sebastian
Gifford
© MapQuest.com, Inc.

11 12 13 14 15 16 17 18 19 20

Florida (south)

"In God We Trust"

	FORT LAUDERDALE	FORT MYERS	FORT PIERCE	KEY WEST	LAKELAND	MELBOURNE	MIAMI	ORLANDO	ST. PETERSBURG	SARASOTA	TAMPA	WEST PALM BEACH
FORT MYERS	139		126	308	113	178	155	155	108	74	123	125
FORT PIERCE	102	126		288	122	57	122	120	197	150	172	57
MIAMI	23	155	122	168	236	179		232	259	225	274	67
ORLANDO	216	155	120	398	56	72	232		107	130	82	169
TAMPA	257	123	172	426	37	142	274	82	25	60		223

DRIVING DISTANCES IN MILES

SEE ALSO MILEAGE AND DRIVING TIME MAP ON PAGE 144

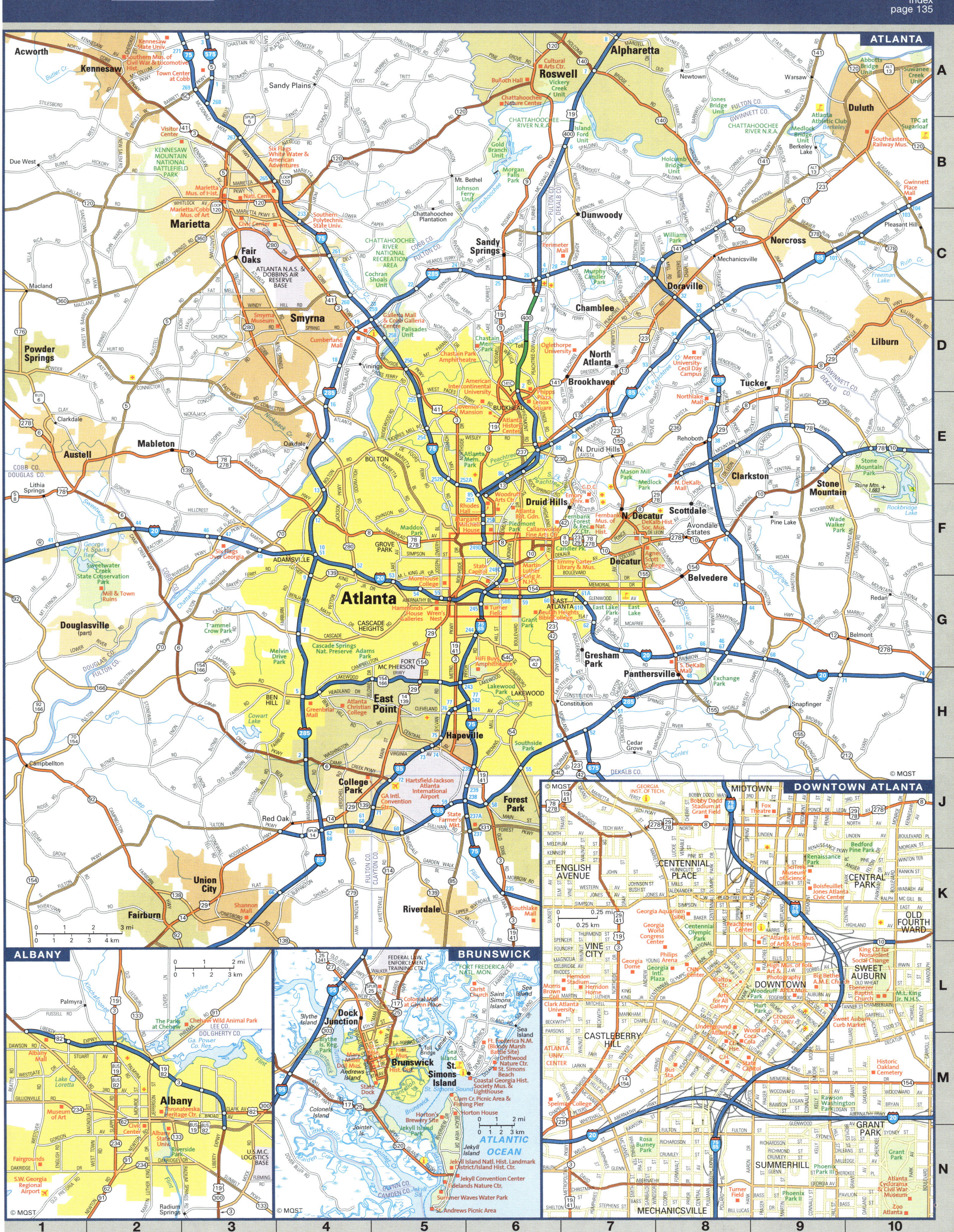
ATLANTA
Acworth
Kennesaw
Alpharetta
Roswell
Duluth
Sandy Plains
Newtown
Warsaw
Due West
Marietta
Fair Oaks
Smyrna
Sandy Springs
Dunwoody
Norcross
Doraville
Chamblee
Macland
Powder Springs
North Atlanta
Brookhaven
Tucker
Lilburn
Austell
Mableton
Clarkston
Stone Mountain
Druid Hills
Decatur
Scottdale
Belvedere
Atlanta
Douglasville
East Point
Hapeville
College Park
Forest Park
Gresham Park
Panthersville
Red Oak
Union City
Fairburn
Riverdale
Campbellton
ALBANY
Albany
Palmyra
BRUNSWICK
Brunswick
St. Simons Island
Dock Junction
Blythe Island
ATLANTIC OCEAN
DOWNTOWN ATLANTA
MIDTOWN
ENGLISH AVENUE
CENTENNIAL PLACE
VINE CITY
CASTLEBERRY HILL
DOWNTOWN
SWEET AUBURN
OLD FOURTH WARD
CENTRAL PARK
GRANT PARK
SUMMERHILL
MECHANICSVILLE
© MQST

Index page 135

	ALBANY	AMERICUS	ATHENS	ATLANTA	AUGUSTA	BAINBRIDGE	BRUNSWICK	CHATTANOOGA, TN	COLUMBUS	DUBLIN	GAINESVILLE	LA GRANGE	MACON	ROME	SAVANNAH	STATESBORO	VALDOSTA	WAYCROSS
ATLANTA	180	129	70		149	236	308	113	106	139	56	69	84	66	249	211	228	253
AUGUSTA	226	206	97	149		282	194	266	249	95	136	212	123	219	135	81	274	184
MACON	102	83	89	84	123	159	225	201	95	55	142	114		154	165	127	151	159
SAVANNAH	246	226	225	249	135	248	78	366	244	114	307	279	165	319		53	168	106
VALDOSTA	90	119	239	228	274	80	120	346	183	139	287	226	151	298	168	173		62

DRIVING DISTANCES IN MILES

SEE ALSO MILEAGE AND DRIVING TIME MAP ON PAGE 144

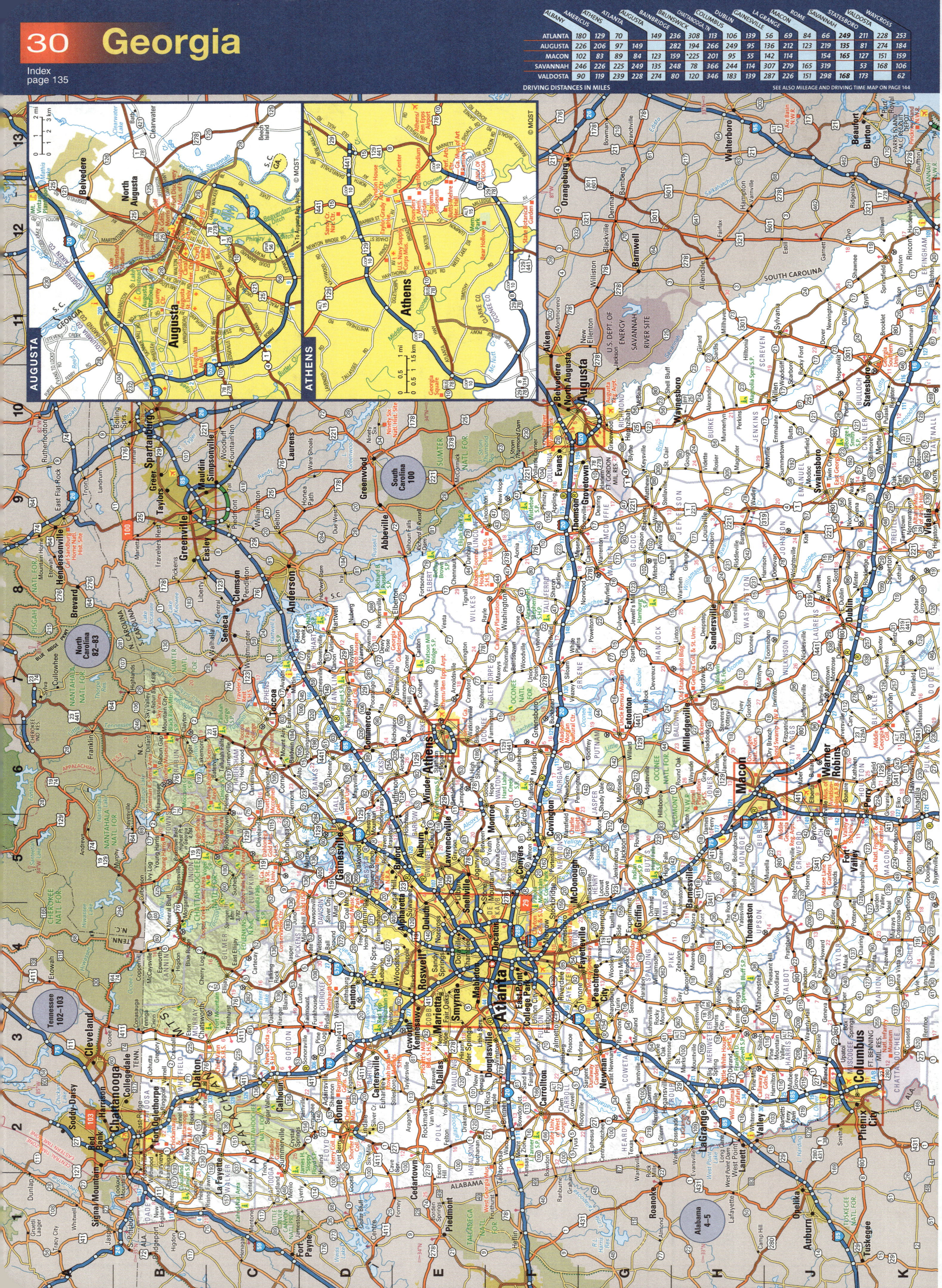

"Wisdom, Justice and Moderation"

Index page 135

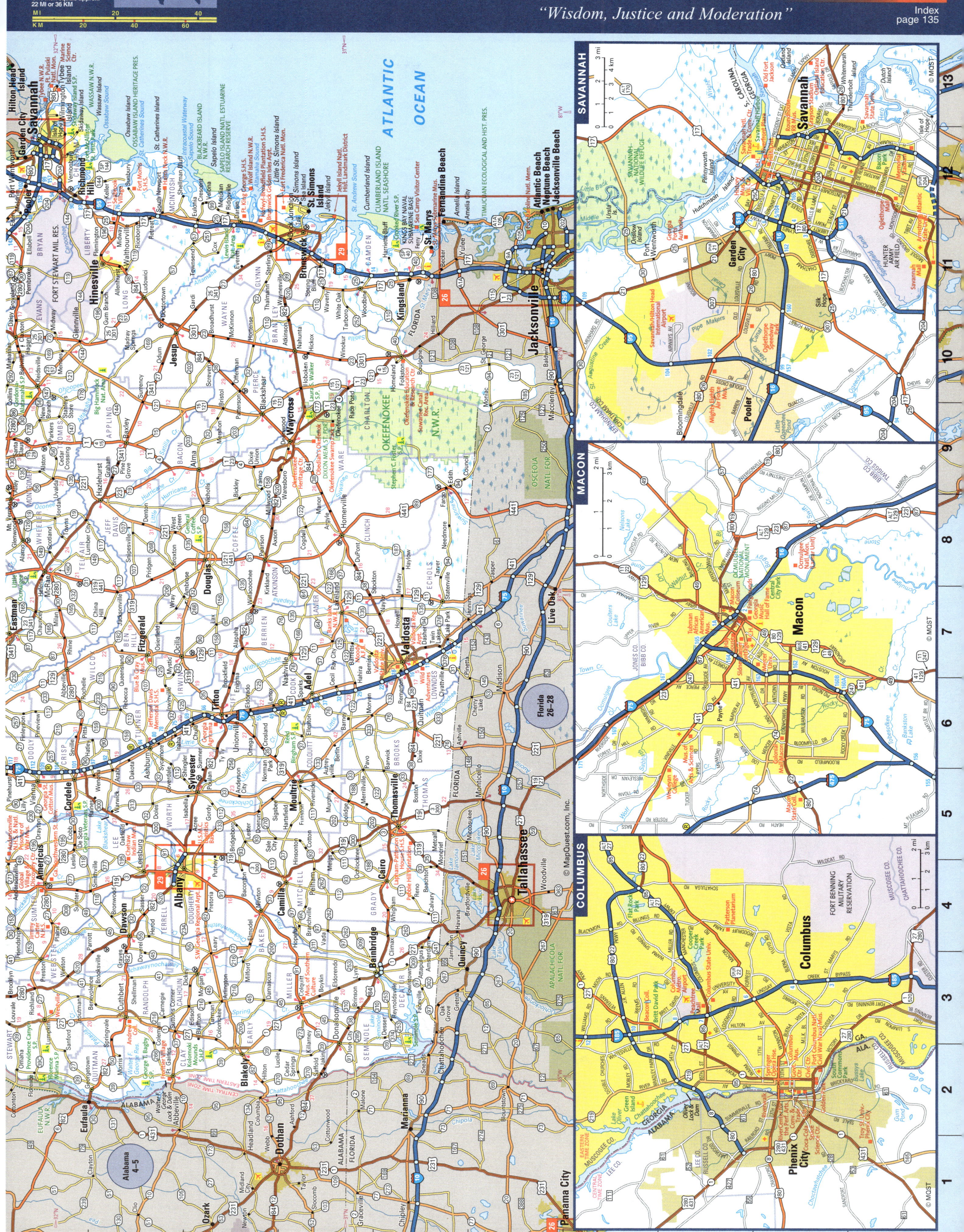

Hawaii

Index page 135

"The Life of the Land Is Perpetuated in Righteousness"

	HĀNA	HILO	HONOLULU	HO'OLEHUA	KAHULUI	KAILUA	KAILUA-KONA	LAHAINA	LANAI CITY	LIHUE	WAHIAWĀ	WAIMEA
HILO	149*		217*	169*	121*	235*	88	142*	155*	319*	234*	54
HONOLULU	129*	217*		54*	101*	14	185*	92*	74*	102*	23	172*
KAHULUI	42	121*	101*	76		119*	109*	23	57	202*	118*	79*
KAILUA-KONA	137*	88	185*	157*	109*	203*		132*	143*	285*	202*	39
LIHUE	230*	319*	102*	156*	202*	120*	285*	225*	176*		119*	174*

DISTANCES IN MILES

* DISTANCE INCLUDES AIR TRAVEL

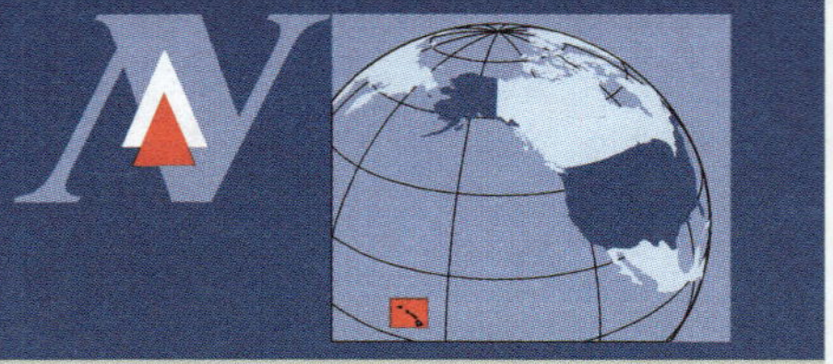

KAUA'I

PACIFIC OCEAN

HAWAI'IAN ISLANDS

PACIFIC OCEAN

MAUI-MOLOKA'I-LĀNA'I

O'AHU

PACIFIC OCEAN

HILO

HONOLULU

PACIFIC OCEAN

HAWAI'I

PACIFIC OCEAN

"It Is Perpetual"

Index page 135

	BOISE	COEUR D'ALENE	GRANGEVILLE	IDAHO FALLS	KETCHUM	LEWISTON	MISSOULA, MT	MOUNTAIN HOME	POCATELLO	SALMON	SANDPOINT	TWIN FALLS
BOISE		406	202	288	163	270	374	49	241	247	452	134
COEUR D'ALENE	406		186	476	485	118	167	499	526	307	48	584
IDAHO FALLS	288	476	483		153	532	311	240	53	168	523	162
LEWISTON	270	118	74	532	477		221	363	555	337	166	448
POCATELLO	241	526	440	53	190	555	360	193		217	572	116

DRIVING DISTANCES IN MILES

SEE ALSO MILEAGE AND DRIVING TIME MAP ON PAGE 144

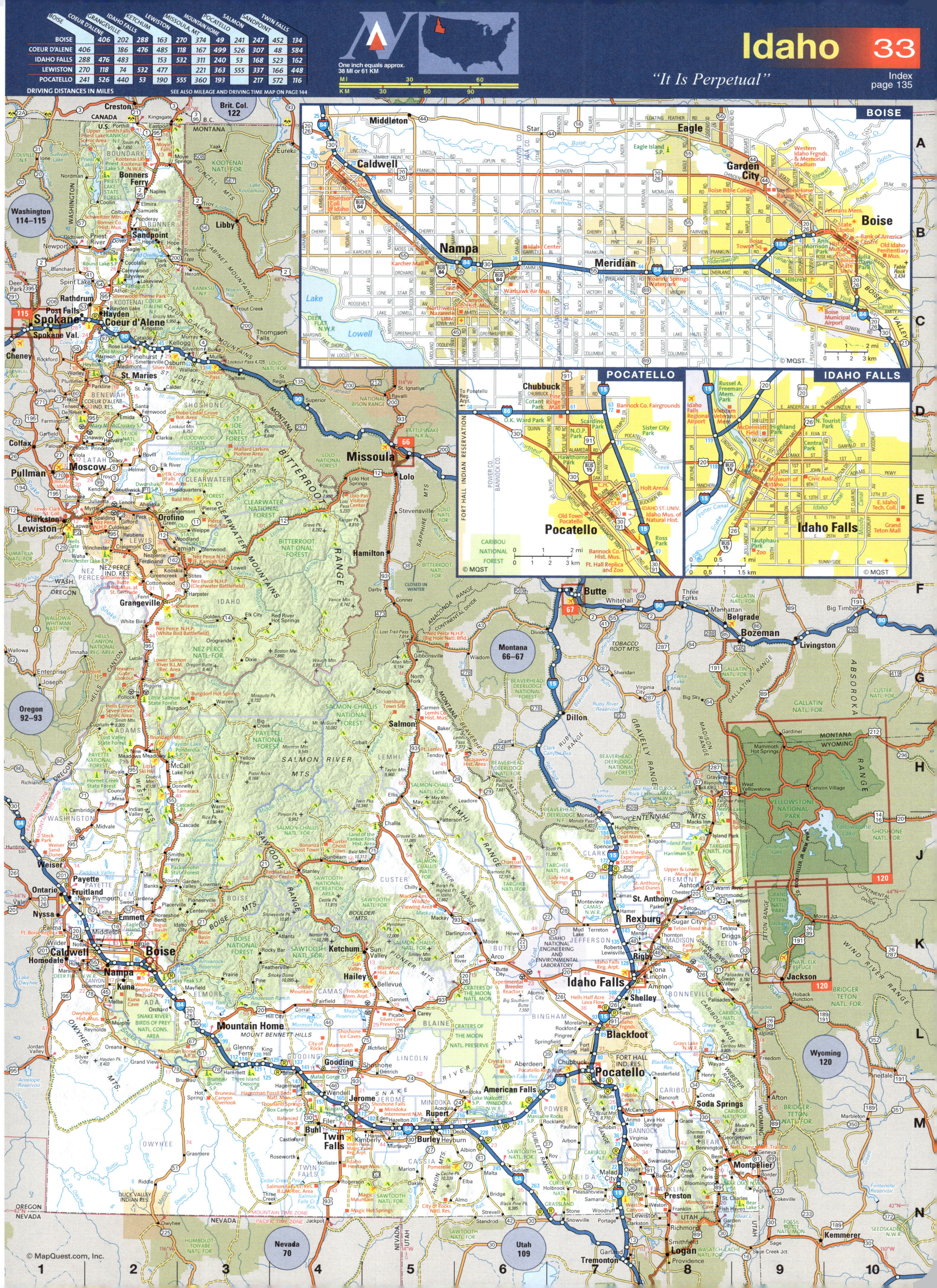

Index page 135

	BLOOMINGTON	CAIRO	CARBONDALE	CHAMPAIGN	CHICAGO	DECATUR	DUBUQUE, IA	EFFINGHAM	GALESBURG	JOLIET	KANKAKEE	MOUNT VERNON	PEORIA	QUINCY	ROCKFORD	ROCK ISLAND	ST. LOUIS, MO	SPRINGFIELD
CHAMPAIGN	54	241	199		141	52	263	77	141	115	79	145	94	197	189	191	179	87
CHICAGO	135	376	334	141		186	180	212	198	40	61	280	168	306	86	169	294	197
ROCKFORD	134	424	382	189	86	184	93	260	153	99	139	328	135	272		124	293	196
ST. LOUIS, MO	160	156	105	179	294	116	342	103	220	257	252	81	172	131	293	270		97
SPRINGFIELD	63	254	182	87	197	40	245	89	123	160	152	158	75	110	196	173	97	

DRIVING DISTANCES IN MILES

SEE ALSO MILEAGE AND DRIVING TIME MAP ON PAGE 144

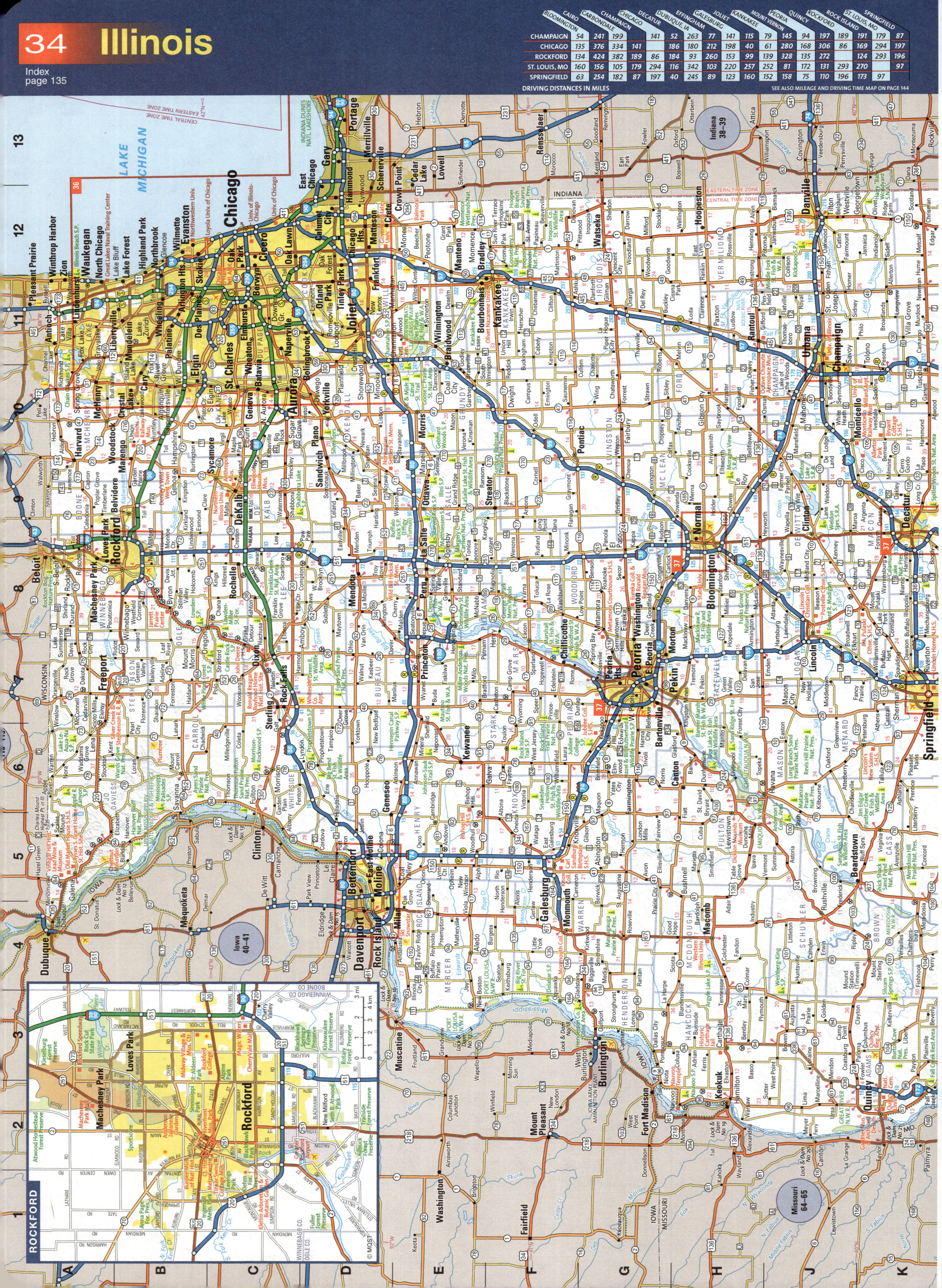

"State Sovereignty—National Unity"

Index page 135

One inch equals approx. 19 MI or 31 KM

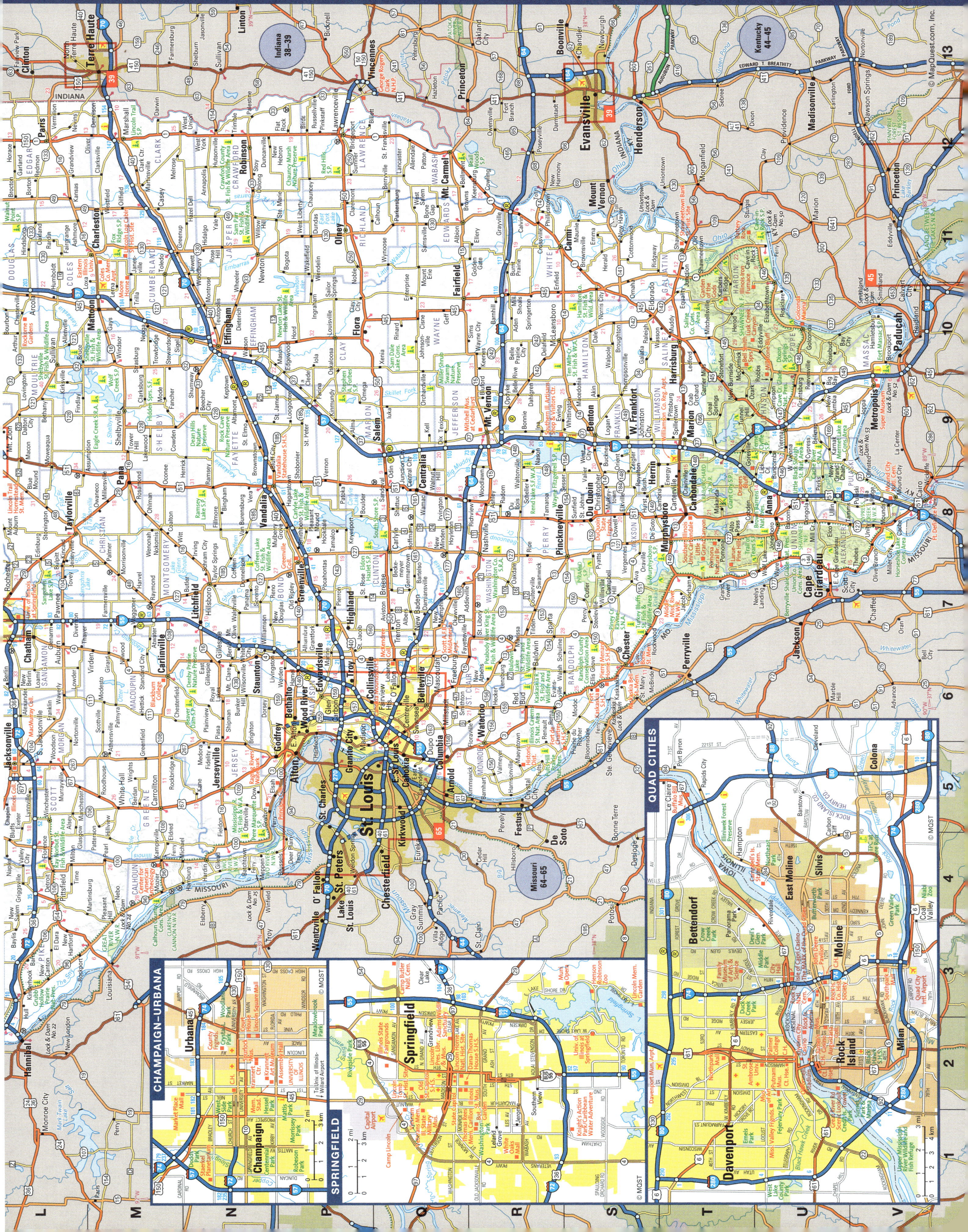

MI 0 10 20 30
KM 0 10 20 30 40

CHAMPAIGN-URBANA

SPRINGFIELD

QUAD CITIES

Chicago (IL)

Index page 135

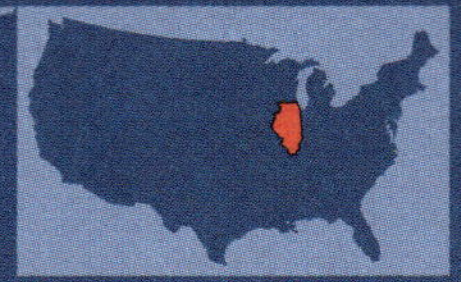

One inch equals approx. 5 MI or 8 KM

MI 4 8
KM 4 8 12

© MQST

LAKE MICHIGAN

Chicago

Waukegan
Gurnee
Park City
North Chicago
Lake Bluff
Lake Forest
Highwood
Highland Park
Deerfield
Northbrook
Glencoe
Winnetka
Wilmette
Kenilworth
Glenview
Northfield
Skokie
Evanston
Morton Grove
Niles
Lincolnwood
Park Ridge
Des Plaines
Mount Prospect
Arlington Heights
Wheeling
Prospect Hts.
Buffalo Grove
Lincolnshire
Vernon Hills
Mundelein
Libertyville
Grayslake
Round Lake Beach
Lake Villa
Fox Lake
Antioch
Johnsburg
McHenry
Crystal Lake
Cary
Algonquin
Carpentersville
Barrington
Palatine
Inverness
Rolling Meadows
Hoffman Estates
Schaumburg
Streamwood
Elgin
South Elgin
Bartlett
Hanover Park
Roselle
Bloomingdale
Itasca
Wood Dale
Elk Grove Village
Bensenville
Schiller Park
Franklin Park
Norridge
Harwood Hts.
River Grove
Elmwood Park
Northlake
Melrose Park
Oak Park
Berwyn
Cicero
Maywood
Bellwood
Berkeley
Hillside
Westchester
Broadview
Forest Park
River Forest
Elmhurst
Addison
Villa Park
Lombard
Glen Ellyn
Wheaton
Winfield
West Chicago
Carol Stream
Glendale Heights
St. Charles
Geneva
Batavia
Warrenville
North Aurora
Aurora
Naperville
Lisle
Downers Grove
Westmont
Woodridge
Darien
Oak Brook
Hinsdale
Clarendon Hills
Burr Ridge
La Grange
Western Springs
Countryside
Riverside
Brookfield
Lyons
Stickney
Summit
Justice
Bridgeview
Burbank
Oak Lawn
Evergreen Park
Hickory Hills
Palos Hills
Chicago Ridge
Worth
Alsip
Blue Island
Calumet Park
Palos Heights
Crestwood
Robbins
Midlothian
Oak Forest
Orland Park
Orland Hills
Tinley Park
Country Club Hills
Markham
Harvey
Riverdale
Dolton
Calumet City
Hammond
East Chicago
Whiting
Lansing
Homewood
Flossmoor
Hazel Crest
S. Holland
Thornton
Glenwood
Chicago Heights
Park Forest
Matteson
Richton Park
University Park
Steger
Sauk Village
Crete
Dyer
Munster
Highland
Griffith
Schererville
St. John
Frankfort
Mokena
New Lenox
Joliet
Shorewood
Plainfield
Romeoville
Bolingbrook
Lemont
Homer Glen
Lockport
Crest Hill
Oswego
Montgomery
Boulder Hill
Plattville

A B C D E F G H J K L M N

1 2 3 4 5 6 7 8 9 10

DOWNTOWN CHICAGO
PEORIA
SOUTH BEND
DECATUR
DOWNTOWN INDIANAPOLIS
BLOOMINGTON-NORMAL
INDIANAPOLIS
LAKE MICHIGAN
© MQST

Index page 136

	ANDERSON	BLOOMINGTON	COLUMBUS	CRAWFORDSVILLE	EVANSVILLE	FORT WAYNE	GARY	GREENSBURG	INDIANAPOLIS	KOKOMO	LAFAYETTE	LOUISVILLE, KY	MUNCIE	PLYMOUTH	RICHMOND	SOUTH BEND	TERRE HAUTE	VINCENNES
EVANSVILLE	211	117	175	164		296	324	195	166	219	194	114	228	281	241	305	107	51
FORT WAYNE	86	175	169	163	296		143	149	128	85	116	236	75	65	95	79	207	253
GARY	180	192	200	122	324	143		210	153	127	91	268	198	66	226	62	161	268
INDIANAPOLIS	43	47	45	47	166	128	153	55		52	66	112	61	114	74	138	77	123
SOUTH BEND	129	187	187	136	305	79	62	187	138	86	104	255	141	24	172		217	263

DRIVING DISTANCES IN MILES

SEE ALSO MILEAGE AND DRIVING TIME MAP ON PAGE 144

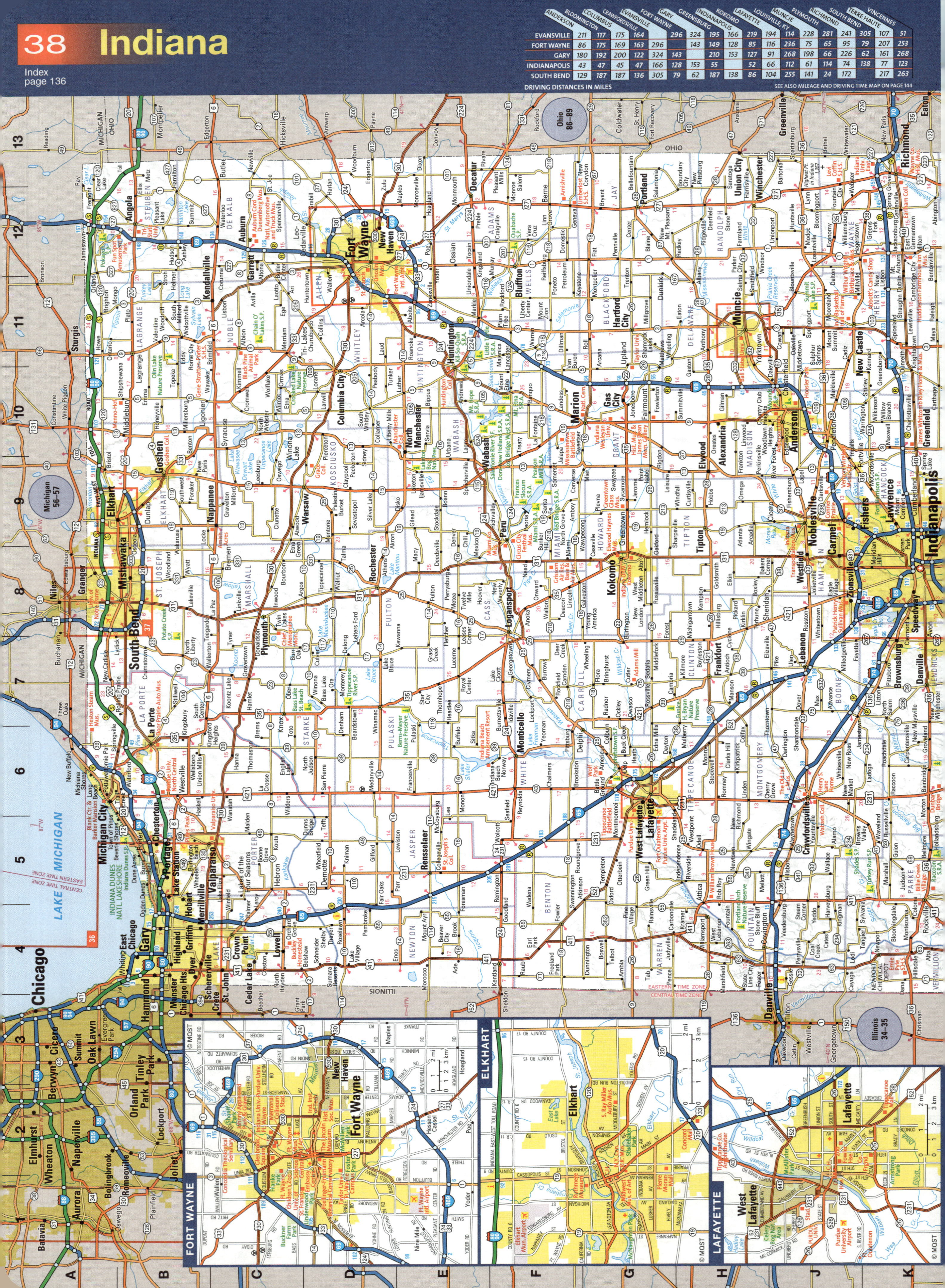

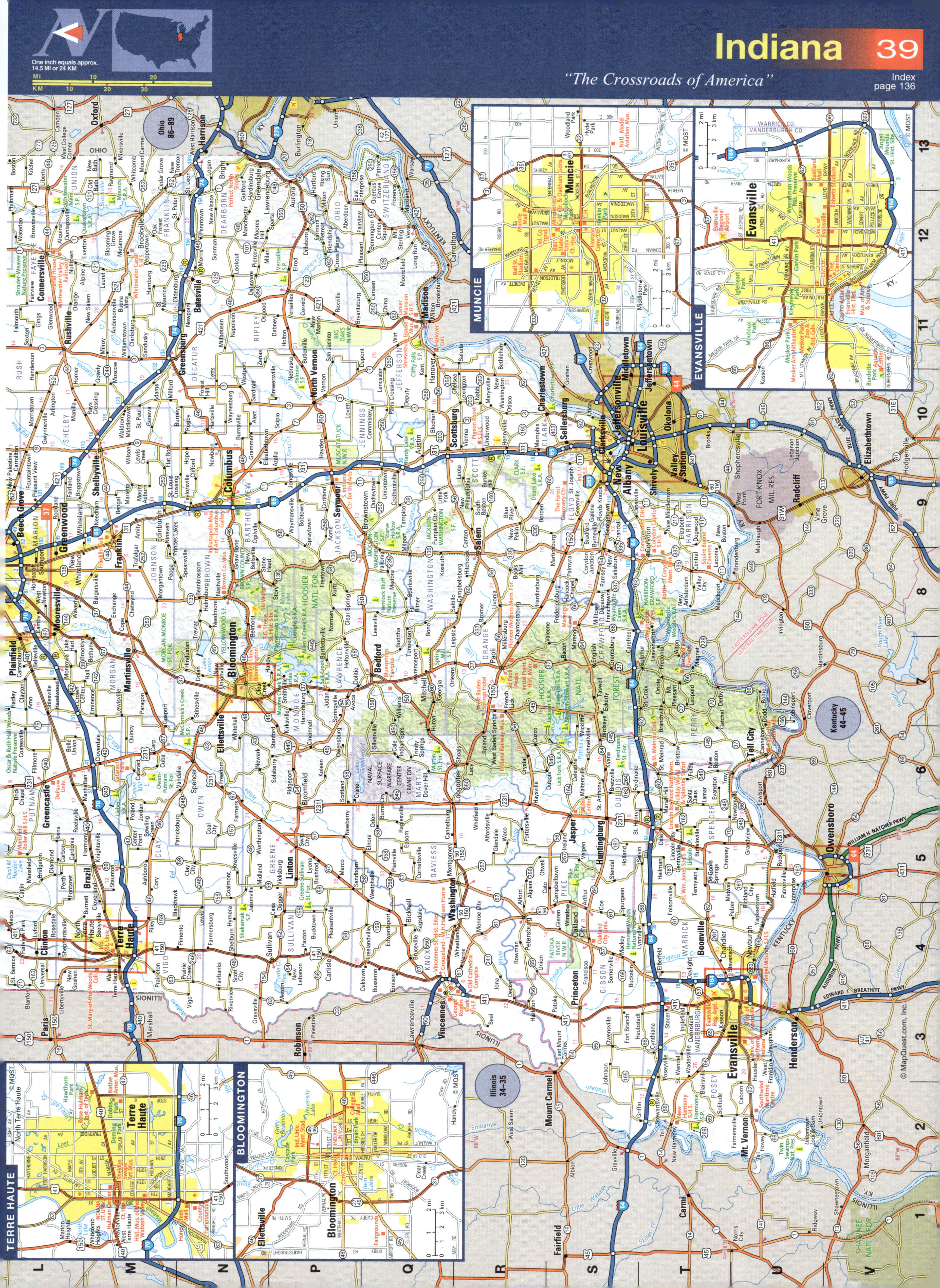

Indiana
39
"The Crossroads of America"
Index page 136
One inch equals approx. 14.5 MI or 24 KM
MI 10 20
KM 10 20 30
Ohio 86–89
Kentucky 44–45
Illinois 34–35
MUNCIE
EVANSVILLE
TERRE HAUTE
BLOOMINGTON
Muncie
Evansville
Terre Haute
Bloomington
Louisville
Owensboro
Henderson
Columbus
Bedford
Seymour
Jasper
Vincennes
Washington
Madison
Greensburg
Batesville
Connersville
Rushville
Shelbyville
Franklin
Martinsville
Greenwood
Mooresville
Plainfield
Brazil
Clinton
Sullivan
Linton
Princeton
Boonville
Mt. Vernon
Salem
Corydon
Scottsburg
North Vernon
New Albany
Jeffersonville
Elizabethtown
Radcliff
Tell City
Huntingburg
Paoli
Spencer
Ellettsville
Greencastle
Paris
Robinson
Mount Carmel
Fairfield
Carmi
Harrison
Oxford
FORT KNOX MIL. RES.
HOOSIER NATL. FOREST
© MapQuest.com, Inc.

Index page 136

	Ames	Burlington	Carroll	Cedar Rapids	Council Bluffs	Creston	Davenport	Decorah	Des Moines	Dubuque	Fort Dodge	Iowa City	Marshalltown	Mason City	Ottumwa	Sioux City	Spencer	Waterloo
COUNCIL BLUFFS	165	323	101	261		99	303	347	130	327	160	245	181	258	216	101	157	238
DES MOINES	34	157	90	129	130	81	171	215		196	94	113	49	126	86	202	188	106
IOWA CITY	136	82	195	28	245	195	59	131	113	84	196		98	157	83	316	267	78
SIOUX CITY	171	394	105	332	101	189	375	303	202	321	120	316	252	218	287		103	228
WATERLOO	95	157	160	53	238	189	137	79	106	93	108	78	58	79	125	228	189	

DRIVING DISTANCES IN MILES

SEE ALSO MILEAGE AND DRIVING TIME MAP ON PAGE 144

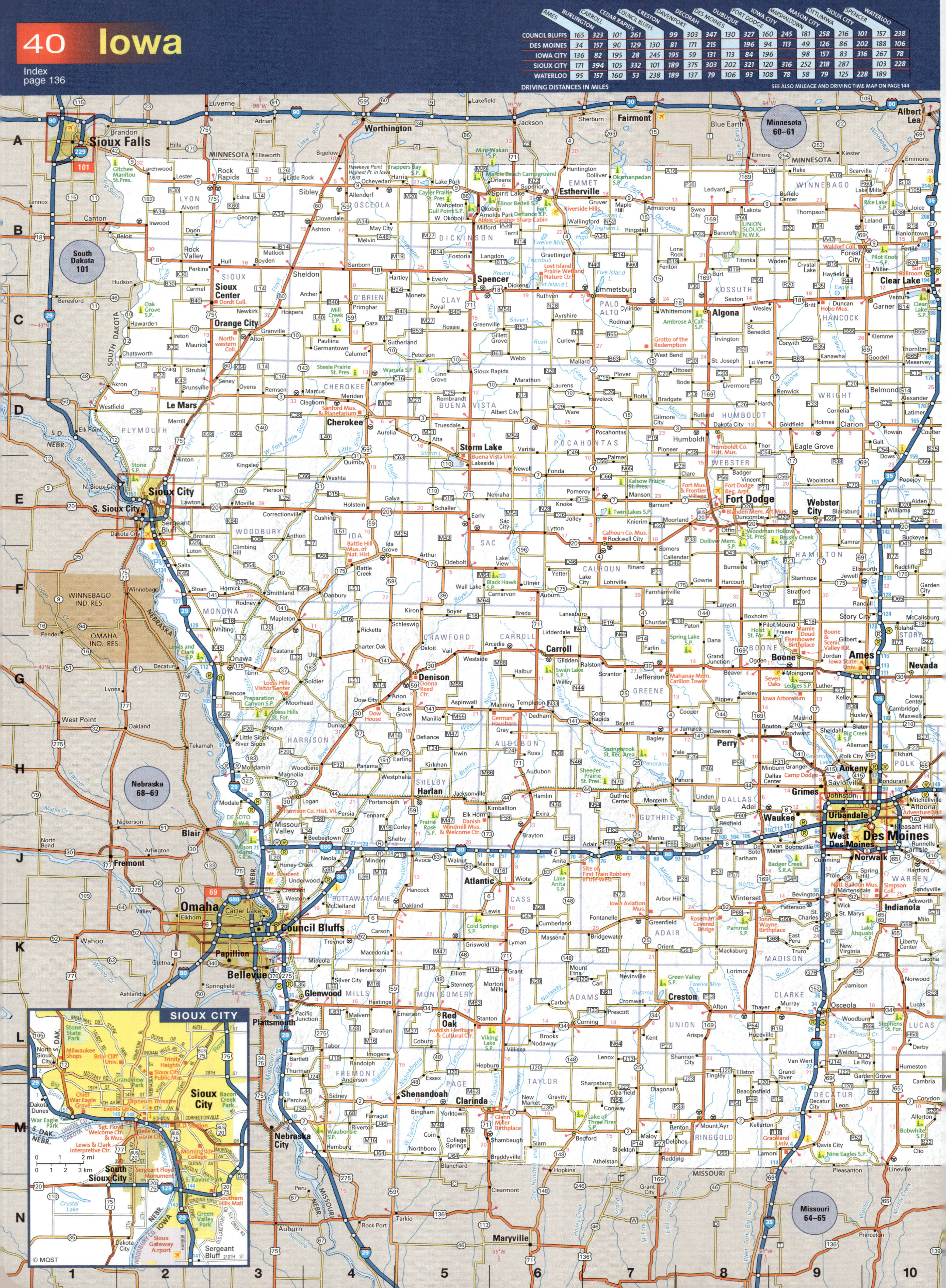

"Our Liberties We Prize and Our Rights We Will Maintain"

Index page 136

One inch equals approx. 17.5 MI or 28.5 KM

MI 0 15 30

KM 0 15 30 45

DES MOINES

CEDAR RAPIDS

Minnesota 60–61

Wisconsin 118–119

Illinois 34–35

Missouri 64–65

	Arkansas City	Atchison	Colby	Dodge City	Emporia	Garden City	Great Bend	Hays	Hutchinson	Independence	Iola	Kansas City	Lawrence	Liberal	Manhattan	Salina	Topeka	Wichita
DODGE CITY	141	107	315		238	52	83	106	120	270	264	333	298	83	232	164	271	153
KANSAS CITY	247	50	369	333	106	373	250	261	240	162	105		35	402	117	172	61	192
SALINA	151	160	200	164	118	204	81	93	68	206	187	172	137	247	72		111	92
TOPEKA	193	49	308	271	58	311	188	200	178	135	100	61	26	347	55	111		137
WICHITA	61	186	289	153	85	205	119	181	51	118	112	192	159	210	131	92	137	

DRIVING DISTANCES IN MILES

SEE ALSO MILEAGE AND DRIVING TIME MAP ON PAGE 144

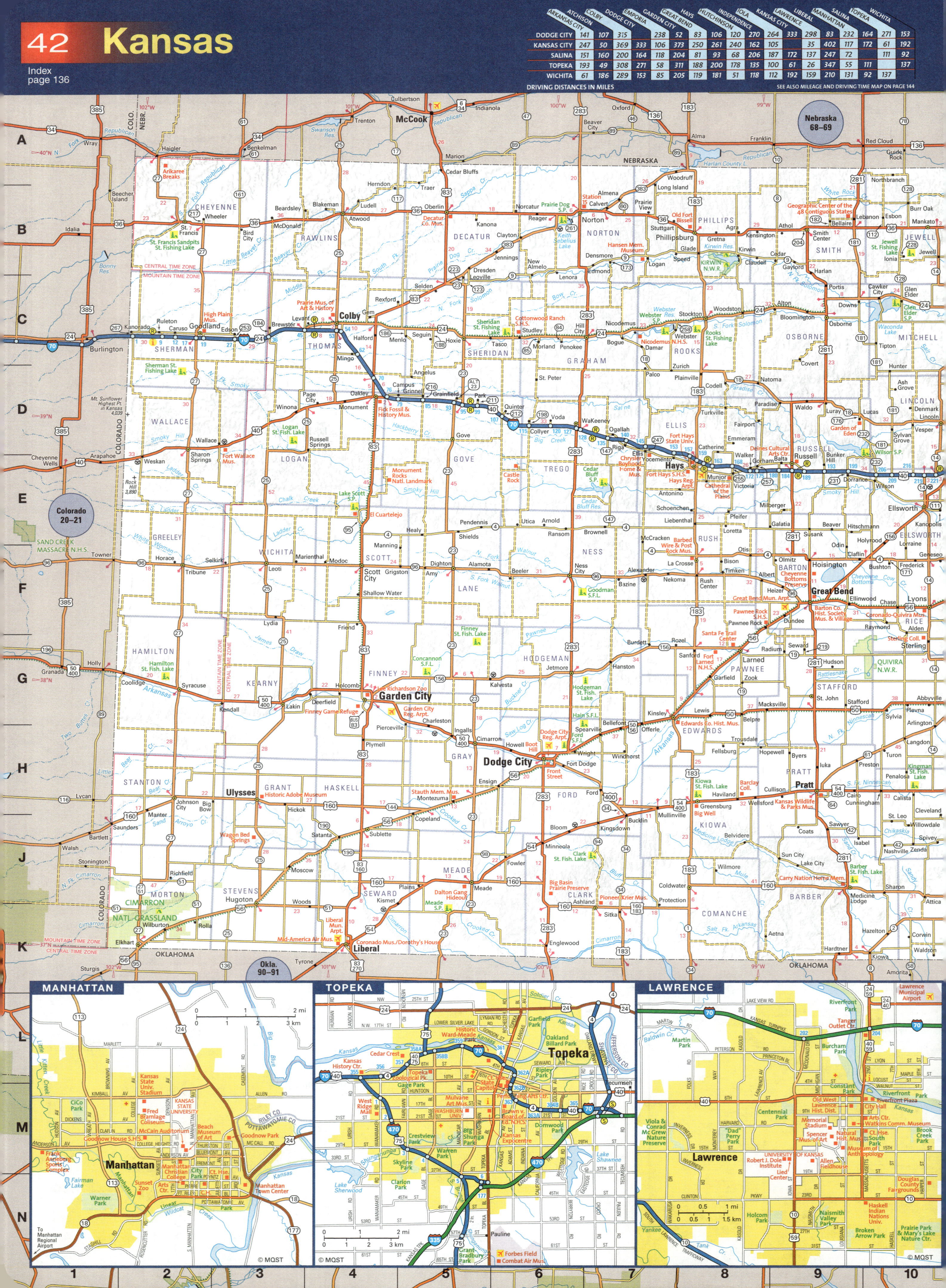

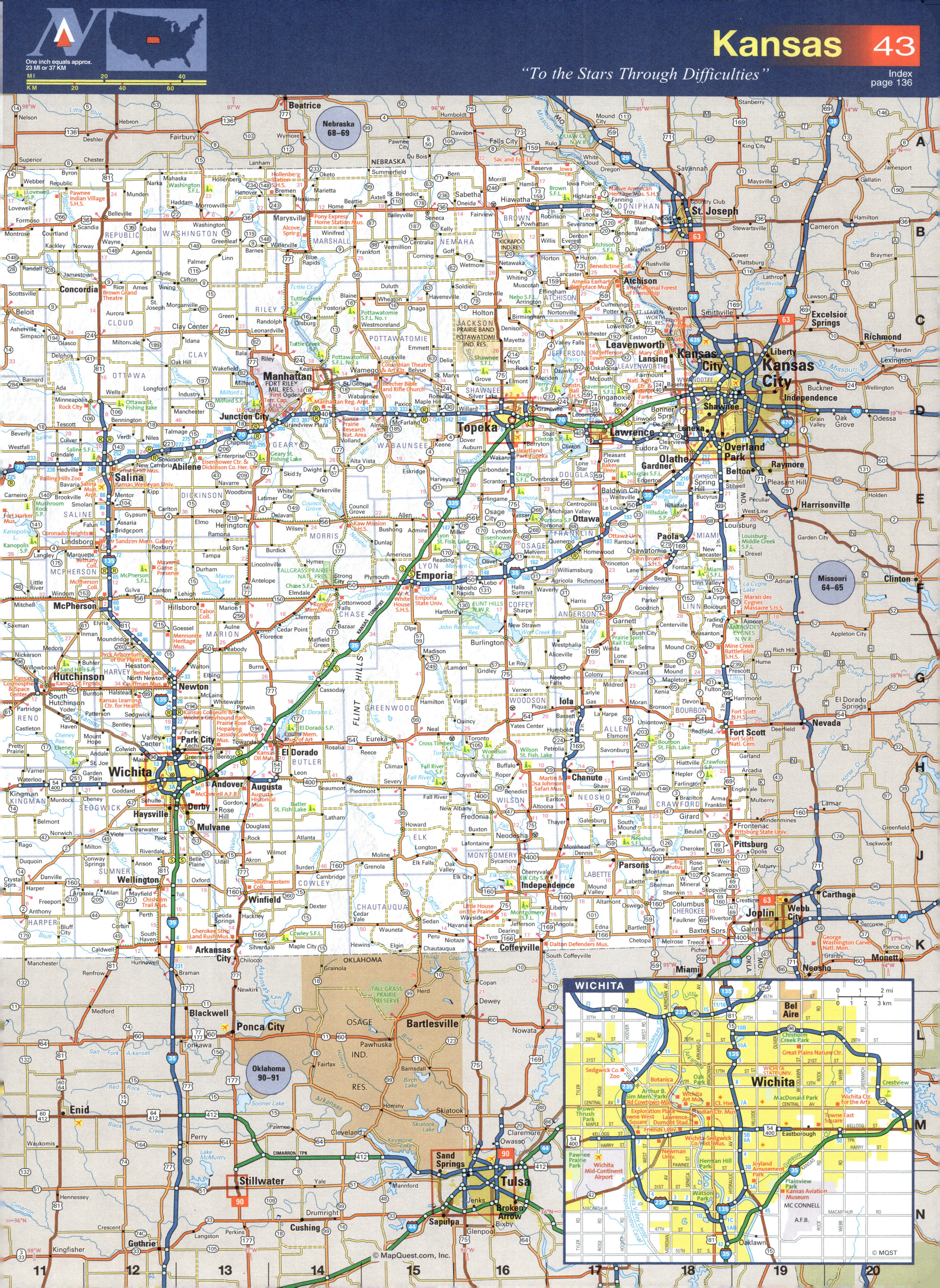

One inch equals approx. 23 MI or 37 KM
Kansas
43
"To the Stars Through Difficulties"
Index page 136
Nebraska 68–69
Missouri 64–65
Oklahoma 90–91
WICHITA
Topeka
Kansas City
Wichita
Manhattan
Salina
Lawrence
Leavenworth
Emporia
Hutchinson
St. Joseph
Joplin
Tulsa
Ponca City
Bartlesville
Stillwater
Enid
© MapQuest.com, Inc.
© MQST

Index page 136

	ASHLAND	BOWLING GREEN	CINCINNATI, OH	ELIZABETHTOWN	FRANKFORT	GLASGOW	HAZARD	HENDERSON	HOPKINSVILLE	LEXINGTON	LONDON	LOUISVILLE	MAYFIELD	MAYSVILLE	MIDDLESBORO	OWENSBORO	PADUCAH	PIKEVILLE
BOWLING GREEN	274		212	70	161	36	200	107	63	157	145	112	146	222	203	76	135	265
LEXINGTON	119	157	85	89	29	138	120	201	215		77	80	273	67	136	183	262	142
LOUISVILLE	194	112	100	44	54	92	194	123	170	80	156		228	141	214	109	217	217
OWENSBORO	300	76	206	95	161	111	275	30	80	183	221	109	138	248	279		127	323
PADUCAH	379	135	317	175	266	173	337	121	72	262	283	217	24	327	373	127		402

DRIVING DISTANCES IN MILES

SEE ALSO MILEAGE AND DRIVING TIME MAP ON PAGE 144

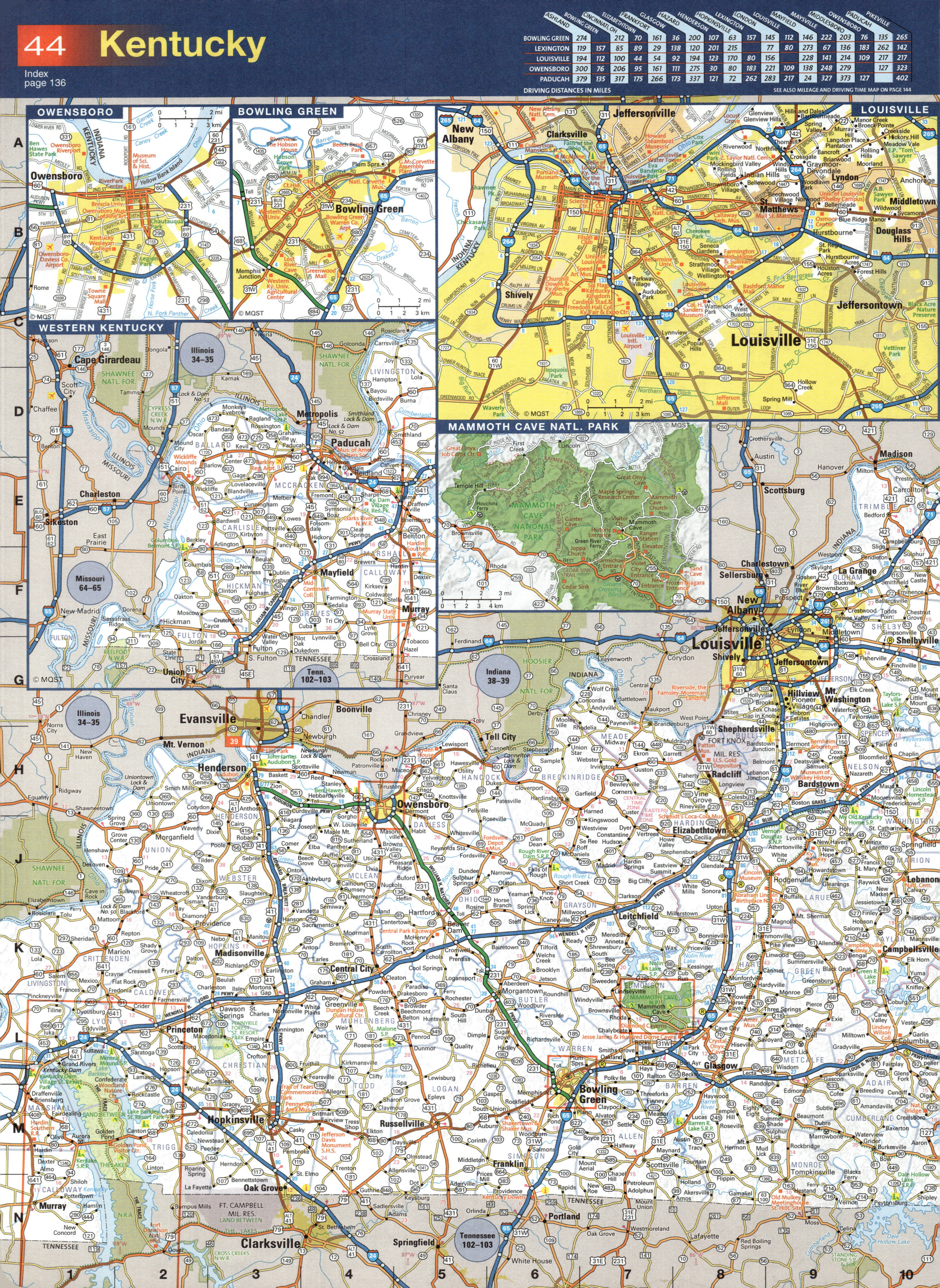

One inch equals approx. 17 MI or 27.5 KM

Kentucky

"United We Stand, Divided We Fall"

Index page 136

LEXINGTON

LAND BETWEEN THE LAKES

FRANKFORT

Indiana 38–39

Ohio 86–89

West Virginia 117

Virginia 112–113

Tennessee 102–103

A B C D E F G H J K L M N

11 12 13 14 15 16 17 18 19 20

Louisiana

Index page 136

	ALEXANDRIA	BATON ROUGE	DE RIDDER	FERRIDAY	HAMMOND	HOUMA	LAFAYETTE	LAKE CHARLES	MONROE	NATCHITOCHES	NEW IBERIA	NEW ORLEANS	OPELOUSAS	RUSTON	SHREVEPORT	SLIDELL	TALLULAH	WINNFIELD
BATON ROUGE	140		176	104	51	101	60	132	188	195	79	91	80	233	261	97	163	188
LAFAYETTE	87	60	119	152	106	101		76	183	142	20	147	27	180	208	152	214	135
MONROE	96	188	170	85	248	283	183	196		100	202	302	156	37	103	298	55	64
NEW ORLEANS	227	91	262	191	57	57	147	219	302	282	166		167	339	348	31	247	275
SHREVEPORT	121	261	137	188	308	309	208	186	103	73	227	348	182	71		354	158	105

DRIVING DISTANCES IN MILES

SEE ALSO MILEAGE AND DRIVING TIME MAP ON PAGE 144

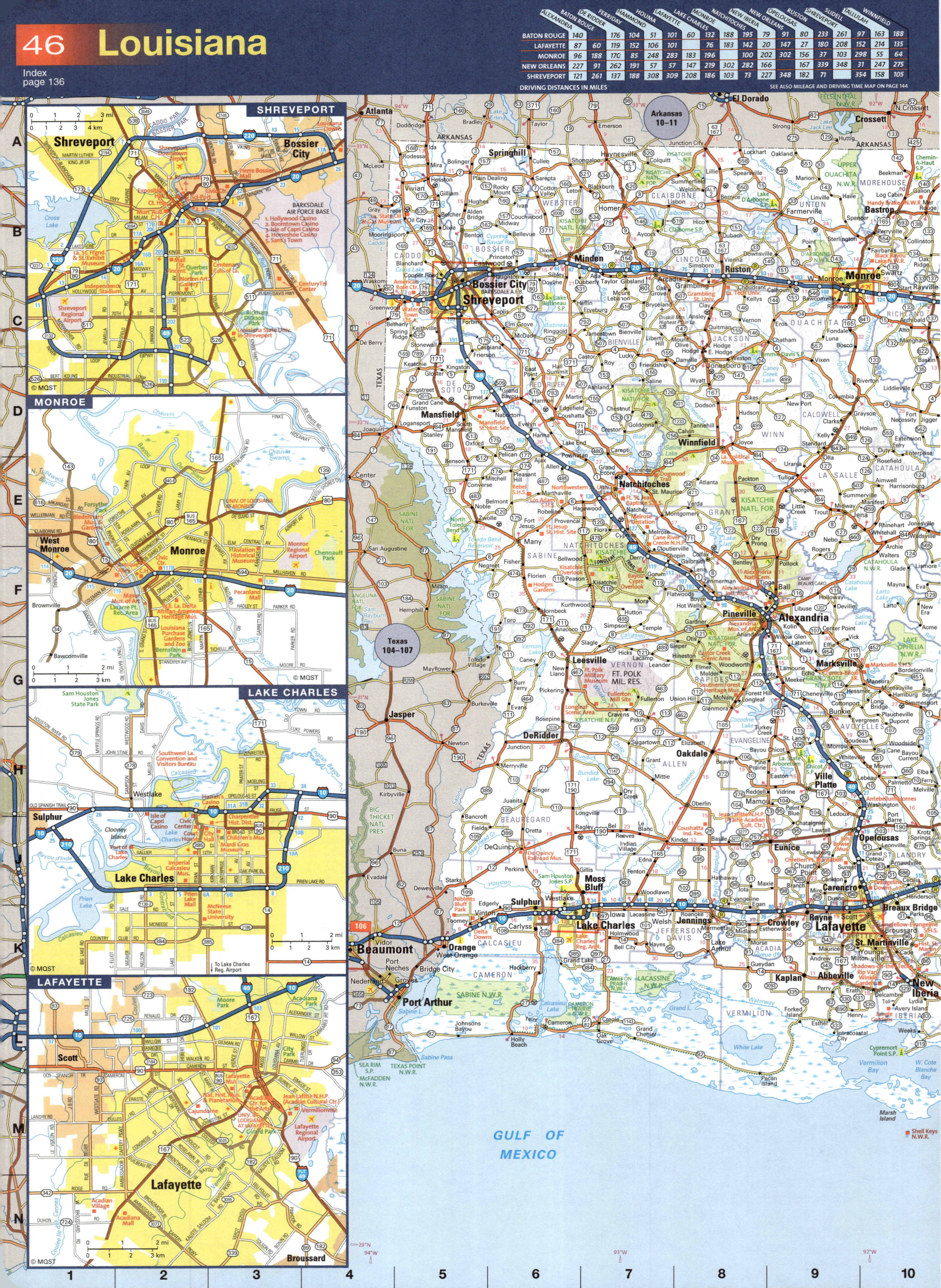

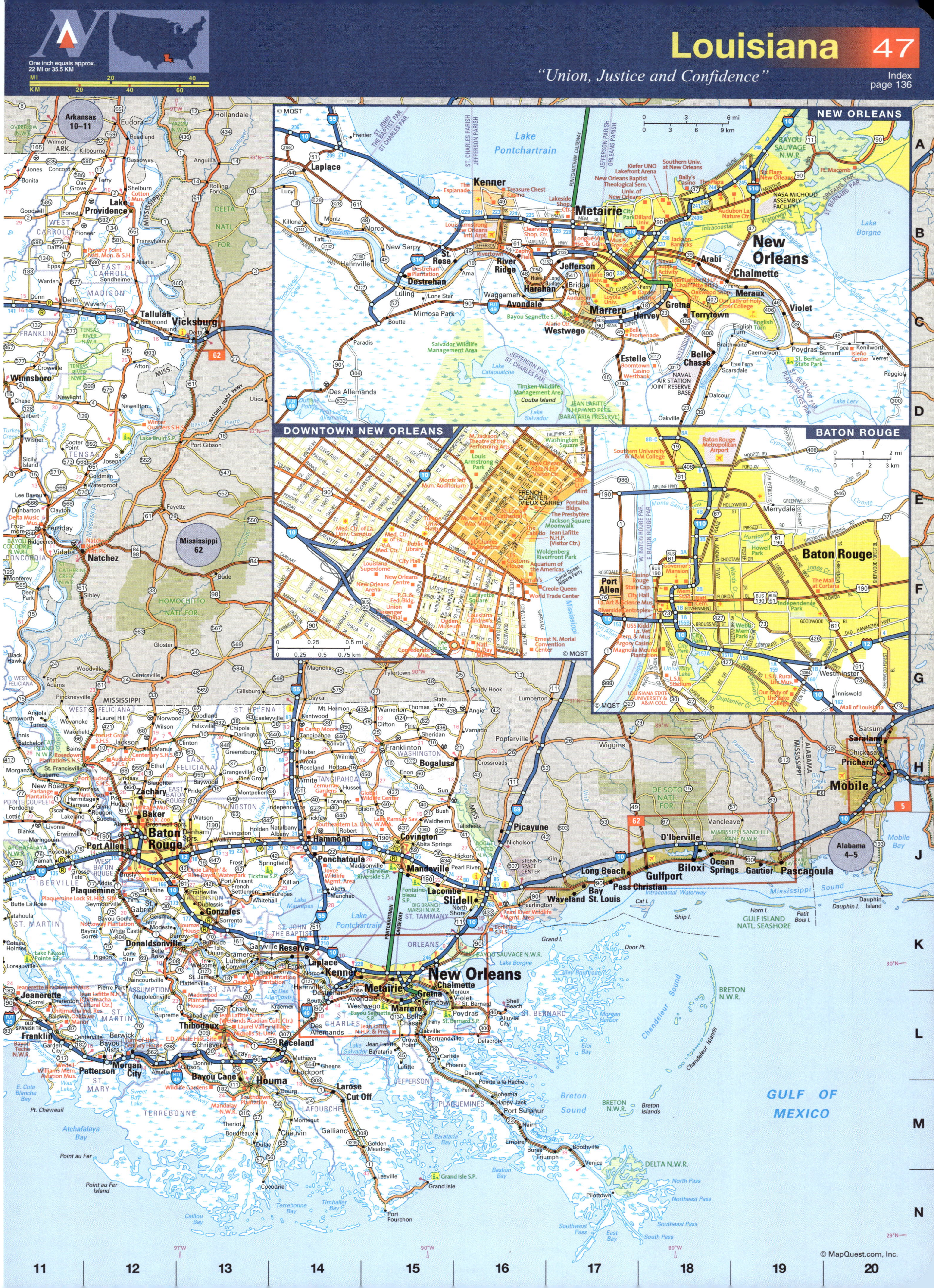
Louisiana
47
"Union, Justice and Confidence"
Index page 136
One inch equals approx. 22 MI or 35.5 KM
NEW ORLEANS
DOWNTOWN NEW ORLEANS
BATON ROUGE
Lake Pontchartrain
Kenner
Metairie
New Orleans
Chalmette
Arabi
Meraux
Violet
Harahan
Jefferson
Gretna
Terrytown
Marrero
Harvey
Westwego
Avondale
River Ridge
Laplace
Destrehan
St. Rose
Norco
Hahnville
Luling
Boutte
Paradis
Des Allemands
Estelle
Belle Chasse
Lake Borgne
Lake Cataouatche
Lake Salvador
Port Allen
Baton Rouge
Merrydale
Westminster
Inniswold
Arkansas 10-11
Mississippi 62
Alabama 4-5
Vicksburg
Tallulah
Natchez
Vidalia
Winnsboro
Ferriday
Lake Providence
Eudora
Hollandale
Homochitto Natl. For.
Delta Natl. For.
De Soto Natl. For.
Zachary
Baker
Denham Springs
Hammond
Ponchatoula
Covington
Mandeville
Slidell
Bogalusa
Picayune
Gulfport
Biloxi
D'Iberville
Ocean Springs
Gautier
Pascagoula
Mobile
Prichard
Saraland
Long Beach
Pass Christian
Bay St. Louis
Waveland
Plaquemine
Gonzales
Donaldsonville
Reserve
Thibodaux
Raceland
Houma
Bayou Cane
Morgan City
Patterson
Franklin
Jeanerette
Larose
Cut Off
Galliano
Port Sulphur
Chandeleur Sound
Breton Sound
Chandeleur Islands
Gulf of Mexico
Atchafalaya Bay
Terrebonne Bay
Timbalier Bay
Barataria Bay
Grand Isle
Port Fourchon
Mississippi Sound
Lake Maurepas
Gulf Islands Natl. Seashore
Delta N.W.R.
Breton N.W.R.
© MapQuest.com, Inc.
A
B
C
D
E
F
G
H
J
K
L
M
N
11
12
13
14
15
16
17
18
19
20

Index page 137

	AUGUSTA	BANGOR	BAR HARBOR	BRUNSWICK	CALAIS	FARMINGTON	FORT KENT	GREENVILLE	HOULTON	LEWISTON	MACHIAS	MILLINOCKET	PORTLAND	PORTSMOUTH, NH	PRESQUE ISLE	ROCKLAND	SACO	WATERVILLE
AUGUSTA		77	120	32	173	65	269	99	196	35	161	149	58	110	236	43	74	20
BANGOR	77		45	106	97	80	195	74	122	108	85	75	131	184	162	58	147	56
CALAIS	173	97	112	203		177	189	160	91	205	55	112	228	281	133	155	244	153
HOULTON	196	122	166	226	91	200	98	155		228	126	73	251	304	42	182	267	176
PORTLAND	58	131	175	27	228	81	324	153	251	36	216	203		53	291	78	16	84

DRIVING DISTANCES IN MILES

SEE ALSO MILEAGE AND DRIVING TIME MAP ON PAGE 144

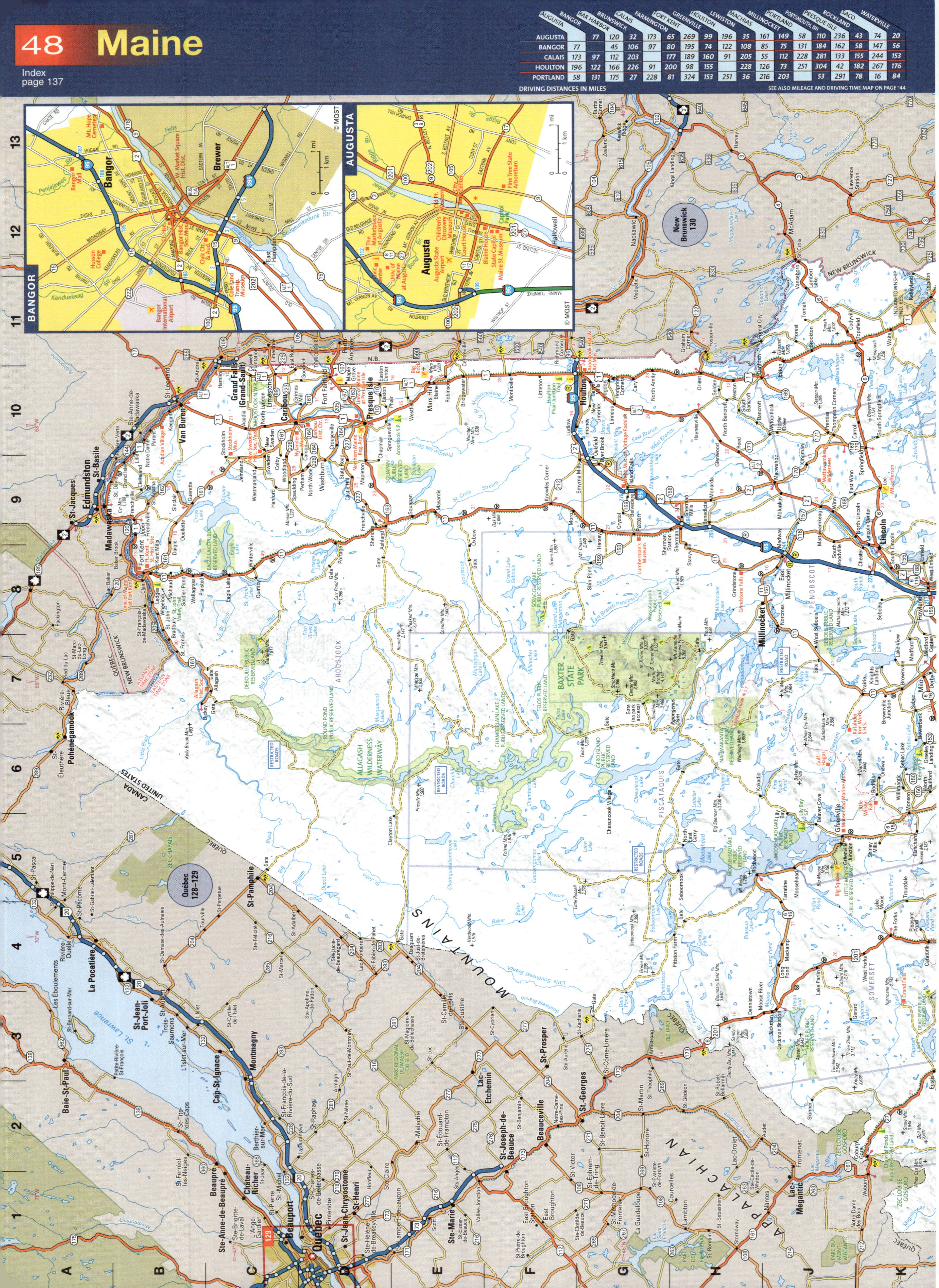

One inch equals approx. 15.5 MI or 25.5 KM

MI 0 10 20 30

KM 0 10 20 30 40

ACADIA NATIONAL PARK

PORTLAND

LEWISTON–AUBURN

ATLANTIC OCEAN

Gulf of Maine

Index page 137

	ABERDEEN	ANNAPOLIS	BALTIMORE	CAMBRIDGE	CHESTERTOWN	CUMBERLAND	EASTON	FREDERICK	HAGERSTOWN	HANCOCK	LEXINGTON PARK	OCEAN CITY	POCOMOKE CITY	ROCKVILLE	ST. CHARLES	SALISBURY	WASHINGTON, DC	WESTMINSTER
ANNAPOLIS	54		25	55	45	162	38	73	98	124	66	108	112	47	47	83	31	56
BALTIMORE	35	25		78	68	140	61	51	76	102	95	131	135	45	57	106	38	39
HAGERSTOWN	109	98	76	153	143	67	136	28		29	142	206	211	54	103	182	70	50
SALISBURY	124	83	106	32	81	246	47	156	182	207	149	30	29	130	130		115	138
WASHINGTON, DC	71	31	38	87	76	134	70	44	70	96	63	139	144	19	25	115		53

DRIVING DISTANCES IN MILES

SEE ALSO MILEAGE AND DRIVING TIME MAP ON PAGE 144

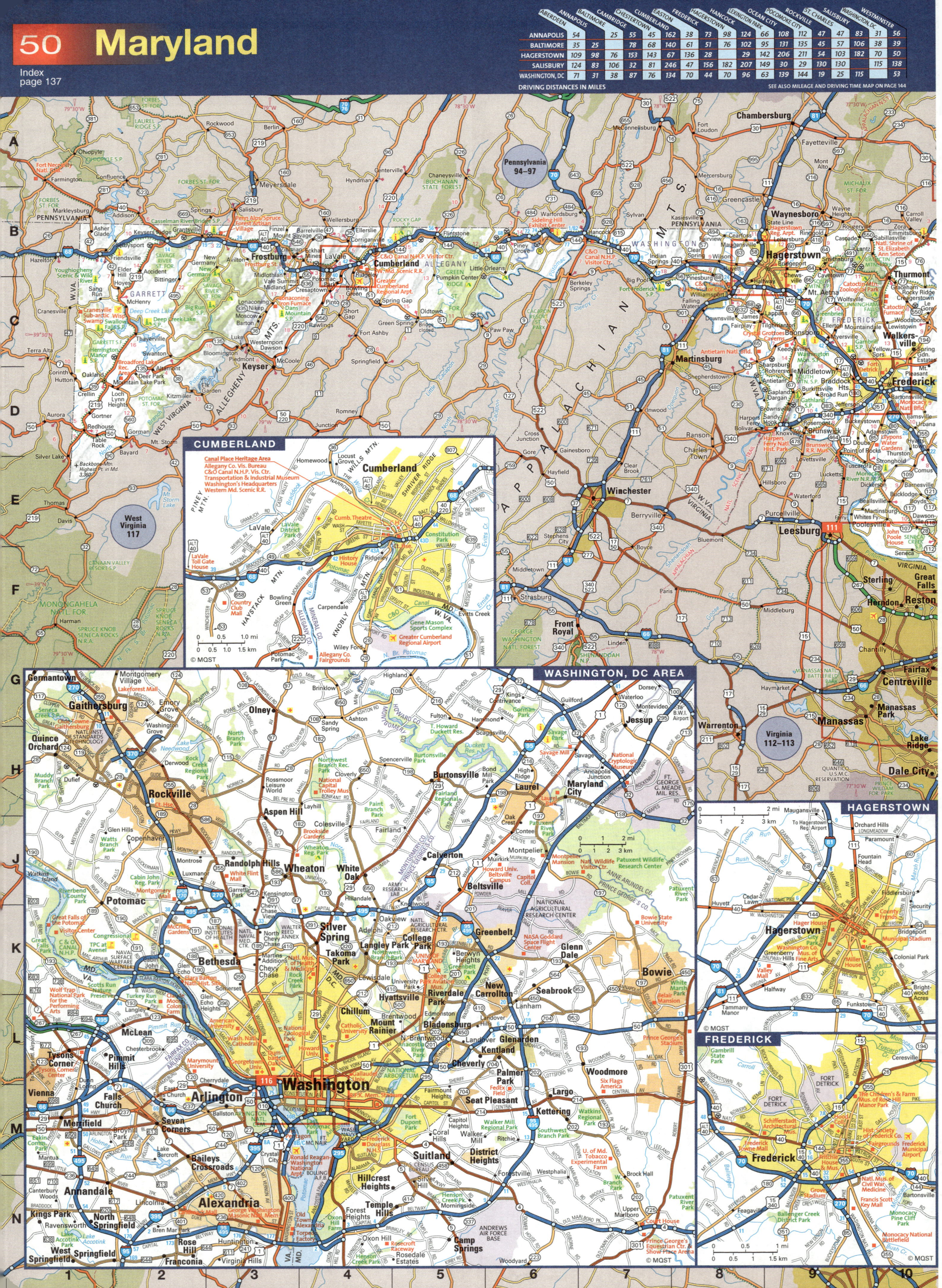

One inch equals approx. 12 MI or 19 KM
"Manly Deeds, Womanly Words"
Philadelphia
Baltimore
Washington
Annapolis
Wilmington
Dover
Salisbury
Pennsylvania 94–97
New Jersey 72–73
Delaware 24
Virginia 112–113
DC 116
Chesapeake Bay
Delaware Bay
ATLANTIC OCEAN
ANNAPOLIS
© MQST
© MapQuest.com, Inc.

Baltimore (MD)

Index page 137

One inch equals approx. 3 MI or 4.5 KM

MI 2 4
KM 2 4 6

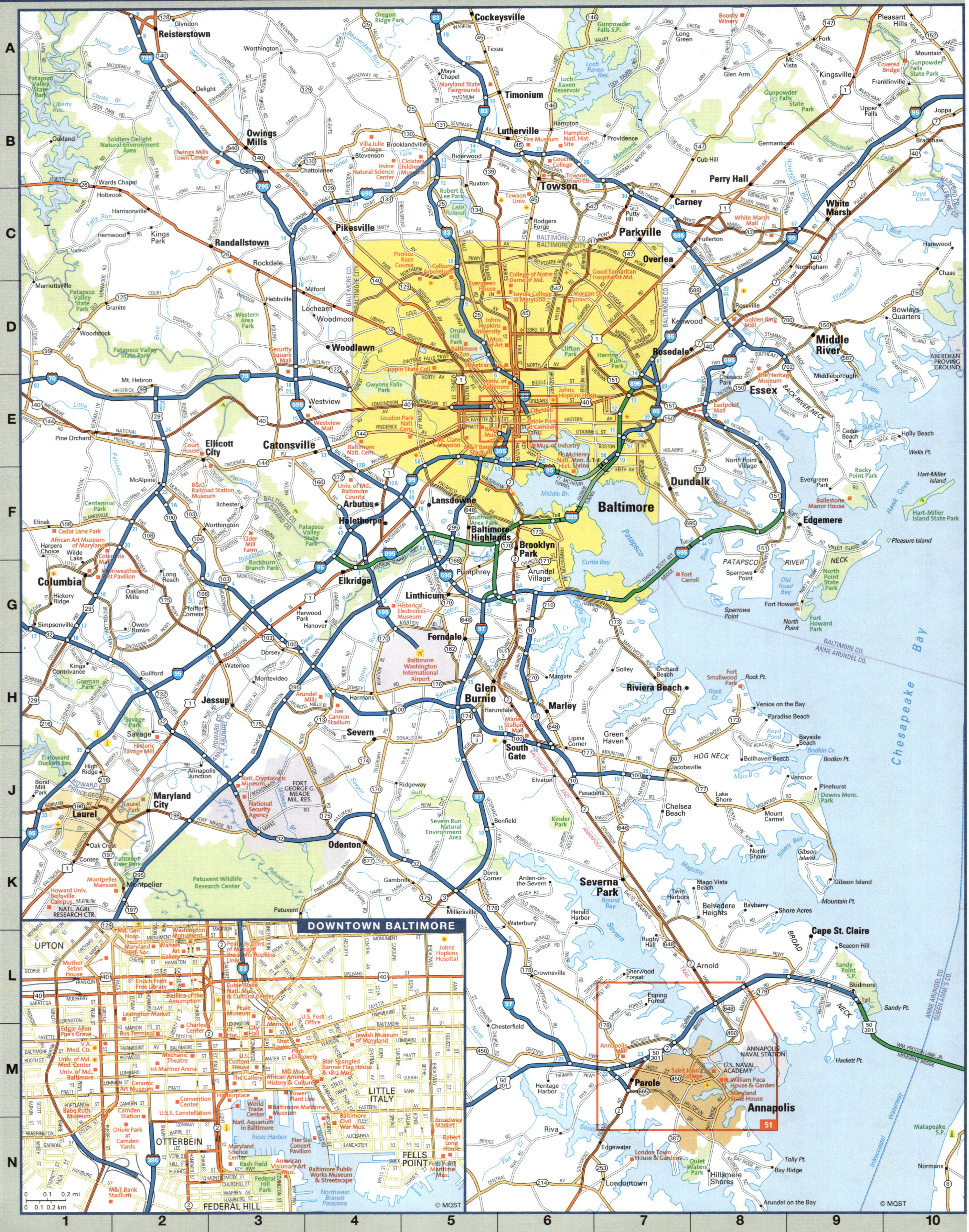

DOWNTOWN BALTIMORE

One inch equals approx. 2.5 MI or 4 KM

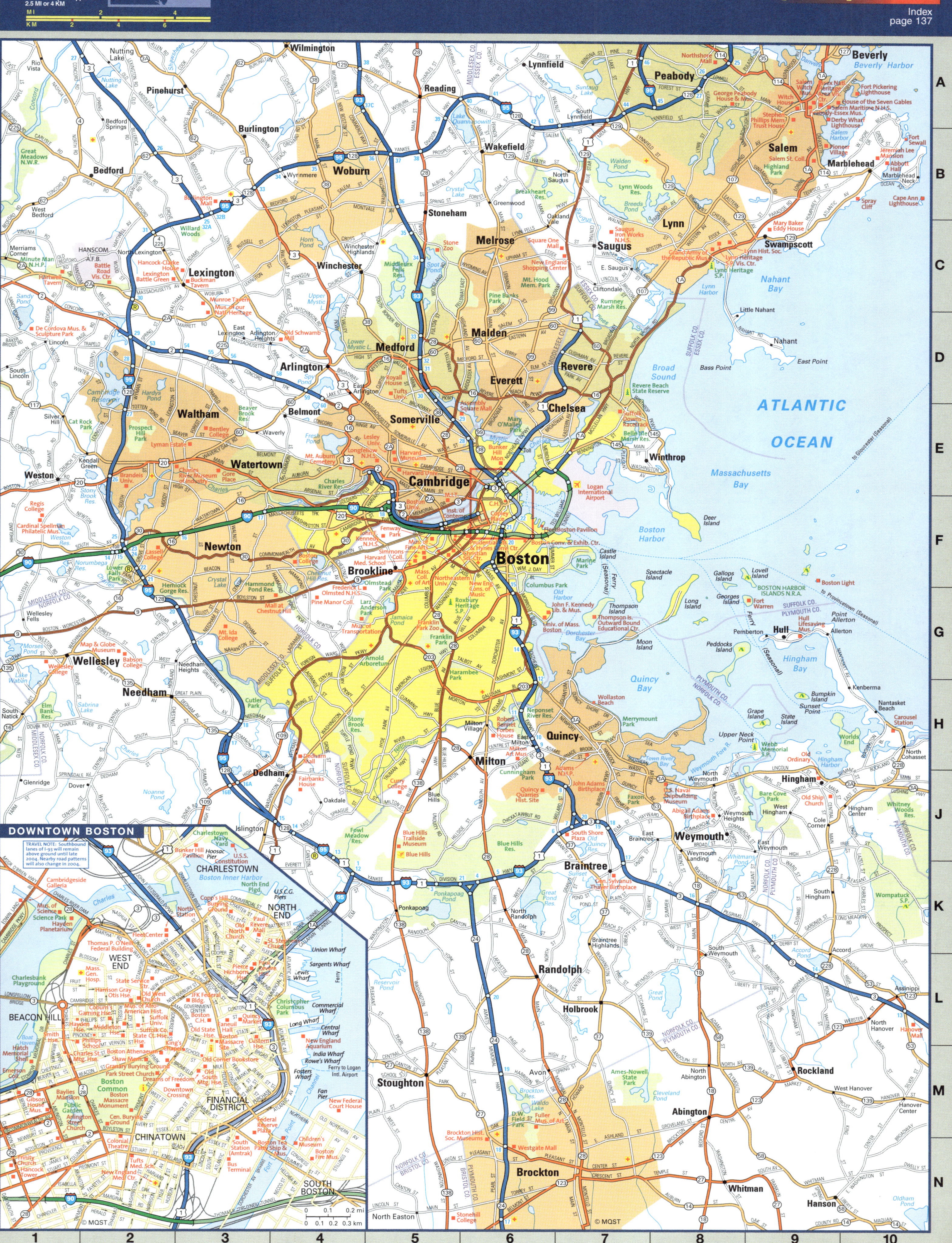

Massachusetts

Index page 137

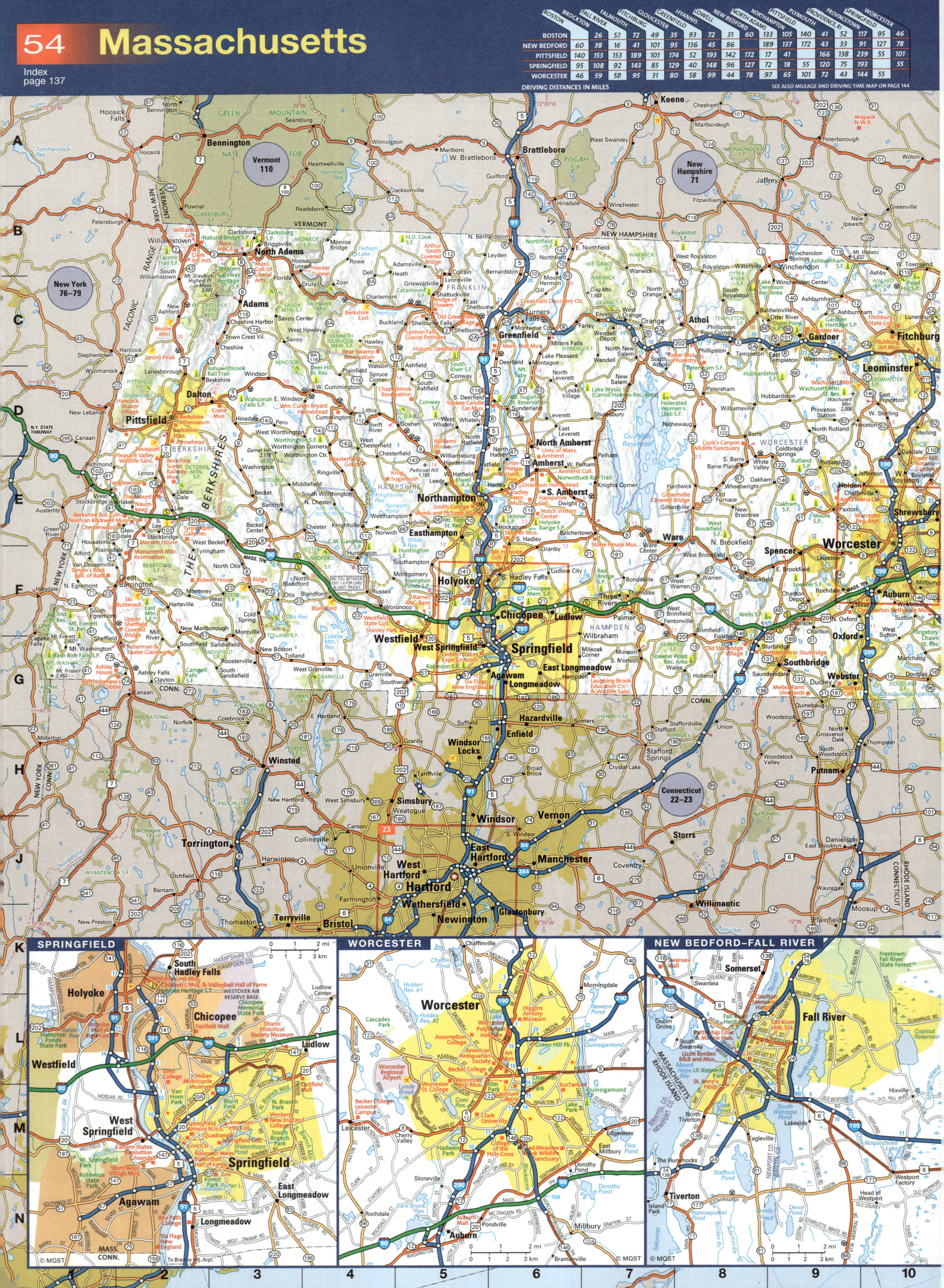

	BOSTON	BROCKTON	FALL RIVER	FALMOUTH	FITCHBURG	GLOUCESTER	GREENFIELD	HYANNIS	LOWELL	NEW BEDFORD	NORTH ADAMS	NORTHAMPTON	PITTSFIELD	PLYMOUTH	PROVIDENCE, RI	PROVINCETOWN	SPRINGFIELD	WORCESTER
BOSTON		26	53	72	49	35	93	72	31	60	133	105	140	41	52	117	95	46
NEW BEDFORD	60	38	16	41	101	95	136	45	86		189	137	172	43	33	91	127	78
PITTSFIELD	140	153	153	189	101	174	52	193	142	172	17	41		166	138	239	55	101
SPRINGFIELD	95	108	92	143	85	129	40	148	96	127	72	18	55	120	75	193		55
WORCESTER	46	59	58	95	31	80	58	99	44	78	97	65	101	72	43	144	55	

DRIVING DISTANCES IN MILES

SEE ALSO MILEAGE AND DRIVING TIME MAP ON PAGE 144

"By the Sword We Seek Peace, but Peace Only Under Liberty"

Index page 137

Index page 137

	Alpena	Ann Arbor	Benton Harbor	Cadillac	Detroit	Escanaba	Flint	Grand Rapids	Houghton	Kalamazoo	Lansing	Mackinaw City	Marquette	Muskegon	Port Huron	Saginaw	Sault Ste. Marie	Traverse City
DETROIT	242	42	186	209		438	62	153	556	136	86	291	455	191	58	97	346	257
GRAND RAPIDS	261	129	78	99	153	391	112		510	53	67	244	408	40	176	144	299	141
LANSING	230	63	126	131	86	375	53	67	493	76		228	391	105	117	86	282	173
MACKINAW CITY	94	281	323	145	291	149	230	244	268	302	228		166	248	293	198	57	106
MARQUETTE	257	444	487	309	455	65	393	408	102	466	391	166		412	457	361	163	269

DRIVING DISTANCES IN MILES

SEE ALSO MILEAGE AND DRIVING TIME MAP ON PAGE 144

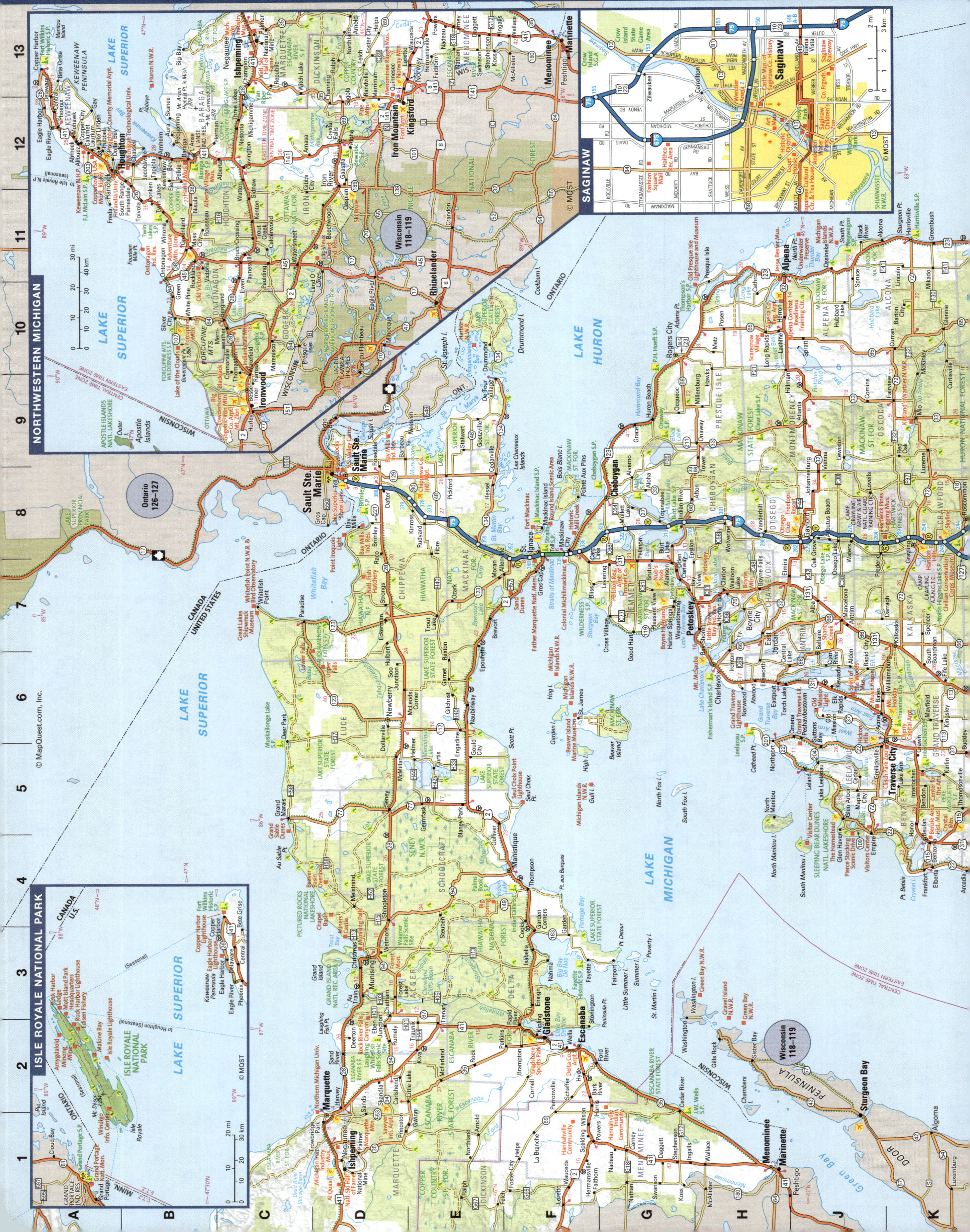

SAGINAW

NORTHWESTERN MICHIGAN

ISLE ROYALE NATIONAL PARK

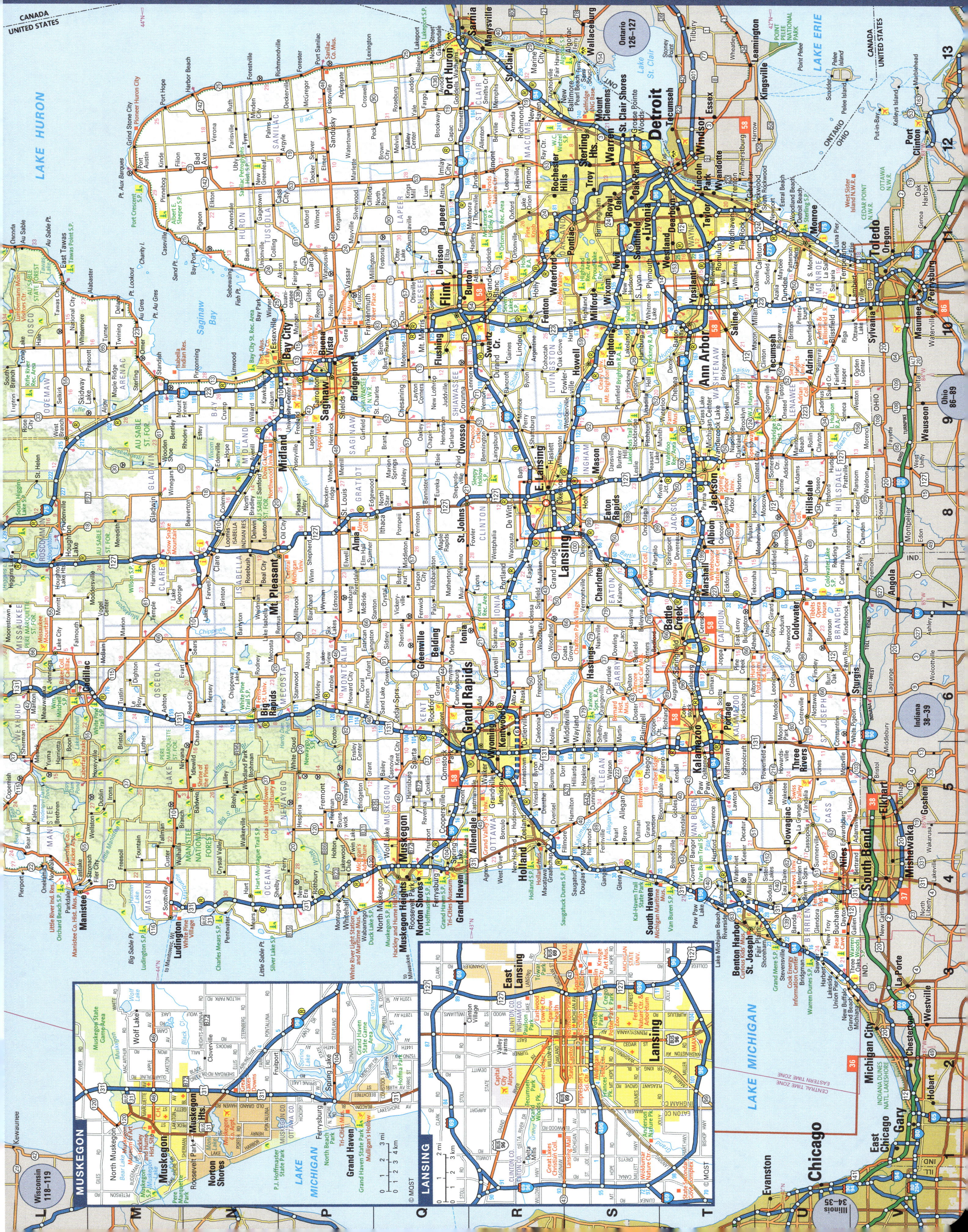

"If You Seek a Pleasant Peninsula, Look About You"

Index page 137

One inch equals approx. 20.5 MI or 33 KM

MI 0 15 30
KM 0 15 30 45

LAKE HURON

LAKE MICHIGAN

LAKE ERIE

Ontario 126–127

Ohio 86–89

Indiana 38–39

Illinois 34–35

Wisconsin 118–119

MUSKEGON

LANSING

© MOST

Index page 137

GRAND RAPIDS

Comstock Park
Grand Rapids
Walker
East Grand Rapids
Jenison
Grandville
Wyoming
Kentwood
Marne
Tallmadge
Ada
Cascade
Gerald R. Ford International Airport
Fifth Third Ballpark
Celebration! Village
Frederik Meijer Gardens & Sculpture Park
Gerald R. Ford Mus.
Public Museum of Grand Rapids
John Ball Zoological Gdn.
Van Andel Arena
DeVos Place
Grand Valley State Univ.
Calvin College
Aquinas College
Cornerstone Univ.
Kendall Coll. of Art & Design
Woodland Shopping Ctr.
Breton Village Shopping Ctr.
RiverTown Crossings
Egypt Valley
Cannonsburg

KALAMAZOO

Kalamazoo
Parchment
Comstock
Portage
Western Michigan Univ.
Kalamazoo College
Kalamazoo Valley Museum
Kalamazoo Inst. of the Arts
Kalamazoo/Battle Creek Intl. Airport
Kalamazoo Air Zoo
Southland Shopping Mall
The Crossroads
Celery Flats Interpretive Center
Maple Hill Mall
Davenport Univ.
Wings Stadium
Milham Park
Asylum Lake
Spring Valley Park

BATTLE CREEK

Battle Creek
Springfield
Bedford
Ft. Custer Training Center
Fort Custer Natl. Cem.
Fort Custer Rec. Area
Lakeview Square Mall
W.K. Kellogg Reg. Airport
Kellogg's Cereal City USA
Full Blast
Kimball Pines Park
Binder Park Zoo
W.K. Kellogg Ctr.
Historic Adventist Village & Kellogg Discovery Ctr.
Brown Stadium
Kellogg Community College
Leila Arboretum

FLINT

Flint
Beecher
Burton
Swartz Creek
Bishop Intl. Airport
Genesee Valley Center
Kettering Univ.
Univ. of Michigan Flint
Mott Community College
Flint Cultural Ctr.
Crossroads Village & Huckleberry R.R.
Stepping Stone Falls
For-Mar Nature Pres. & Arboretum
Davenport Univ.
Hasselbring Park
Forest Park
Bassett Park
Kearsley Park
Courtland Ctr.
Hockey World Arena

ANN ARBOR

Ann Arbor
Ypsilanti
Barton Hills
Saline
Delhi Mills
Dixboro
Ann Arbor Municipal Airport
Univ. of Michigan
Univ. of Michigan Stadium
Eastern Michigan University
Cleary Univ.
Concordia Univ.
Washtenaw Comm. Coll.
Domino's Farms
Matthaei Botanical Gardens
Briarwood Mall
Ypsilanti Historical Mus.

DOWNTOWN DETROIT

Comerica Park
Ford Field
Fox Theatre
Detroit Opera House
Music Hall
Greektown Casino
MGM Grand Detroit Casino
MotorCity Casino
Renaissance Center
Cobo Center
Joe Louis Arena
Hart Plaza
Greyhound Bus Terminal
Federal Office Building
Detroit Police Hdqtrs.
Frank Murphy Hall of Justice
Trappers Alley
Wayne State Univ.
Lafayette Park
Masonic Temple
Detroit River

DETROIT

Detroit
Pontiac
Waterford
Clarkston
Rochester
Rochester Hills
Auburn Hills
Troy
Sterling Heights
Warren
Utica
Mount Clemens
Macomb
Washington
Waldenburg
Disco
Roseville
Fraser
St. Clair Shores
Eastpointe
Harper Woods
Grosse Pointe Woods
Grosse Pointe Shores
Grosse Pointe Farms
Grosse Pointe
Grosse Pointe Park
Hamtramck
Highland Park
Center Line
Madison Heights
Royal Oak
Clawson
Birmingham
Bloomfield Hills
Beverly Hills
Berkley
Huntington Woods
Oak Park
Ferndale
Hazel Park
Southfield
Farmington Hills
Farmington
Franklin
Bingham Farms
Lathrup Village
Novi
Northville
Wolverine Lake
Walled Lake
Livonia
Redford
Plymouth
Westland
Garden City
Dearborn Heights
Dearborn
Inkster
Wayne
Romulus
Taylor
Allen Park
Melvindale
Ecorse
River Rouge
Lincoln Park
Southgate
Wyandotte
Riverview
Trenton
Grosse Ile
Woodhaven
Flat Rock
Gibraltar
New Boston
Belleville
Drayton Plains
Clintonville
Lake Angelus
Union Lake
Oxbow
Keego Harbor
Orchard Lake
West Acres
Sylvan Lake
Huron Heights
Detroit Metro. Wayne County Airport
Oakland-Pontiac Intl. Airport
Windsor
Tecumseh
Lakeshore
St. Clair Beach
Oldcastle
LaSalle
Amherstburg
Essex
McGregor
Maidstone
Paquette Corners
Windsor Intl. Airport
Univ. of Windsor
Ambassador Bridge
Detroit-Windsor Tunnel
Casino Windsor
Fort Malden Natl. Hist. Site
Bois Blanc Island Lighthouse Natl. Hist. Site
Ojibway Prairie Provincial Nature Res.
Belle Isle
The Henry Ford (Greenfield Village)
Henry Ford Estate
Univ. of Michigan Dearborn
Fairlane Town Center
Detroit River Intl. Wildlife Refuge
Fighting Island
Oakland Univ.
Oakland Mall
Somerset Collection
Twelve Oaks Mall
Laurel Park Place Mall
Westland Shopping Center
Northland Shopping Center
Eastland Center
Lakeside Center
Southland Shopping Center
The Palace of Auburn Hills
Great Lakes Crossing
Pine Knob
DTE Energy Music Center
Bald Mountain Rec. Area
Stony Creek Metro Park
Wolcott Mill Metro Park
Lower Huron Metropark
Willow Metropark
Oakwoods Metropark
Holocaust Memorial Center
Detroit City Airport
Detroit Zoo
Marygrove College
Univ. of Detroit Mercy
Lawrence Tech. Univ.
Cranbrook Educational Community
Walsh College
Madonna Univ.
Schoolcraft College
Henry Ford Comm. College
Macomb Ctr. for the Performing Arts
Lake St. Clair
U.S. / CANADA
MICHIGAN / ONTARIO

Ramsey
Andover
Anoka
Ham Lake
Forest Lake
Dayton
Lino Lakes
Hugo
Coon Rapids
Champlin
Blaine
Centerville
Brooklyn Park
Maple Grove
Osseo
Spring Lake Park
Mounds View
Shoreview
Circle Pines
Lexington
Withrow
Bald Eagle
Grant
Dellwood
Mahtomedi
Brooklyn Center
Fridley
Arden Hills
North Oaks
Vadnais Heights
Gem Lake
White Bear Lake
Birchwood Village
Willernie
Plymouth
Crystal
Columbia Hts.
New Brighton
Stillwater
Oak Park Heights
Houlton
Robbinsdale
New Hope
St. Anthony
Roseville
Little Canada
Maplewood
North St. Paul
Pine Springs
Golden Valley
Lauderdale
Falcon Heights
Oakdale
Lake Elmo
Siegel
Wayzata
St. Louis Park
St. Paul
Landfall
Woodland
Minneapolis
Minnetonka
Deephaven
Hopkins
Lilydale
Mendota Heights
West St. Paul
South St. Paul
Woodbury
Afton
Edina
Richfield
Mendota
Sunfish Lake
Eden Prairie
Newport
St. Paul Park
Bloomington
Eagan
Inver Grove Heights
Basswood Grove
Cottage Grove
Shakopee
Burnsville
Savage
Apple Valley
Rosemount
Prior Lake
Coates
Hastings
Lakeville
Prescott
SHAKOPEE MDEWAKANTON SIOUX IND. COMM.
Mississippi
© MQST
DOWNTOWN MINNEAPOLIS
DOWNTOWN ST. PAUL
0 0.25 0.5 mi
0 0.25 0.5 0.75 km
© MQST
A B C D E F G H J K L M N
1 2 3 4 5 6 7 8 9 10

Minnesota

Index page 137

	ALBERT LEA	BEMIDJI	BRAINERD	DULUTH	FERGUS FALLS	GRAND FORKS, ND	INTERNATIONAL FALLS	MANKATO	MARSHALL	MINNEAPOLIS	MOORHEAD	ROCHESTER	ST. CLOUD	ST. PAUL	VIRGINIA	WILLMAR	WINONA	WORTHINGTON
DULUTH	251	153	116		210	264	157	239	274	158	257	239	149	154	61	206	216	362
MINNEAPOLIS	96	225	129	158	176	312	290	78	148		230	88	64	10	193	92	120	207
MOORHEAD	325	133	141	257	55	80	242	294	220	230		317	172	239	229	168	351	298
ROCHESTER	62	311	215	239	262	399	371	80	185	88	317		151	80	274	177	51	174
ST. CLOUD	159	157	62	149	117	254	251	128	131	64	172	151		73	184	63	185	201

DRIVING DISTANCES IN MILES

SEE ALSO MILEAGE AND DRIVING TIME MAP ON PAGE 144

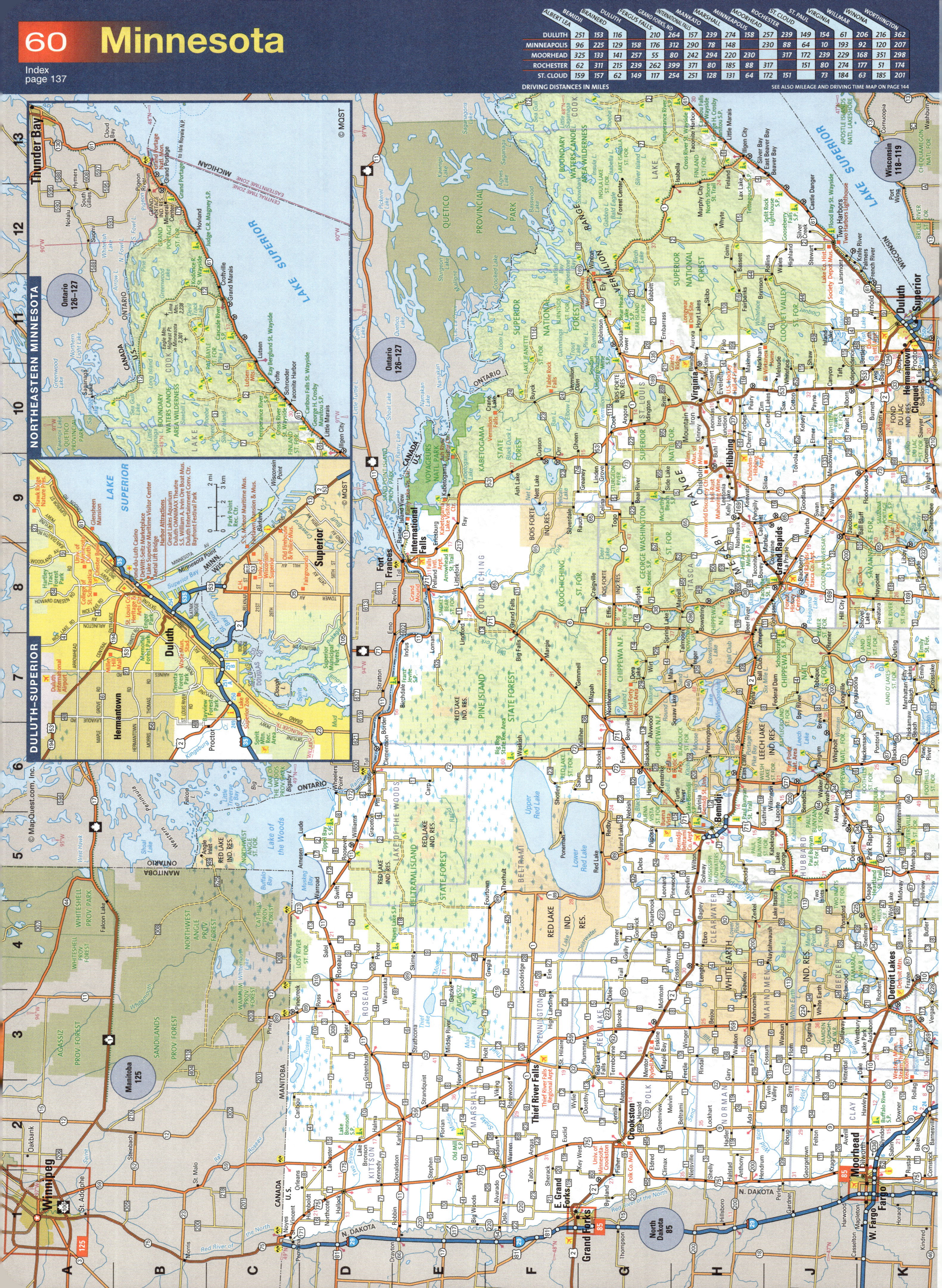

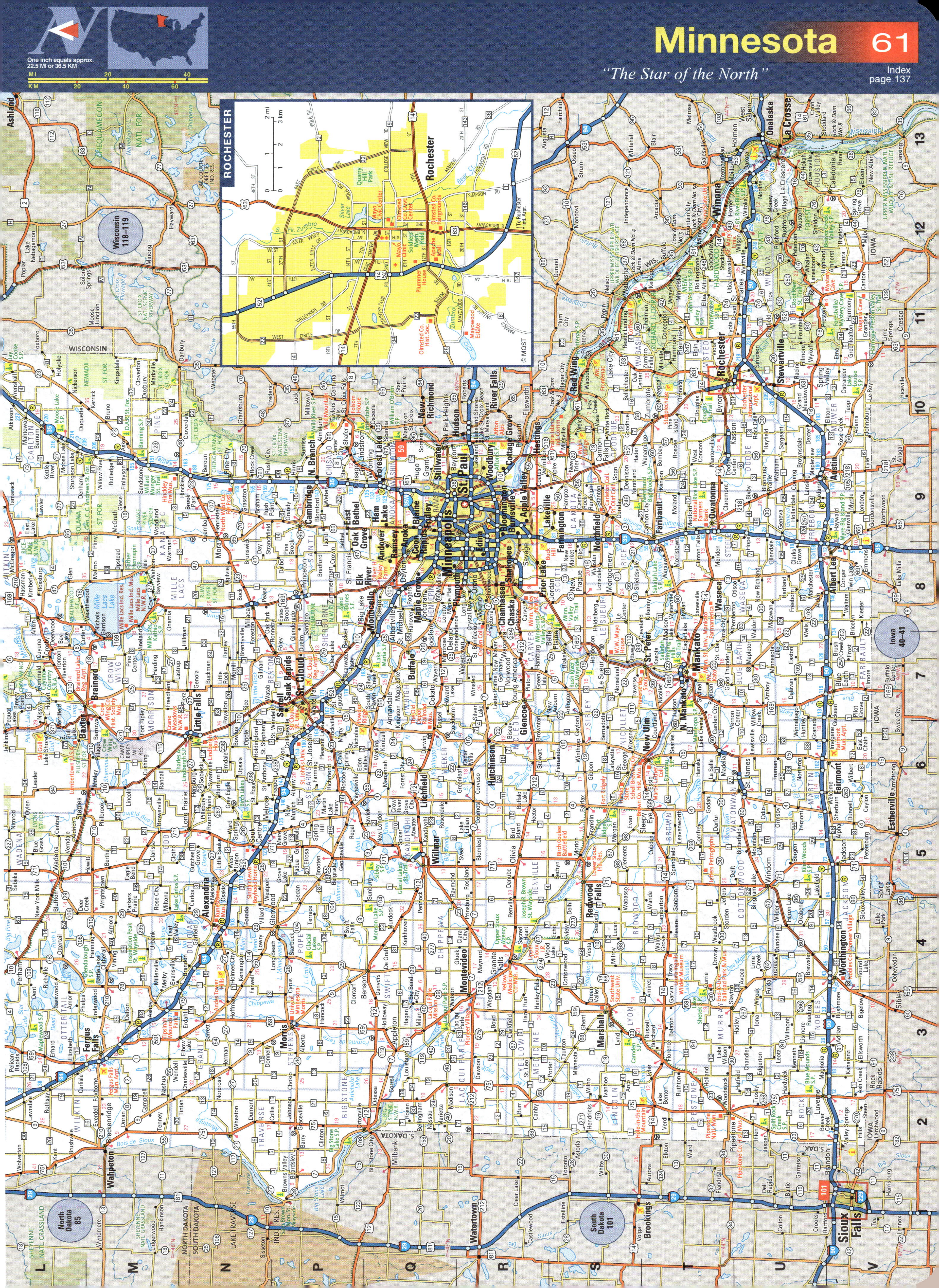

Minnesota
61
"The Star of the North"
Index
page 137
One inch equals approx.
22.5 MI or 36.5 KM
ROCHESTER

Mississippi

"By Valor and Arms"

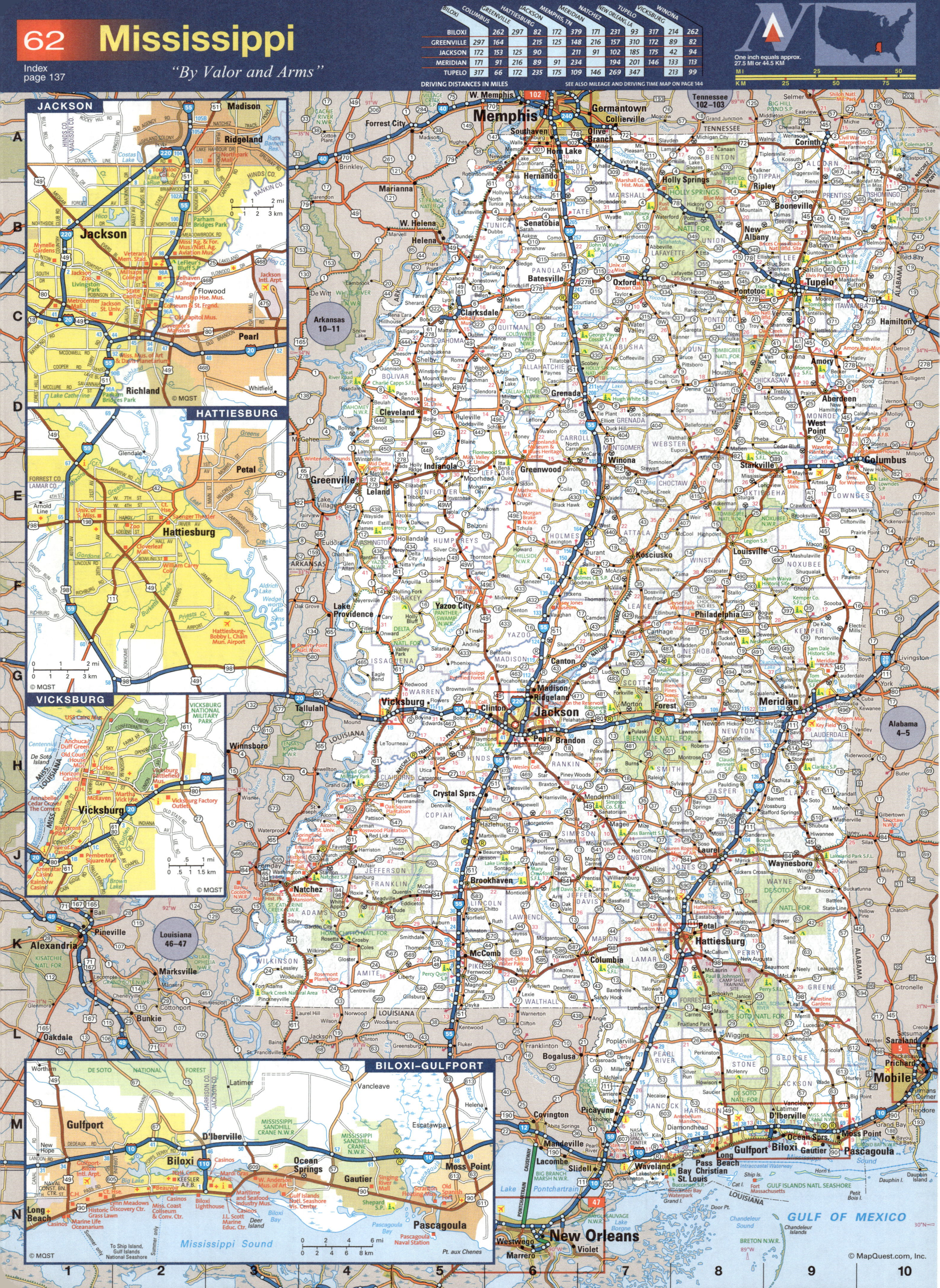

	BILOXI	COLUMBUS	GREENVILLE	HATTIESBURG	JACKSON	MEMPHIS, TN	MERIDIAN	NATCHEZ	NEW ORLEANS, LA	TUPELO	VICKSBURG	WINONA
BILOXI		262	297	82	172	379	171	231	93	317	214	262
GREENVILLE	297	164		215	125	148	216	157	310	172	89	82
JACKSON	172	153	125	90		211	91	102	185	175	42	94
MERIDIAN	171	91	216	89	91	234		194	201	146	133	113
TUPELO	317	66	172	235	175	109	146	269	347		213	99

DRIVING DISTANCES IN MILES

SEE ALSO MILEAGE AND DRIVING TIME MAP ON PAGE 144

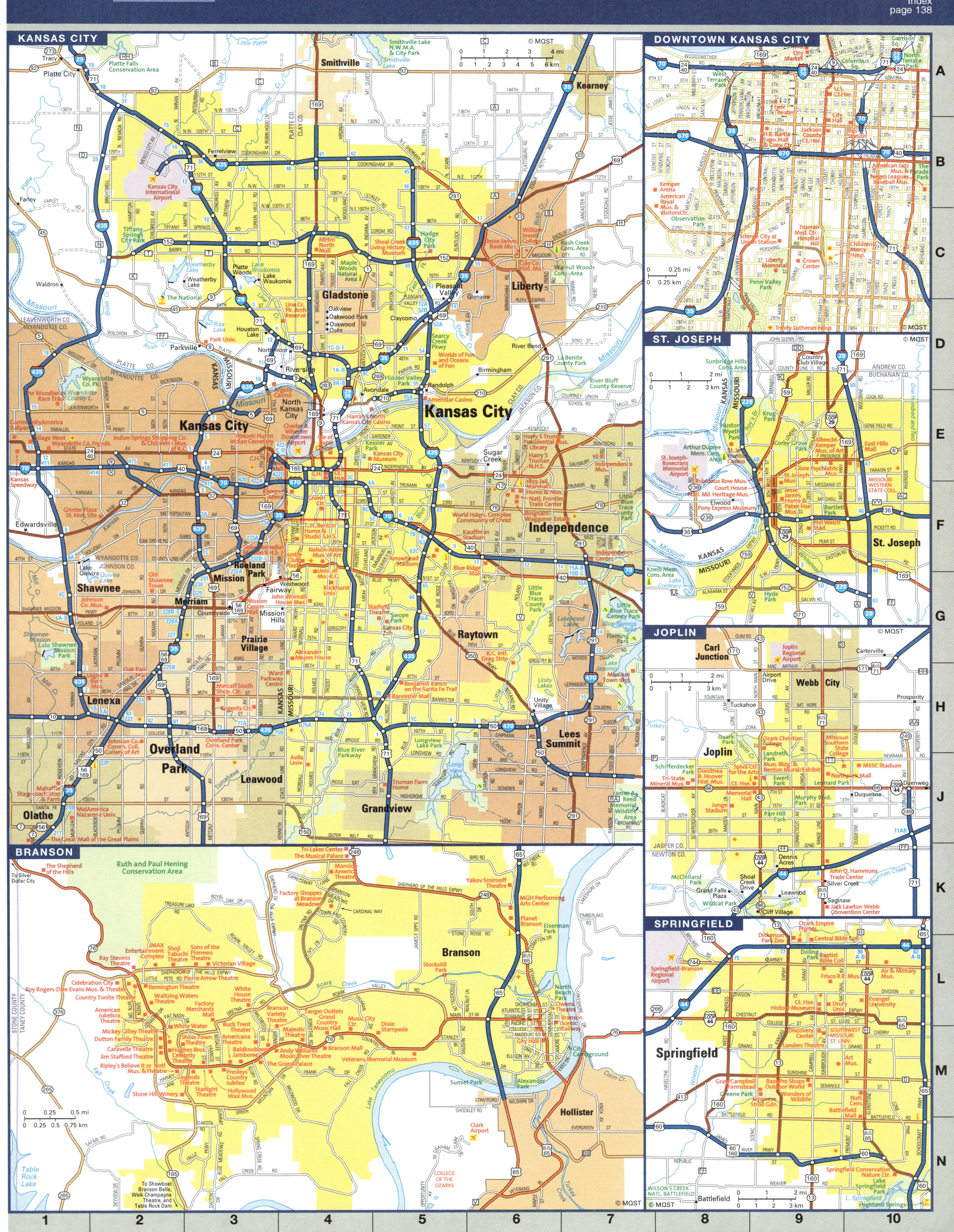
KANSAS CITY
DOWNTOWN KANSAS CITY
ST. JOSEPH
JOPLIN
BRANSON
SPRINGFIELD

Index page 138

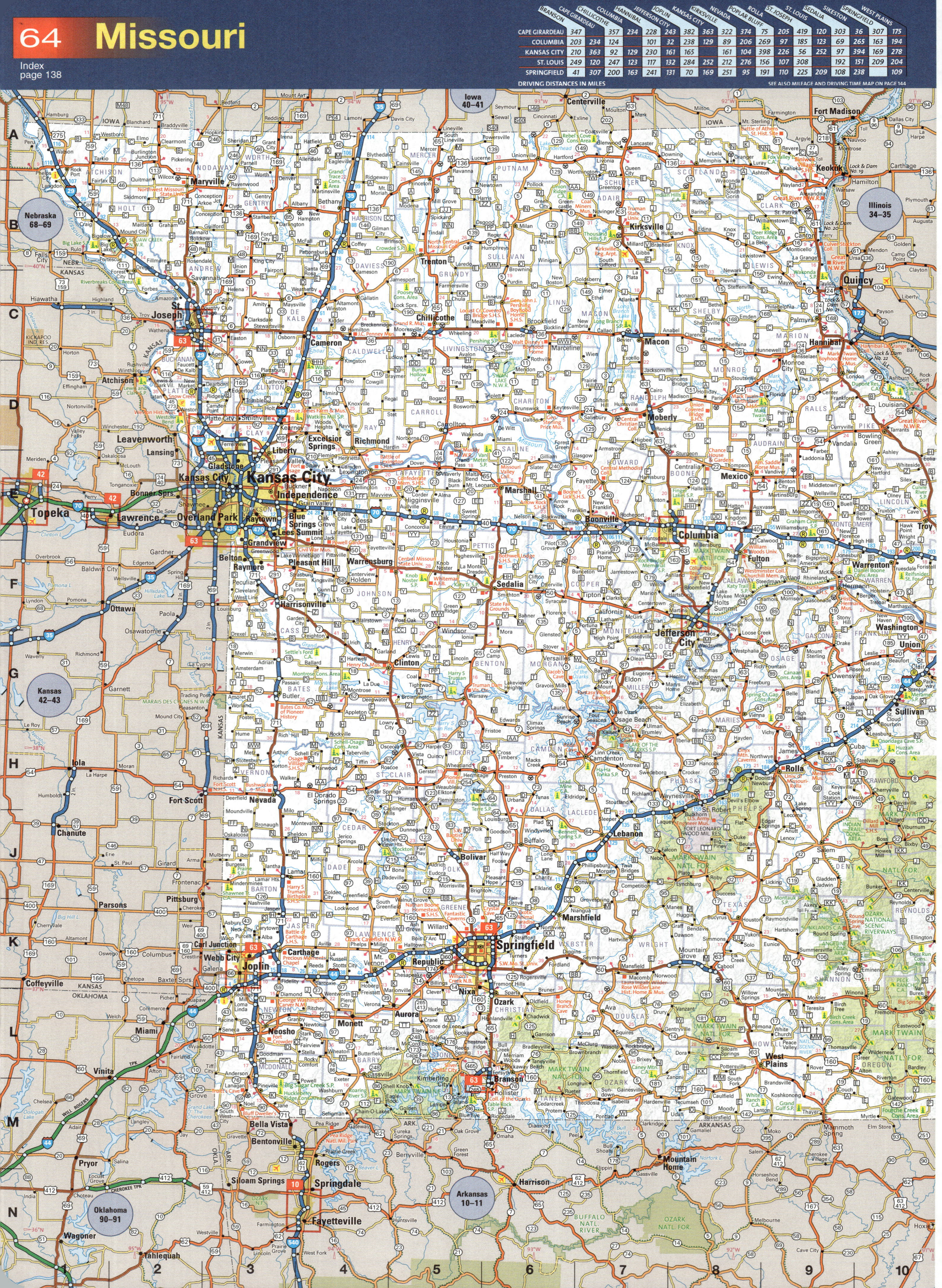

	Branson	Cape Girardeau	Chillicothe	Columbia	Hannibal	Jefferson City	Joplin	Kansas City	Kirksville	Nevada	Poplar Bluff	Rolla	St. Joseph	St. Louis	Sedalia	Sikeston	Springfield	West Plains
CAPE GIRARDEAU	347		357	234	228	243	382	363	322	374	75	205	419	120	303	36	307	175
COLUMBIA	203	234	124		101	32	238	129	89	206	269	97	185	123	69	265	163	194
KANSAS CITY	210	363	92	129	230	161	165		161	104	398	226	56	252	97	394	169	278
ST. LOUIS	249	120	247	123	117	132	284	252	212	276	156	107	308		192	151	209	204
SPRINGFIELD	41	307	200	163	241	131	70	169	251	95	191	110	225	209	108	238		109

DRIVING DISTANCES IN MILES

SEE ALSO MILEAGE AND DRIVING TIME MAP ON PAGE 144

"The Welfare of the People Shall Be the Supreme Law"

Index page 138

One inch equals approx. 25 MI or 40 KM

MI 0 20 40

KM 0 20 40 60

ST. LOUIS

0 2 4 mi

0 2 4 6 km

© MQST

DOWNTOWN ST. LOUIS

0 0.25 0.5 mi

0 0.25 0.5 0.75 km

© MQST

JEFFERSON CITY

0 0.5 1 mi

0 0.5 1 km

© MQST

COLUMBIA

0 1 2 mi

0 1 2 3 km

© MQST

Illinois 34–35

Kentucky 44–45

Tennessee 102–103

Arkansas 10–11

Index page 138

	BILLINGS	BOZEMAN	BROWNING	BUTTE	DILLON	GLASGOW	GLENDIVE	GREAT FALLS	HAVRE	HELENA	KALISPELL	LEWISTOWN	MILES CITY	MISSOULA	SHELBY	SHERIDAN, WY	WEST GLACIER	WEST YELLOWSTONE
BILLINGS		141	346	223	253	277	217	222	249	235	454	125	144	340	304	131	474	232
BUTTE	223	81	241		63	430	439	153	271	71	232	247	367	118	235	354	252	162
GREAT FALLS	222	176	124	153	215	277	351		118	85	222	109	329	199	82	353	192	257
HELENA	235	94	174	71	132	362	452	85	203		195	192	379	114	168	366	216	174
MISSOULA	340	199	201	118	171	476	557	199	317	114	116	306	484		227	471	136	279

DRIVING DISTANCES IN MILES

SEE ALSO MILEAGE AND DRIVING TIME MAP ON PAGE 144

One inch equals approx. 29 MI or 47.5 KM

MI 0 25 50

KM 0 25 50 75

Saskatchewan 124

North Dakota 85

South Dakota 101

Wyoming 120

CENTRAL TIME ZONE

MOUNTAIN TIME ZONE

CANADA

UNITED STATES

SASKATCHEWAN

N. DAK.

S. DAK.

WYOMING

Havre

Glasgow

Wolf Point

Williston

Sidney

Glendive

Lewistown

Miles City

Billings

Laurel

Hardin

Sheridan

Powell

Cody

Belle Fourche

FORT BELKNAP IND. RES.

FORT PECK IND. RES.

CROW INDIAN RESERVATION

NORTHERN CHEYENNE INDIAN RES.

CHARLES M. RUSSELL NATIONAL WILDLIFE REFUGE

CUSTER NATL. FOR.

BIGHORN NATL. FOR.

SHOSHONE NATL. FOR.

BUTTE

HELENA

GREAT FALLS

BILLINGS

© MQST

Index page 138

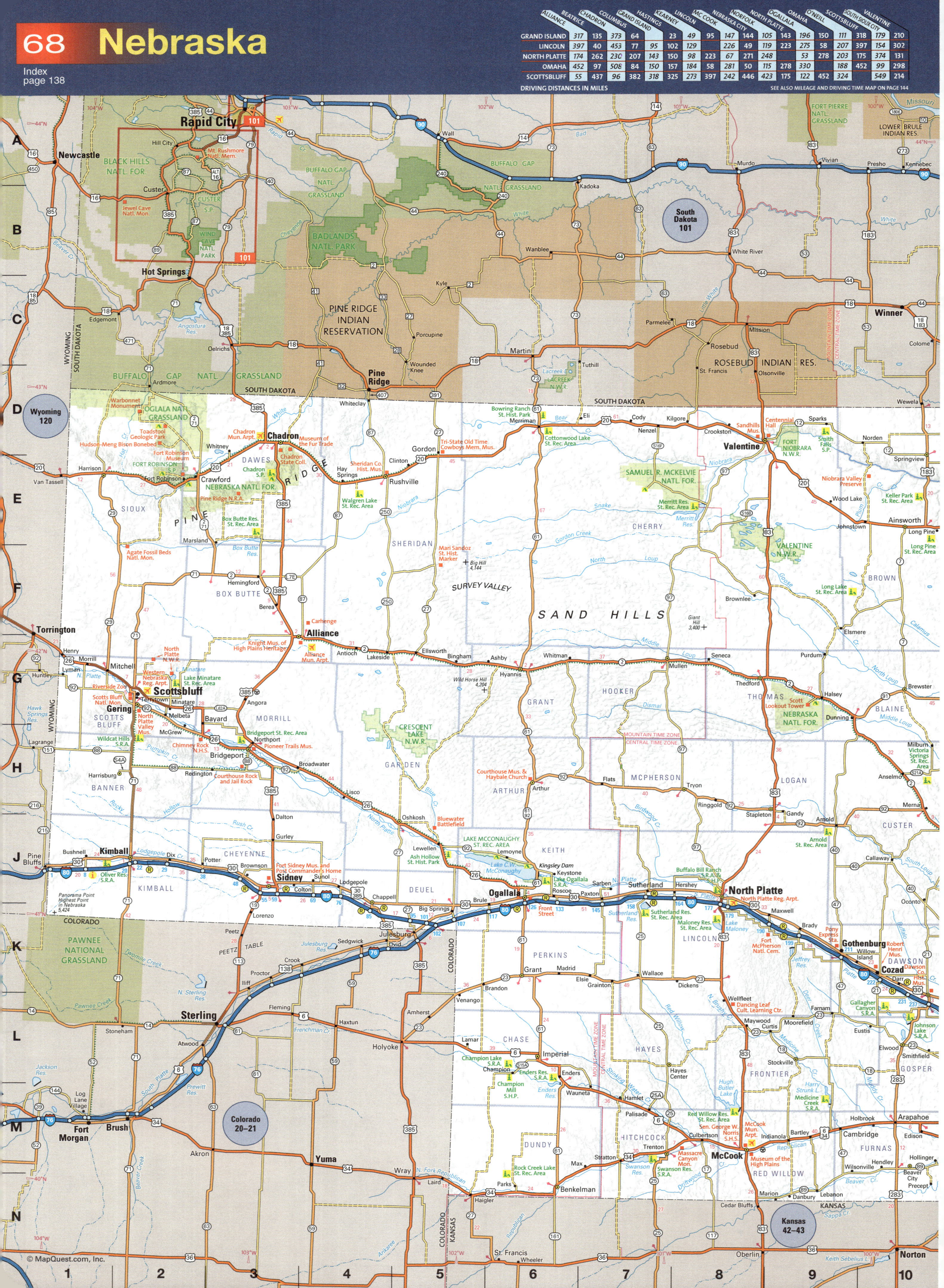

	ALLIANCE	BEATRICE	CHADRON	COLUMBUS	GRAND ISLAND	HASTINGS	KEARNEY	LINCOLN	MC COOK	NEBRASKA CITY	NORFOLK	NORTH PLATTE	OGALLALA	OMAHA	O'NEILL	SCOTTSBLUFF	SOUTH SIOUX CITY	VALENTINE
GRAND ISLAND	317	135	373	64		23	49	95	147	144	105	143	196	150	111	318	179	210
LINCOLN	397	40	453	77	95	102	129		226	49	119	223	275	58	207	397	154	302
NORTH PLATTE	174	262	230	207	143	150	98	223	67	271	248		53	278	203	175	374	131
OMAHA	452	97	508	84	150	157	184	58	281	50	115	278	330		188	452	99	298
SCOTTSBLUFF	55	437	96	382	318	325	273	397	242	446	423	175	122	452	324		549	214

DRIVING DISTANCES IN MILES

SEE ALSO MILEAGE AND DRIVING TIME MAP ON PAGE 144

One inch equals approx. 22.5 MI or 36 KM

MI 0 20 40

KM 0 20 40 60

GRAND ISLAND

LINCOLN

OMAHA–COUNCIL BLUFFS

© MQST

SOUTH DAKOTA

South Dakota 101

Iowa 40–41

Missouri 64–65

Kansas 42–43

KANSAS

IOWA

MISSOURI

A B C D E F G H J K L M N

11 12 13 14 15 16 17 18 19 20

Omaha

Lincoln

Council Bluffs

Grand Island

Kearney

Hastings

Norfolk

Columbus

Fremont

Sioux City

Bellevue

Papillion

La Vista

Beatrice

Nebraska City

Yankton

O'Neill

Lexington

Holdrege

Falls City

Marysville

Nevada

Index page 138

"All for Our Country"

	BEATTY	CARSON CITY	ELKO	ELY	FALLON	HAWTHORNE	LAS VEGAS	LAUGHLIN	RENO	TONOPAH	WEST WENDOVER	WINNEMUCCA
CARSON CITY	316		320	319	62	128	429	522	30	232	431	194
ELKO	349	320		180	255	300	424	517	291	257	111	127
ELY	259	319	180		257	299	244	338	317	167	120	273
LAS VEGAS	113	429	424	244	381	309		94	442	205	364	465
RENO	329	30	291	317	61	133	442	536		237	402	166

DRIVING DISTANCES IN MILES

SEE ALSO MILEAGE AND DRIVING TIME MAP ON PAGE 144

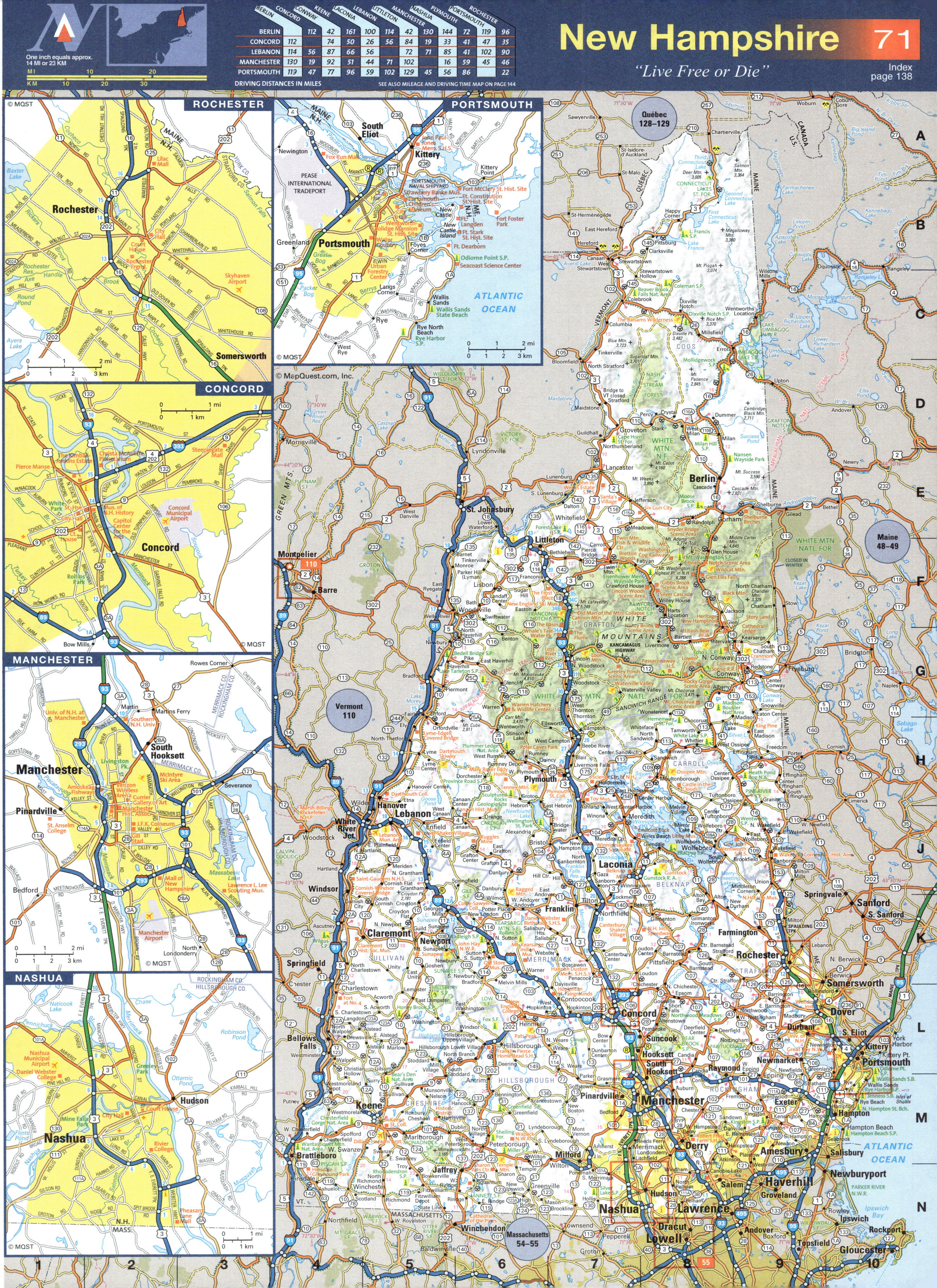

	BERLIN	CONCORD	CONWAY	KEENE	LACONIA	LEBANON	LITTLETON	MANCHESTER	NASHUA	PLYMOUTH	PORTSMOUTH	ROCHESTER
BERLIN		112	42	161	100	114	42	130	144	72	119	96
CONCORD	112		74	50	26	56	84	19	33	41	47	35
LEBANON	114	56	87	66	56		72	71	85	41	102	90
MANCHESTER	130	19	92	51	44	71	102		16	59	45	46
PORTSMOUTH	119	47	77	96	59	102	129	45	56	86		22

DRIVING DISTANCES IN MILES

SEE ALSO MILEAGE AND DRIVING TIME MAP ON PAGE 144

Index
page 138

	ATLANTIC CITY	CAMDEN	CAPE MAY	HACKENSACK	JERSEY CITY	LONG BRANCH	MORRISTOWN	NEW BRUNSWICK	NEW YORK, NY	NEWARK	NEWTON	PATERSON	PHILADELPHIA, PA	PHILLIPSBURG	TOMS RIVER	TRENTON	VINELAND	WILMINGTON, DE
ATLANTIC CITY		61	41	133	120	82	126	94	125	114	159	128	62	120	54	77	47	86
NEW YORK, NY	125	92	155	12	5	55	32	34		11	54	16	91	67	75	55	119	120
NEWARK	114	82	144	15	5	45	18	23	11		51	18	80	57	65	45	109	109
PHILADELPHIA, PA	62	2	92	98	86	77	82	55	91	80	94	94		58	58	34	36	30
TRENTON	77	35	107	63	50	53	47	22	55	45	63	58	34	50	48		68	68

DRIVING DISTANCES IN MILES

SEE ALSO MILEAGE AND DRIVING TIME MAP ON PAGE 144

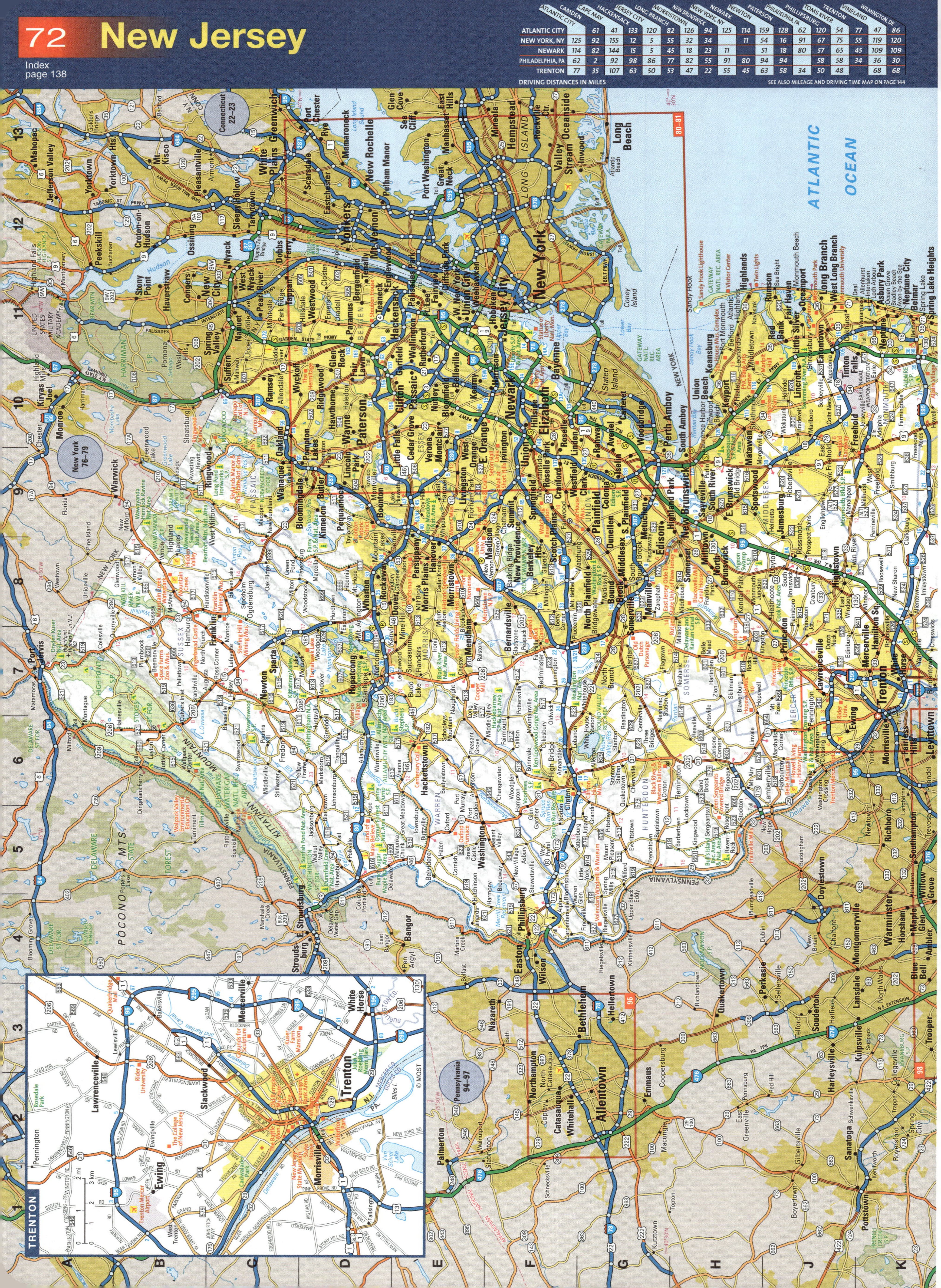

One inch equals approx. 8.5 MI or 13.5 KM

New Mexico

Index
page 138

	ALAMOGORDO	ALBUQUERQUE	CARLSBAD	CLOVIS	EL PASO, TX	FARMINGTON	GALLUP	HOBBS	LAS CRUCES	LAS VEGAS	LOS ALAMOS	RATON	ROSWELL	SANTA FE	SILVER CITY	SOCORRO	TAOS	TUCUMCARI
ALBUQUERQUE	213		275	220	263	181	141	316	220	115	92	221	199	55	234	77	123	174
FARMINGTON	399	181	455	401	450		120	496	407	264	196	300	379	205	361	263	211	355
LAS CRUCES	65	220	203	293	42	407	338	250		335	312	441	182	275	111	146	343	394
ROSWELL	117	199	76	110	203	379	340	117	182	178	228	284		191	293	164	248	161
SANTA FE	220	55	267	213	319	205	197	308	275	65	37	171	191		290	132	68	167

DRIVING DISTANCES IN MILES

SEE ALSO MILEAGE AND DRIVING TIME MAP ON PAGE 144

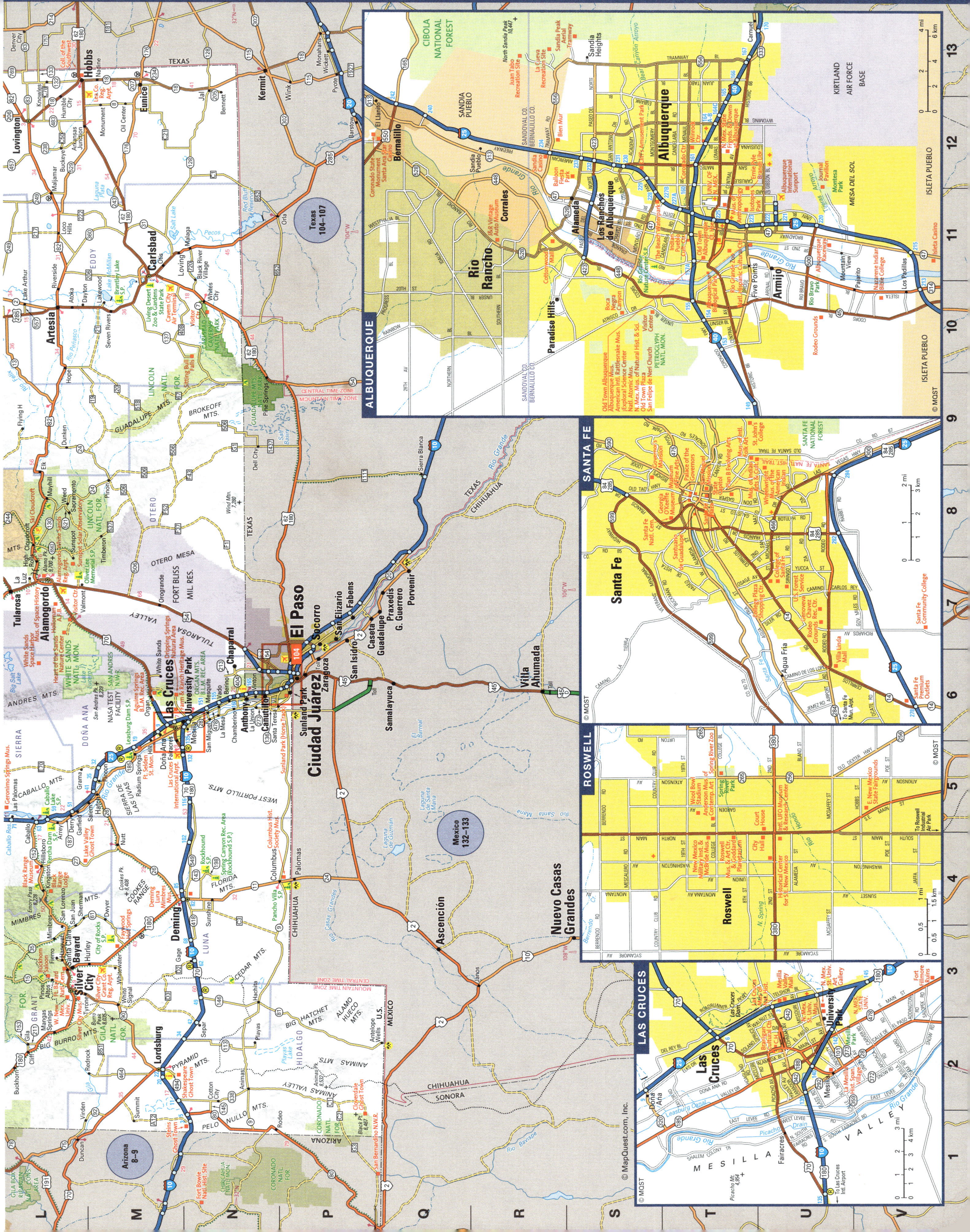

One inch equals approx. 29 MI or 46 KM

MI 25 50

KM 25 50 75

ALBUQUERQUE

SANTA FE

ROSWELL

LAS CRUCES

© MapQuest.com, Inc.

Index page 138

	ALBANY	BINGHAMTON	BUFFALO	COOPERSTOWN	GENEVA	ITHACA	JAMESTOWN	KINGSTON	LAKE PLACID	NEW YORK	NIAGARA FALLS	OLEAN	PLATTSBURGH	ROCHESTER	SARATOGA SPRINGS	SYRACUSE	UTICA	WATERTOWN
ALBANY		135	292	89	197	186	361	56	138	151	306	297	160	228	32	146	94	179
BINGHAMTON	135		225	78	97	53	214	125	253	176	239	164	276	161	160	76	95	139
BUFFALO	292	225		239	103	153	74	346	337	400	20	74	374	74	293	152	199	210
ROCHESTER	228	161	74	175	39	89	142	282	273	336	88	113	310		229	88	135	146
SYRACUSE	146	76	152	93	56	59	220	201	192	250	166	163	228	88	147		53	65

DRIVING DISTANCES IN MILES

SEE ALSO MILEAGE AND DRIVING TIME MAP ON PAGE 144

One inch equals approx. 16.5 MI or 26.5 KM
New York (north)
77
"Ever Upward"
Index page 138
BINGHAMTON
Ontario 126–127
Québec 128–129
Vermont 110
Massachusetts 54–55
Connecticut 22–23
Pennsylvania 94–97
CANADA
UNITED STATES
ADIRONDACK PARK
ADIRONDACK MOUNTAINS
CATSKILL MTS.
CATSKILL PARK
ST. LAWRENCE
FRANKLIN
CLINTON
ESSEX
HAMILTON
HERKIMER
LEWIS
JEFFERSON
OSWEGO
ONEIDA
ONONDAGA
MADISON
OTSEGO
CHENANGO
CORTLAND
TOMPKINS
TIOGA
BROOME
DELAWARE
SCHOHARIE
ALBANY
GREENE
SARATOGA
FULTON
MONTGOMERY
SCHENECTADY
RENSSELAER
WASHINGTON
COLUMBIA
ULSTER
SULLIVAN
DUTCHESS
Cornwall
Massena
Malone
Plattsburgh
Burlington
S. Burlington
Winooski
Ogdensburg
Potsdam
Canton
Saranac Lake
Lake Placid
Tupper Lake
Kingston
Watertown
Oswego
Fulton
Syracuse
N. Syracuse
Rome
Utica
Oneida
Herkimer
Little Falls
Gloversville
Johnstown
Amsterdam
Saratoga Springs
Glens Falls
Hudson Falls
Ballston Spa
Schenectady
Rotterdam
Troy
Cohoes
Albany
Rensselaer
Delmar
Colonie
Cortland
Ithaca
Oneonta
Norwich
Binghamton
Johnson City
Endicott
Hudson
Catskill
Pittsfield
Middlebury
Ticonderoga
Sayre

Index page 138

	ALBANY	BINGHAMTON	BUFFALO	HEMPSTEAD	KINGSTON	MIDDLETOWN	MONTAUK	MONTICELLO	NEWBURGH	NEW YORK	PEEKSKILL	PORT JEFFERSON	PORT JERVIS	POUGHKEEPSIE	RIVERHEAD	ROCHESTER	SYRACUSE	WHITE PLAINS
ALBANY		135	292	182	56	105	276	103	89	151	107	214	121	79	234	228	146	148
BINGHAMTON	135		225	203	125	116	296	87	134	176	144	235	117	127	254	161	76	167
KINGSTON	56	125	346	132		55	225	53	39	101	57	164	71	20	183	282	201	98
NEWBURGH	89	134	357	74	39	26	167	47		56	18	106	42	22	125	294	208	42
NEW YORK	151	176	400	26	101	72	120	95	56		45	58	87	96	78	336	250	29

DRIVING DISTANCES IN MILES

SEE ALSO MILEAGE AND DRIVING TIME MAP ON PAGE 144

One inch equals approx. 9 MI or 14.5 KM
MI 5 10 15
KM 5 10 15 20
UTICA
Rome
Oriskany
Whitesboro
Yorkville
New York Mills
Utica
Clark Mills
New Hartford
Washington Mills
Clinton
Franklin Springs
Hamilton College
Oneida County Airport
ALBANY–SCHENECTADY–TROY
Scotia
Schenectady
Rotterdam
Niskayuna
Cohoes
Troy
Latham
Watervliet
Colonie
Loudonville
Roessleville
Albany
Rensselaer
Menands
Delmar
Elsmere
Voorheesville
Guilderland
Westmere
McKownville
Slingerlands
Glenmont
East Greenbush
Defreestville
Wynantskill
Connecticut 22–23
Mass. 54–55
Rhode Island 99
Waterbury
Naugatuck
Danbury
Bethel
New Milford
Torrington
Thomaston
Terryville
Bristol
Plainville
Southington
Meriden
Wallingford
Cheshire
Prospect
Wolcott
Oakville
Watertown
Middlebury
Southbury
Oxford
Seymour
Ansonia
Derby
Shelton
Woodbridge
Hamden
New Haven
West Haven
East Haven
North Haven
Branford
North Branford
Guilford
Madison
Clinton
Old Saybrook
Essex
Deep River
Chester
Niantic
New London
Groton
Waterford
Mystic
Pawcatuck
Westerly
Orange
Milford
Stratford
Bridgeport
Fairfield
Westport
Norwalk
New Canaan
Darien
Stamford
Trumbull
Ridgefield
Wilton
Long Island Sound
LONG ISLAND
ATLANTIC OCEAN
Block Island Sound
Orient Pt.
Greenport
Southold
Riverhead
Hampton Bays
Southampton
Montauk
Amagansett
East Hampton
Sag Harbor
Port Jefferson
Stony Brook
Smithtown
Huntington
Hauppauge
Commack
Centereach
Selden
Coram
Medford
Holbrook
Patchogue
Shirley
Brentwood
Islip
Bay Shore
Babylon
Lindenhurst
Copiague
Massapequa
Hicksville
Levittown
Hempstead
Freeport
Oceanside
Merrick
Plainview
Deer Park
FIRE ISLAND NATL. SEASHORE
ATLANTIC OCEAN
CONNECTICUT
Q
R
S
T
U
V
W
X
Y
24
25
26
27
28
29
30
© MapQuest.com, Inc.

Index page 138

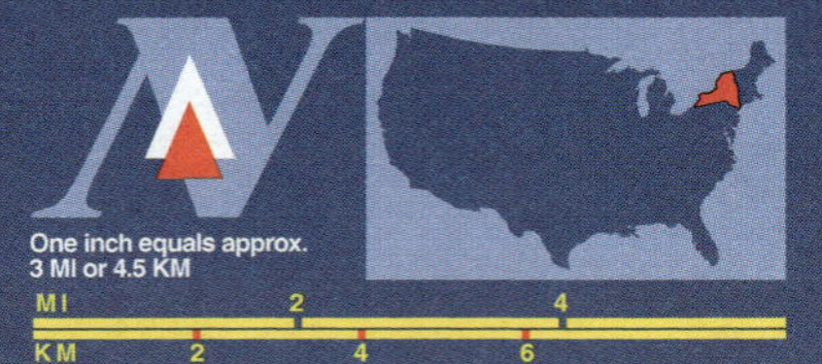

Bloomingdale
Butler
Pompton Lakes
Riverdale
Kinnelon
Pompton Plains
Oakland
Franklin Lakes
Wyckoff
Waldwick
Midland Park
Ho-Ho-Kus
Woodcliff Lake
Hillsdale
Westwood
Washington Township
Old Tappan
Harrington Park
Northvale
Norwood
Rockleigh
Dobbs Ferry
Hastings-on-Hudson
Greenville
Ridgewood
North Haledon
Hawthorne
Glen Rock
Emerson
Oradell
Haworth
Closter
Demarest
Tuckahoe
Bronxville
Pequannock
Packanack Lake
Wayne
Prospect Pk.
Haledon
Fair Lawn
Paramus
Dumont
New Milford
Bergenfield
Cresskill
Alpine
Towaco
Lincoln Park
Mountain View
Totowa
Paterson
Elmwood Park
River Edge
Tenafly
Yonkers
Mount Vernon
Rochelle Park
Maywood
Saddle Brook
Hackensack
Teaneck
Englewood
West Paterson
Little Falls
Garfield
Lodi
Bogota
Englewood Cliffs
Fairfield
North Caldwell
Clifton
Passaic
Hasbrouck Hts.
Leonia
Pine Brook
West Caldwell
Cedar Grove
Wood-Ridge
Wallington
Little Ferry
Ridgefield Park
Palisades Park
Caldwell
Verona
Essex Fells
East Rutherford
Rutherford
Carlstadt
Moonachie
Fort Lee
Ridgefield
Cliffside Park
Edgewater
Roseland
Montclair
Glen Ridge
Nutley
Lyndhurst
Fairview
North Bergen
Bronx
West Orange
Morristown
Bloomfield
Belleville
North Arlington
Guttenberg
West New York
Livingston
Secaucus
Weehawken
Orange
East Orange
Kearny
Union City
Hoboken
Manhattan
South Orange
Harrison
Maplewood
Millburn
Irvington
Summit
Newark
Jersey City
New York
Springfield
Union
Hillside
Mountainside
Kenilworth
Elizabeth
Roselle Park
Roselle
Westfield
Cranford
Garwood
Bayonne
Brooklyn
Linden
Clark
Rahway
Staten Island
Colonia
Avenel
Carteret
Iselin
Woodbridge
Sewaren
Menlo Park
Port Reading
Fords
Perth Amboy
South Amboy
Sayreville
Keasbey
Raritan Bay
Lower New York Bay
Upper New York Bay
Jamaica Bay
Rockaway Inlet
Rockaway Pt.

A
B
C
D
E
F
G
H
J
K
L
M
N

1
2
3
4
5
6
7
8
9
10

MANHATTAN
Hartsdale
Scarsdale
White Plains
Rye Brook
Port Chester
Harrison
Eastchester
New Rochelle
Mamaroneck
Rye
Larchmont
Pelham
Pelham Manor
Long Island Sound
Glen Cove
Sands Point
Manorhaven
Port Washington
Sea Cliff
Kings Point
Great Neck
Manhasset
Great Neck Plaza
Roslyn
Roslyn Hts.
Lake Success
North Hills
Searingtown
Williston Park
Mineola
North New Hyde Park
New Hyde Park
Garden City
Floral Park
Elmont
Franklin Square
North Valley Stream
Lakeview
Valley Stream
Malverne
Lynbrook
Rockville Centre
South Valley Stream
Hewlett
East Rockaway
Woodmere
Cedarhurst
Inwood
Lawrence
Long Beach
Queens
ATLANTIC OCEAN
West New York
Union City
Weehawken
NEW JERSEY
NEW YORK
Hudson
UPPER WEST SIDE
Central Park
UPPER EAST SIDE
THEATER DISTRICT
CLINTON
MIDTOWN
TURTLE BAY
FASHION CENTER
MURRAY HILL
CHELSEA
Manhattan
GRAMERCY PARK
WEST VILLAGE
GREENWICH VILLAGE
STUYVESANT TOWN
SOHO
NOHO
EAST VILLAGE
NOLITA
TRIBECA
LITTLE ITALY
CHINATOWN
LOWER EAST SIDE
BATTERY PARK CITY
FINANCIAL DISTRICT
SOUTH ST. SEAPORT
D.U.M.B.O.
Brooklyn
BROOKLYN HEIGHTS
BROOKLYN NAVY YARD
FORT GREENE
WILLIAMSBURG
GREENPOINT
LONG ISLAND CITY
East River
Roosevelt Island
© MQST

Index page 139

	ASHEVILLE	BOONE	CHARLOTTE	DURHAM	ELIZABETH CITY	FAYETTEVILLE	GREENSBORO	GREENVILLE	HICKORY	JACKSONVILLE	KINSTON	MOREHEAD CITY	NAGS HEAD	RALEIGH	ROCKINGHAM	ROCKY MOUNT	WILMINGTON	WINSTON-SALEM
ASHEVILLE		198	116	224	404	264	176	324	78	354	316	383	444	242	190	297	368	146
CHARLOTTE	116	95		139	319	139	91	239	48	269	232	298	359	158	74	213	205	79
GREENSBORO	176	117	91	49	228	90		148	98	179	141	207	268	67	83	122	193	30
RALEIGH	242	183	158	24	160	62	67	80	164	113	76	142	200		96	54	127	96
WILMINGTON	368	309	205	150	211	92	193	123	290	52	93	95	241	127	131	153		222

DRIVING DISTANCES IN MILES

SEE ALSO MILEAGE AND DRIVING TIME MAP ON PAGE 144

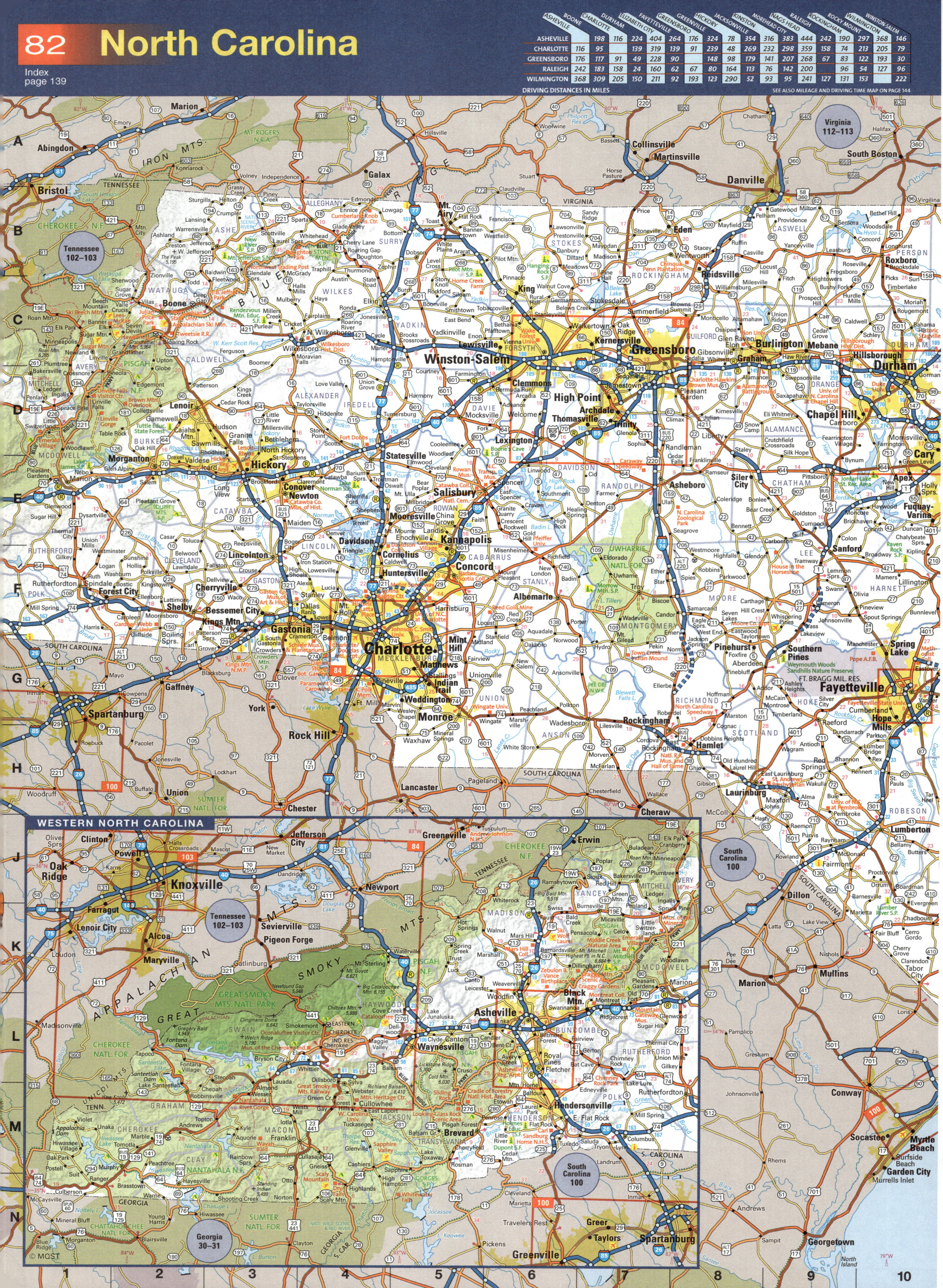

North Carolina
83
"To Be, Rather than to Seem"
Index page 139
One inch equals approx. 18.5 MI or 29.5 KM
Virginia 112–113
ATLANTIC OCEAN
Onslow Bay
Long Bay
OUTER BANKS
Pamlico Sound
Albemarle Sound
FAYETTEVILLE
ASHEVILLE
WILMINGTON
Raleigh
Greenville
Rocky Mount
Wilson
Goldsboro
Kinston
New Bern
Jacksonville
Wilmington
Fayetteville
Asheville
Elizabeth City
Chesapeake
Suffolk
Emporia
Roanoke Rapids
Washington
Williamston
Edenton
Havelock
Morehead City
Clinton
Whiteville
Henderson
Oxford
Smithfield
Selma
Kill Devil Hills
Nags Head
North Myrtle Beach
Oak Island
© MapQuest.com, Inc.

Index
page 139

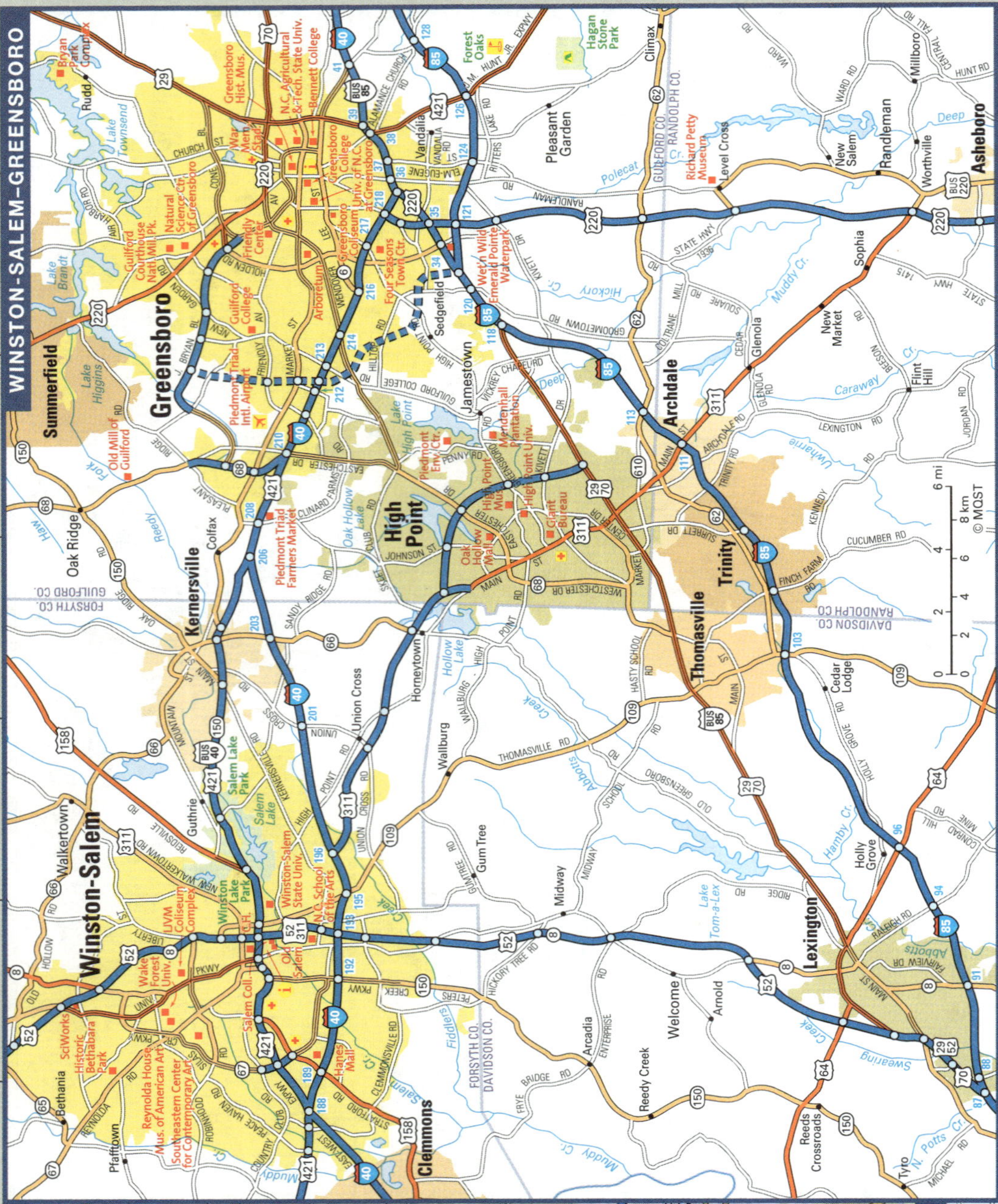

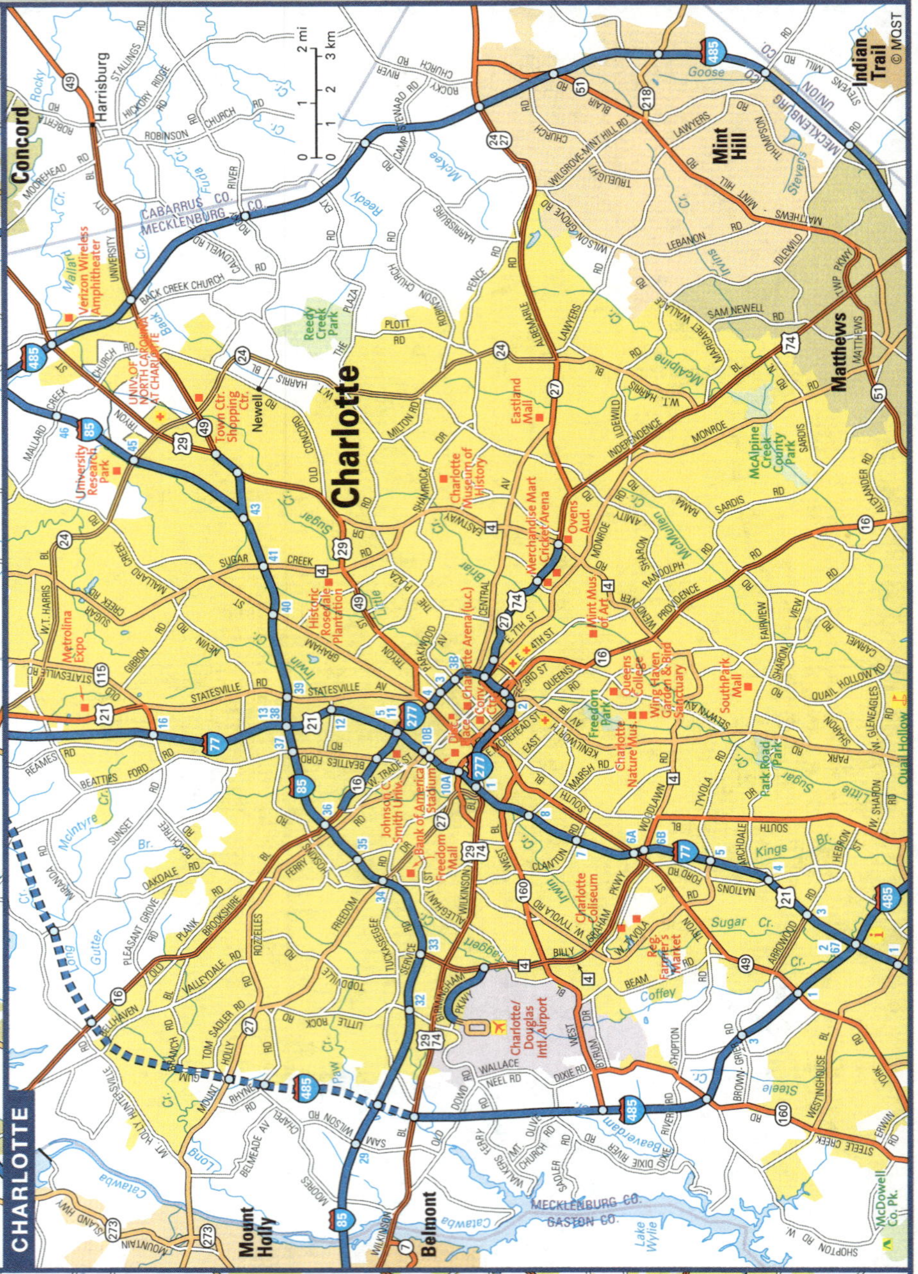

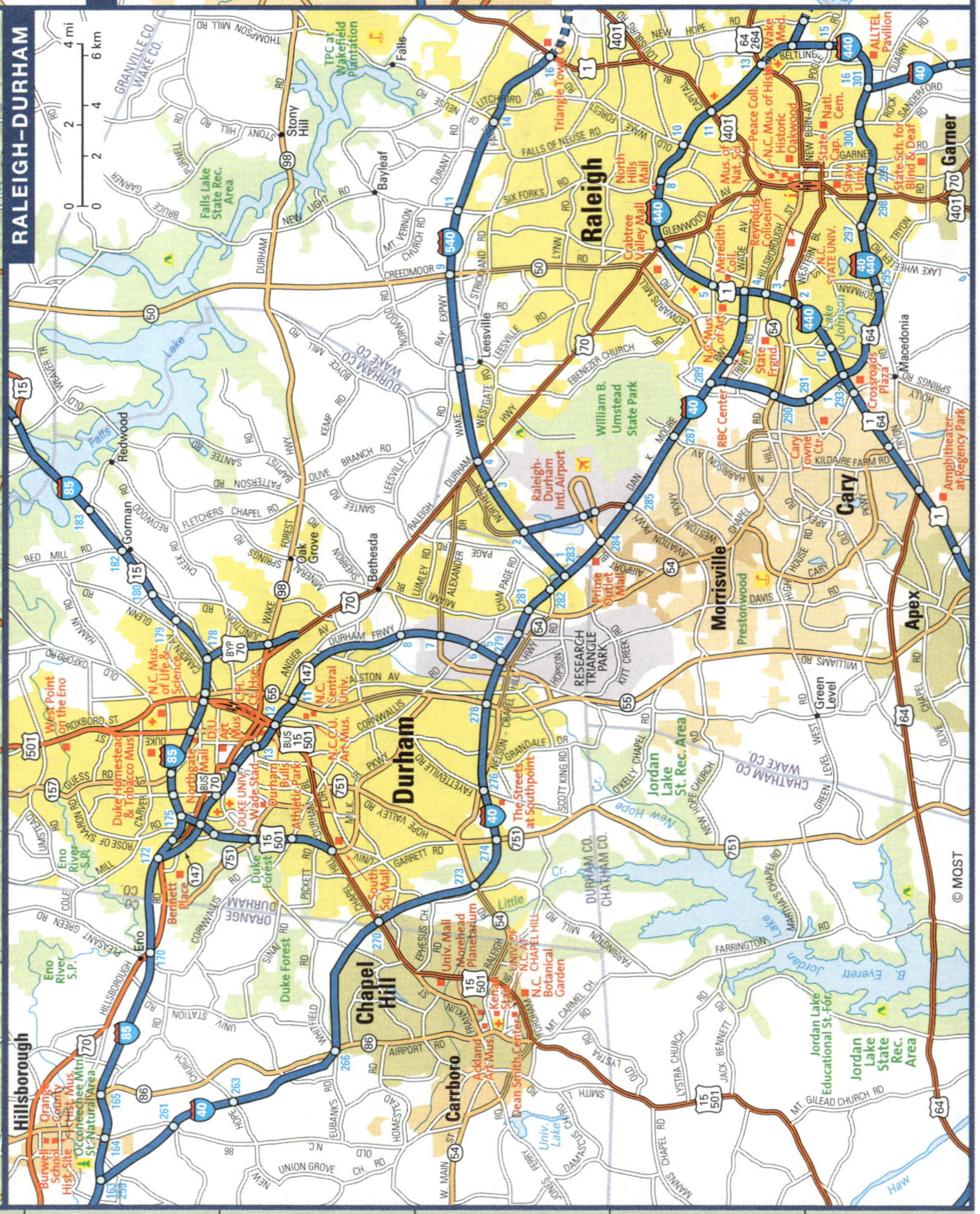

WINSTON-SALEM-GREENSBORO

CHARLOTTE

GREAT SMOKY MTS. AREA

RALEIGH-DURHAM

"Liberty and Union, Now and Forever, One and Inseparable"

Index page 139

	BISMARCK	DEVILS LAKE	DICKINSON	FARGO	GRAND FORKS	JAMESTOWN	MINOT	PEMBINA	RUGBY	VALLEY CITY	WAHPETON	WILLISTON
BISMARCK		186	97	199	274	105	116	347	153	141	249	229
DICKINSON	97	278		291	367	197	178	440	245	234	341	133
FARGO	199	163	291		79	97	268	152	221	58	55	424
GRAND FORKS	274	91	367	79		173	212	77	148	133	130	340
MINOT	116	122	178	268	212	171		238	64	210	318	128

DRIVING DISTANCES IN MILES

SEE ALSO MILEAGE AND DRIVING TIME MAP ON PAGE 144

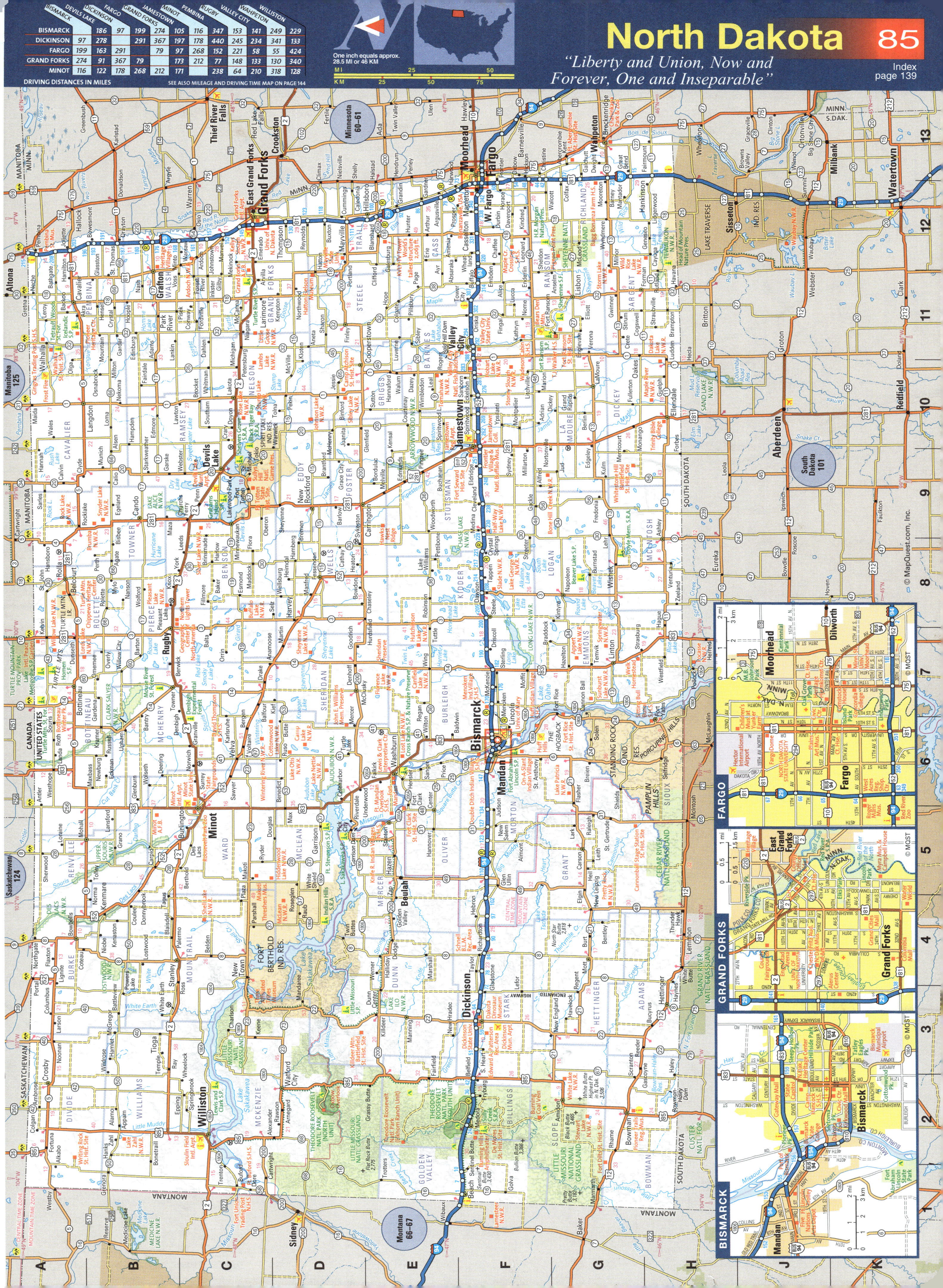

Ohio (north)

Index page 139

	AKRON	CAMBRIDGE	CANTON	CHILLICOTHE	CINCINNATI	CLEVELAND	COLUMBUS	DAYTON	DEFIANCE	FINDLAY	LIMA	MANSFIELD	MARION	NEW PHILADELPHIA	SANDUSKY	SPRINGFIELD	TOLEDO	YOUNGSTOWN
AKRON		83	23	184	243	38	129	198	186	140	157	66	101	46	84	172	142	49
CAMBRIDGE	83		61	98	187	124	80	155	228	178	175	108	126	37	169	128	228	129
CLEVELAND	38	124	64	199	259		144	213	163	126	163	81	116	87	61	187	119	75
COLUMBUS	129	80	143	47	110	144		70	146	101	96	67	50	117	119	44	148	175
TOLEDO	142	228	168	189	209	119	148	156	63	51	83	105	100	191	62	169		179

DRIVING DISTANCES IN MILES

SEE ALSO MILEAGE AND DRIVING TIME MAP ON PAGE 144

One inch equals approx. 12.5 MI or 20 KM
CLEVELAND
DOWNTOWN CLEVELAND
LAKE ERIE
© MapQuest.com, Inc.
Cleveland
Lakewood
Euclid
East Cleveland
Cleveland Hts.
Shaker Hts.
Parma
Westlake
North Olmsted
Strongsville
North Royalton
Brecksville
Mentor
Painesville
Willoughby
Lorain
Elyria
Sandusky
Ashtabula
Conneaut
Geneva
Medina
Akron
Cuyahoga Falls
Kent
Stow
Barberton
Wadsworth
Canton
Massillon
North Canton
Alliance
Warren
Niles
Youngstown
Boardman
Sharon
Wooster
Ashland
Mansfield
Mt. Vernon
Coshocton
New Philadelphia
Dover
Cambridge
Newark
Zanesville
Steubenville
Wheeling
East Liverpool
Aliquippa
Beaver
New Castle
Greenville
Pennsylvania 94–97
West Virginia 117
PENNSYLVANIA

Ohio (south)

Index page 139

	Akron	Athens	Cambridge	Chillicothe	Cincinnati	Cleveland	Columbus	Dayton	Gallipolis	Hillsboro	Huntington, WV	Lancaster	Marietta	Portsmouth	Springfield	Toledo	Wheeling, WV	Zanesville
CAMBRIDGE	83	81		98	187	124	80	155	128	145	185	63	49	142	128	228	50	23
CHILLICOTHE	184	57	98		108	199	47	77	69	40	89	35	107	44	85	189	147	75
CINCINNATI	243	152	187	108		259	110	53	154	61	148	134	236	104	79	209	236	164
COLUMBUS	129	74	80	47	110	144		70	114	69	135	30	129	91	44	148	130	58
DAYTON	198	146	155	77	53	213	70		145	57	160	102	204	116	26	156	204	132

DRIVING DISTANCES IN MILES

SEE ALSO MILEAGE AND DRIVING TIME MAP ON PAGE 144

One inch equals approx. 12.5 MI or 20 KM

MI 0 10 20

KM 0 10 20 30

"With God All Things Are Possible"

Index page 139

Pennsylvania 94–97

West Virginia 117

Kentucky 44–45

YOUNGSTOWN–WARREN

COLUMBUS

SPRINGFIELD

© MQST

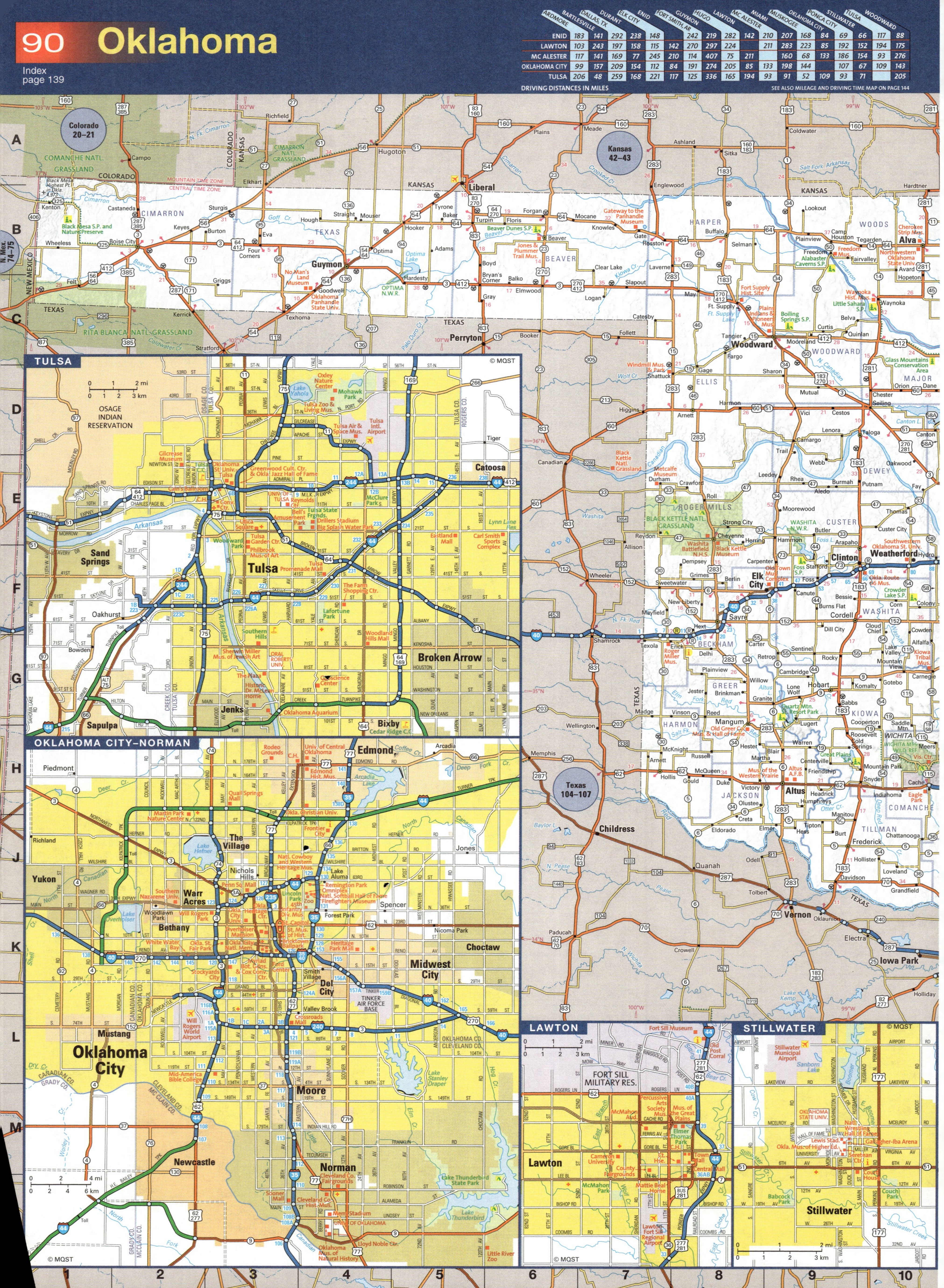

	ARDMORE	BARTLESVILLE	DALLAS, TX	DURANT	ELK CITY	ENID	FORT SMITH, AR	GUYMON	HUGO	LAWTON	MC ALESTER	MIAMI	MUSKOGEE	OKLAHOMA CITY	PONCA CITY	STILLWATER	TULSA	WOODWARD
ENID	183	141	292	238	148		242	219	282	142	210	207	168	84	69	66	117	88
LAWTON	103	243	197	158	115	142	270	297	224		211	283	223	85	192	152	194	175
MC ALESTER	117	141	169	77	245	210	114	407	75	211		160	68	133	186	154	93	276
OKLAHOMA CITY	99	157	209	154	112	84	191	274	205	85	133	198	144		107	67	109	143
TULSA	206	48	259	168	221	117	125	336	165	194	93	91	52	109	93	71		205

DRIVING DISTANCES IN MILES

SEE ALSO MILEAGE AND DRIVING TIME MAP ON PAGE 144

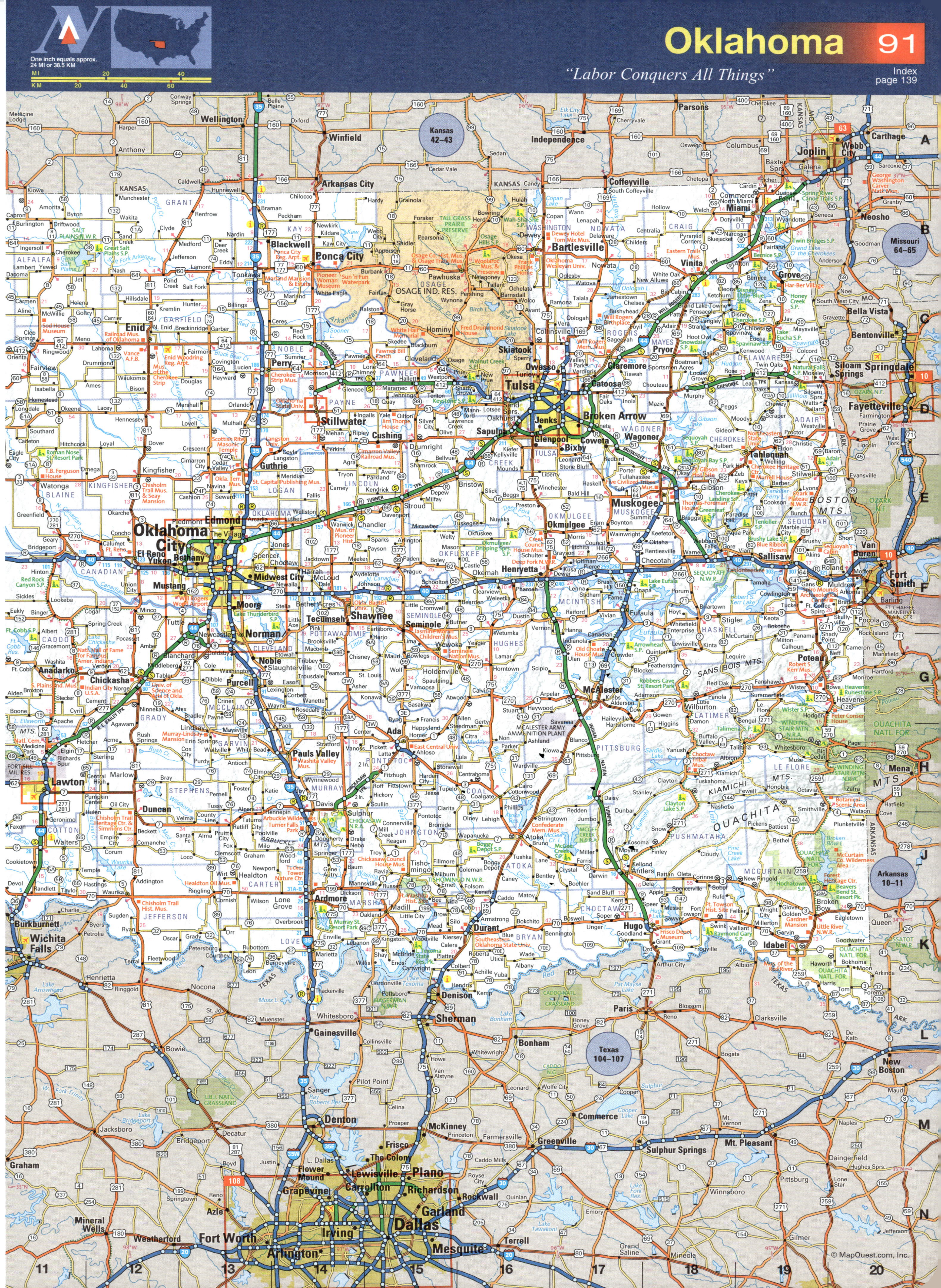

Oklahoma
91
"Labor Conquers All Things"
Index page 139
One inch equals approx. 24 MI or 38.5 KM
MI 20 40
KM 20 40 60
Kansas 42–43
Missouri 64–65
Arkansas 10–11
Texas 104–107
Wellington
Winfield
Independence
Coffeyville
Parsons
Joplin
Carthage
Arkansas City
Blackwell
Ponca City
Bartlesville
Miami
Vinita
Grove
Enid
Stillwater
Tulsa
Broken Arrow
Sapulpa
Muskogee
Tahlequah
Bentonville
Siloam Springs
Springdale
Fayetteville
Guthrie
Edmond
Oklahoma City
El Reno
Yukon
Bethany
Mustang
Midwest City
Moore
Norman
Shawnee
Tecumseh
Seminole
Okmulgee
Henryetta
Sallisaw
Fort Smith
Van Buren
Chickasha
Anadarko
Lawton
Duncan
Purcell
Pauls Valley
Ada
McAlester
Ardmore
Durant
Hugo
Idabel
Denison
Sherman
Paris
Gainesville
Bonham
Wichita Falls
Burkburnett
Denton
McKinney
Frisco
Greenville
Sulphur Springs
Mt. Pleasant
Lewisville
Plano
Carrollton
Richardson
Garland
Irving
Dallas
Grapevine
Fort Worth
Arlington
Mesquite
Rockwall
Terrell
Mineral Wells
Weatherford
New Boston
Flower Mound
The Colony
OSAGE IND. RES.
BOSTON MTS.
OUACHITA NATL. FOR.
SANS BOIS MTS.
KIAMICHI MTS.
© MapQuest.com, Inc.

Index page 140

	ASTORIA	BAKER CITY	BEND	BURNS	COOS BAY	CORVALLIS	CRATER LAKE N.P.	EUGENE	GRANTS PASS	KLAMATH FALLS	LAKEVIEW	MEDFORD	NEWPORT	ONTARIO	PENDLETON	PORTLAND	SALEM	THE DALLES
BEND	252	228		142	227	128	110	115	196	139	177	178	183	272	246	158	134	137
EUGENE	216	423	115	257	105	46	146		137	175	265	164	101	491	328	112	65	198
MEDFORD	375	406	178	311	170	205	80	164	28	76	171		260	441	487	271	224	357
PENDLETON	307	96	246	195	440	298	355	328	460	385	335	487	328	164		212	265	131
PORTLAND	97	307	158	299	224	82	253	112	244	282	335	271	116	375	212		48	82

DRIVING DISTANCES IN MILES

SEE ALSO MILEAGE AND DRIVING TIME MAP PAGE 144

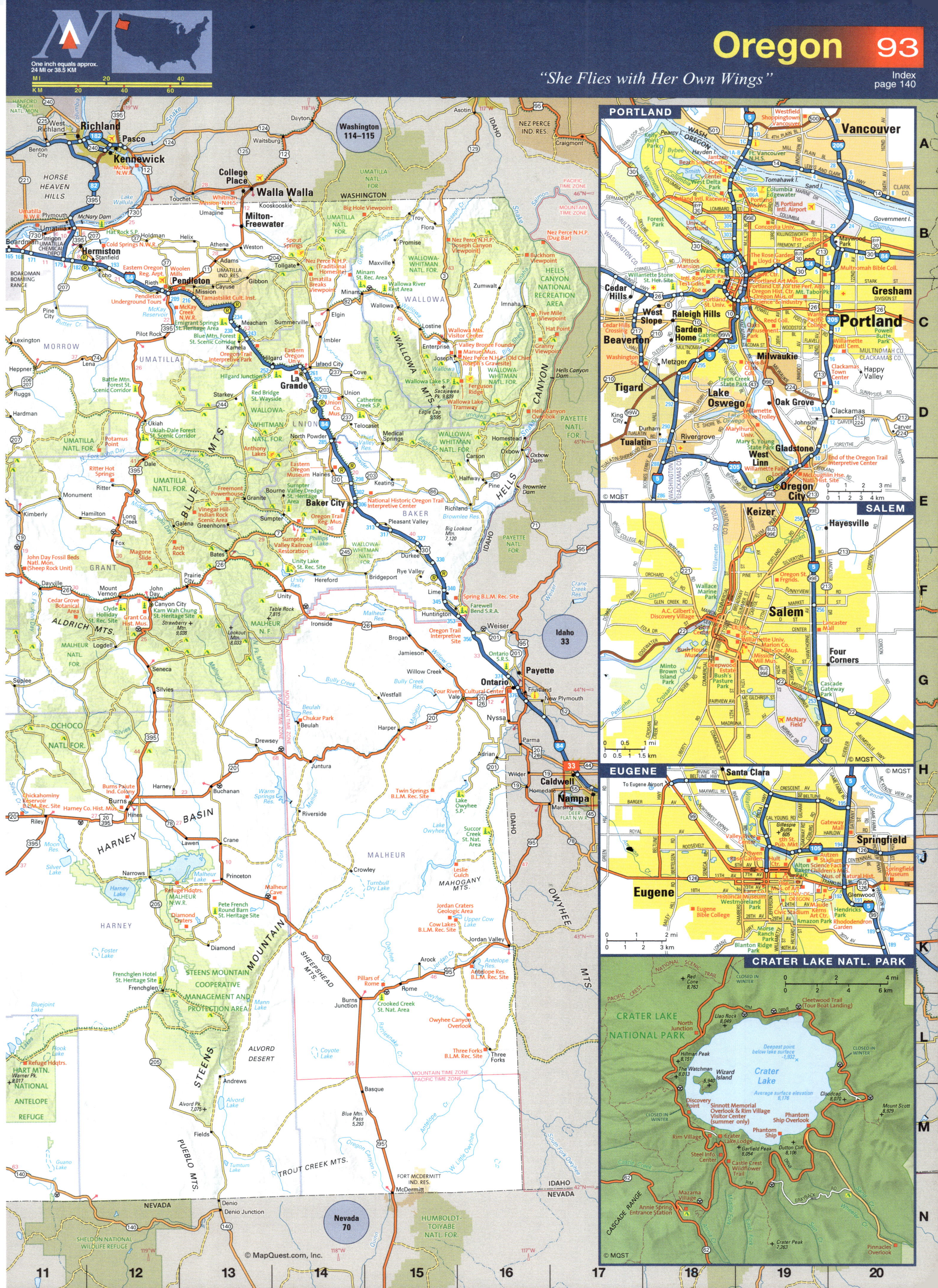

Oregon
93
"She Flies with Her Own Wings"
Index page 140
One inch equals approx. 24 MI or 38.5 KM
PORTLAND
SALEM
EUGENE
CRATER LAKE NATL. PARK
Vancouver
Portland
Gresham
Beaverton
Tigard
Lake Oswego
Milwaukie
Oregon City
West Linn
Tualatin
Gladstone
Oak Grove
Keizer
Salem
Hayesville
Four Corners
Eugene
Springfield
Santa Clara
Crater Lake
Wizard Island
CRATER LAKE NATIONAL PARK
Richland
Pasco
Kennewick
Walla Walla
College Place
Milton-Freewater
Hermiston
Pendleton
La Grande
Baker City
Ontario
Payette
Caldwell
Nampa
Burns
Hines
John Day
Washington 114–115
Idaho 33
Nevada 70
WALLOWA
HARNEY BASIN
MALHEUR
ALVORD DESERT
STEENS MOUNTAIN
HELLS CANYON
BLUE MTS.
© MapQuest.com, Inc.

Index page 140

	ALLENTOWN	ALTOONA	CHAMBERSBURG	ERIE	HARRISBURG	INDIANA	JOHNSTOWN	LEWISTOWN	MEADVILLE	NEW CASTLE	PHILADELPHIA	PITTSBURGH	SCRANTON	STATE COLLEGE	UNIONTOWN	WARREN	WASHINGTON	WILLIAMSPORT
ALTOONA	218		95	205	140	55	48	71	168	129	241	99	185	40	109	147	123	99
ERIE	361	205	282		298	150	195	242	40	95	405	126	317	210	183	66	153	259
HARRISBURG	82	140	54	298		179	138	58	261	250	109	205	119	88	200	224	213	83
PITTSBURGH	284	99	160	126	205	56	73	155	88	49	306		301	139	48	145	30	215
STATE COLLEGE	165	40	105	210	88	95	87	32	172	167	195	139	149		148	136	163	63

DRIVING DISTANCES IN MILES

SEE ALSO MILEAGE AND DRIVING TIME MAP ON PAGE 144

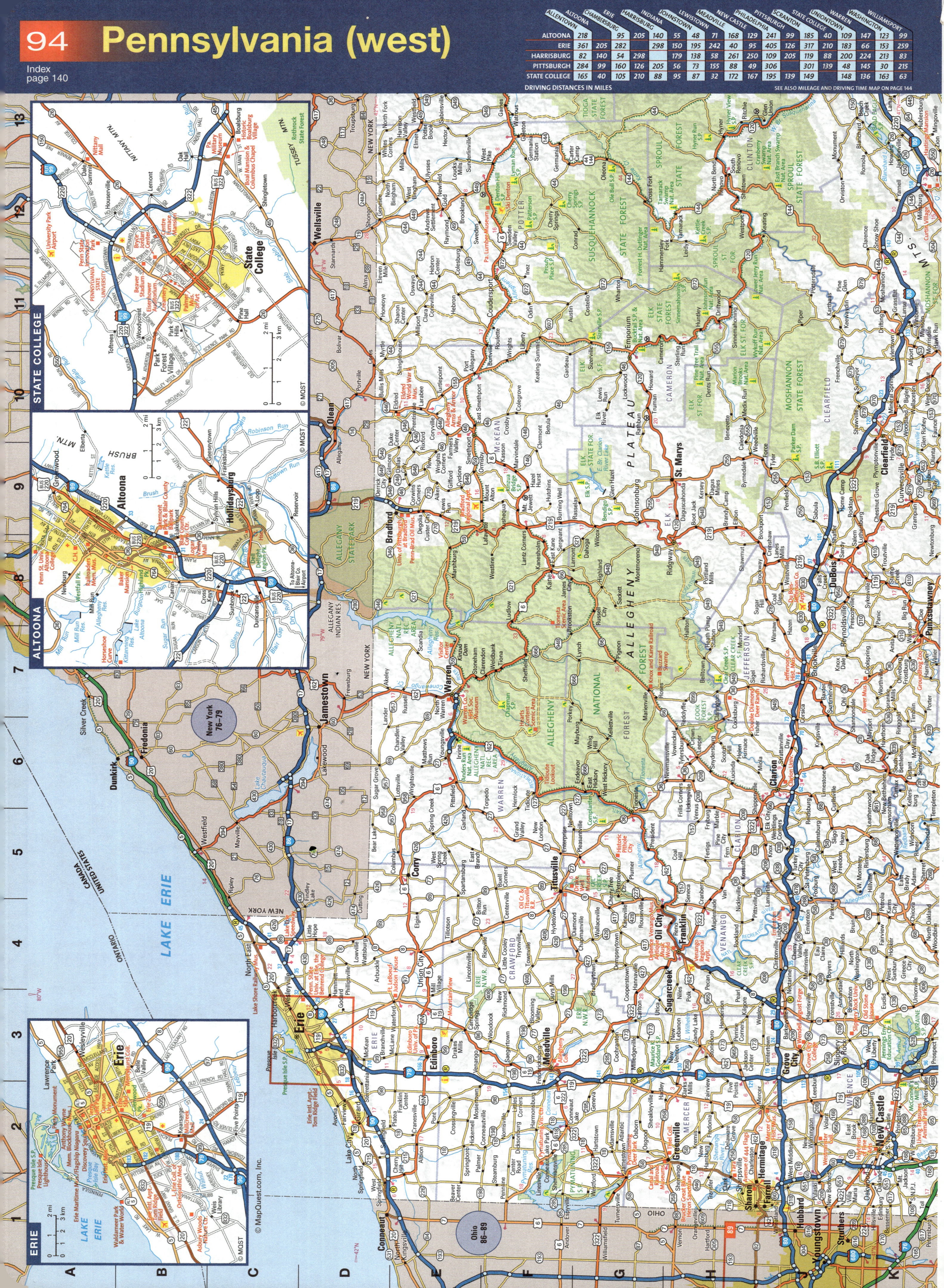

"Virtue, Liberty and Independence"

Index page 140

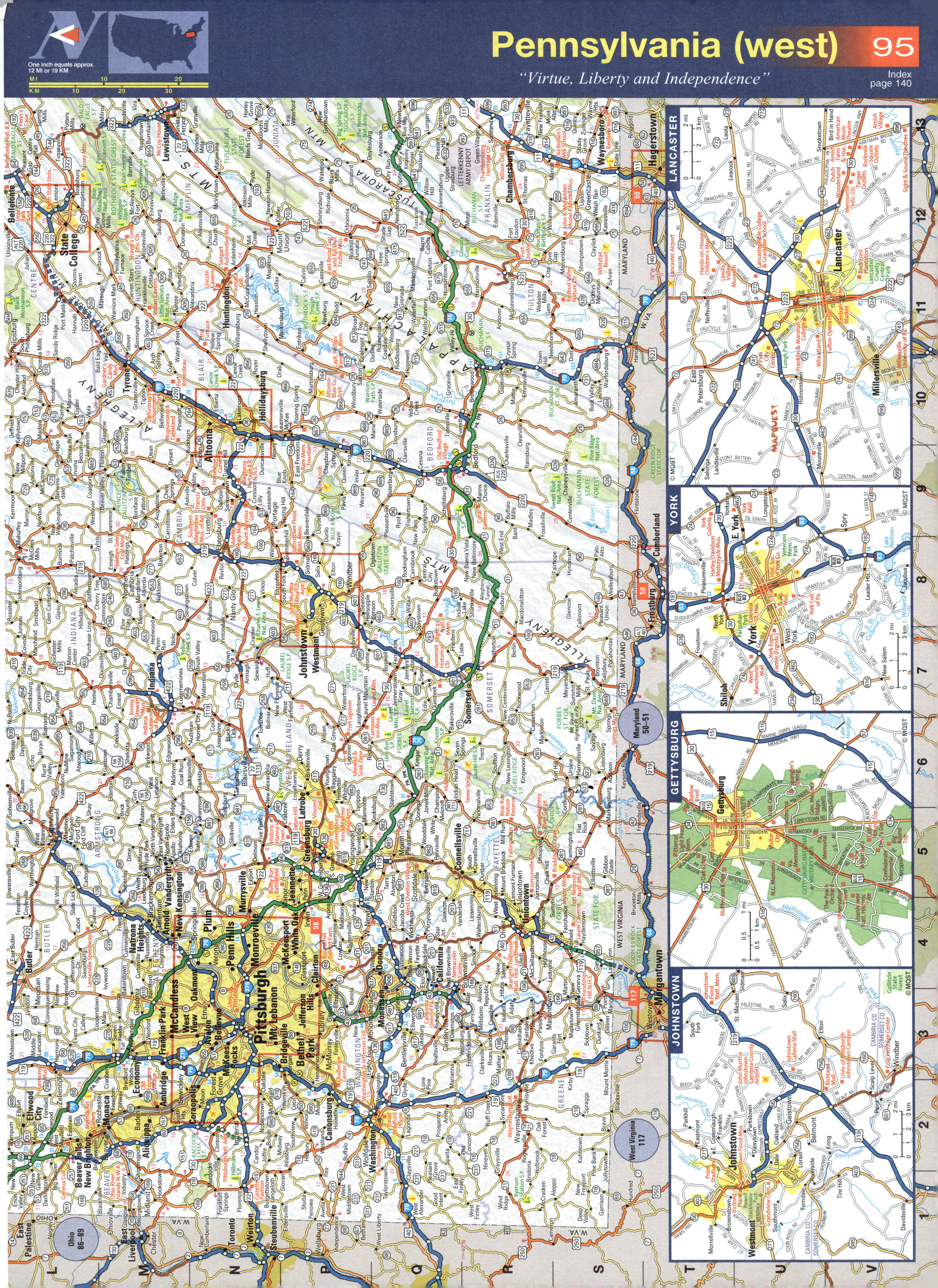

	ALLENTOWN	ALTOONA	CHAMBERSBURG	EAST STROUDSBURG	ERIE	GETTYSBURG	HARRISBURG	LANCASTER	LEWISTOWN	PHILADELPHIA	PITTSBURGH	READING	SCRANTON	STATE COLLEGE	SUNBURY	WILKES-BARRE	WILLIAMSPORT	YORK
ALLENTOWN		218	133	39	361	125	82	71	137	63	284	37	76	165	93	64	116	91
HARRISBURG	82	140	54	121	298	42		44	58	109	205	65	119	88	52	105	83	25
PHILADELPHIA	63	241	154	87	405	131	109	79	164		306	63	128	195	144	117	169	100
SCRANTON	76	185	170	50	317	162	119	130	130	128	301	103		149	84	17	83	143
WILLIAMSPORT	116	99	134	118	259	125	83	124	83	169	215	110	83	63	34	66		108

DRIVING DISTANCES IN MILES

SEE ALSO MILEAGE AND DRIVING TIME MAP ON PAGE 144

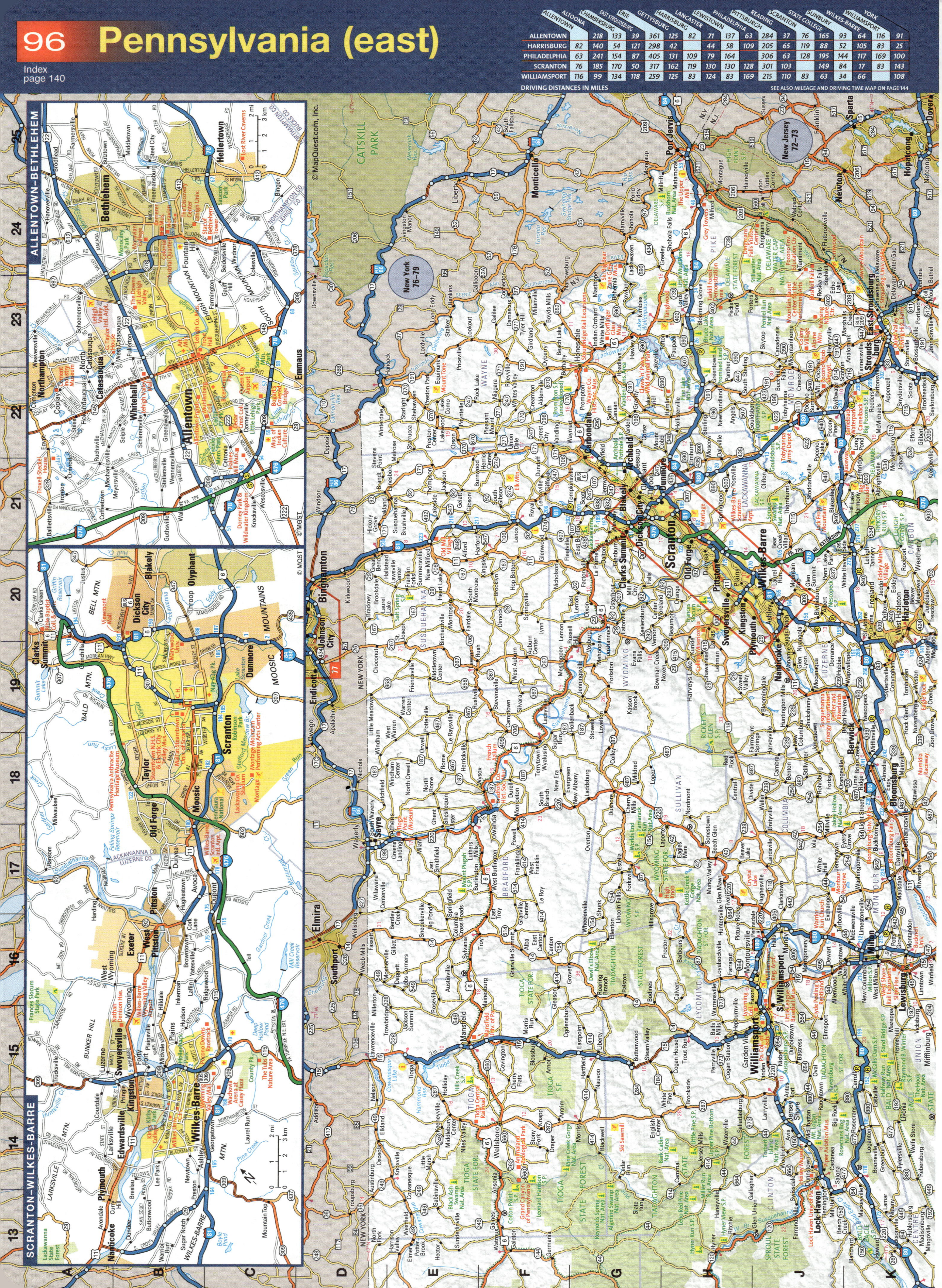

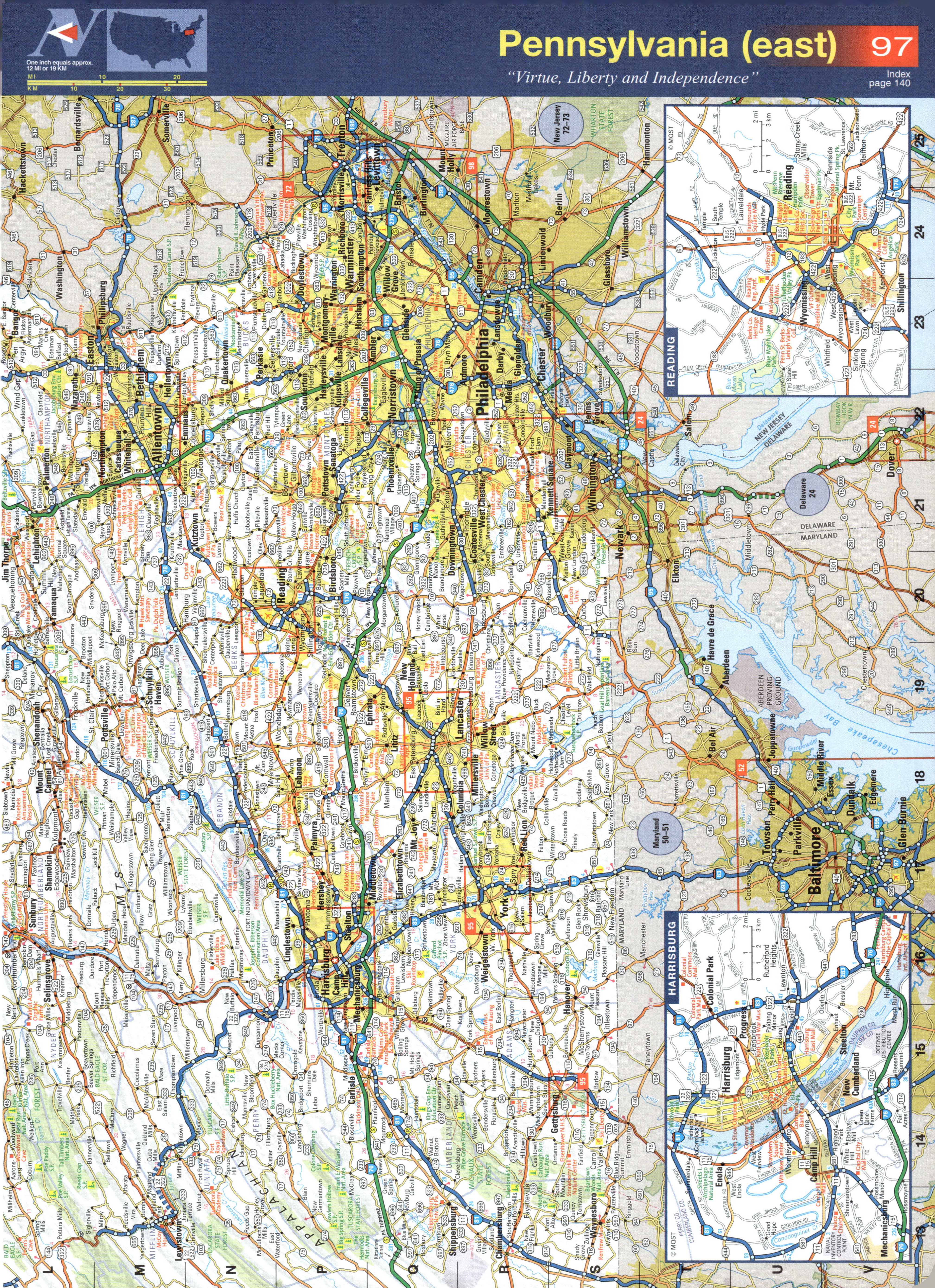

One inch equals approx. 12 MI or 19 KM
MI 10 20
KM 10 20 30
Pennsylvania (east)
97
“Virtue, Liberty and Independence”
Index page 140
READING
HARRISBURG
New Jersey 72-73
Delaware 24
Maryland 50-51
Philadelphia
Allentown
Bethlehem
Reading
Lancaster
York
Harrisburg
Wilmington
Baltimore
Trenton
Camden
Chester
Norristown
Easton
Lebanon
Hershey
Gettysburg
Carlisle
Chambersburg
Pottsville
Sunbury
Lewistown

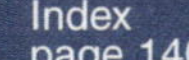

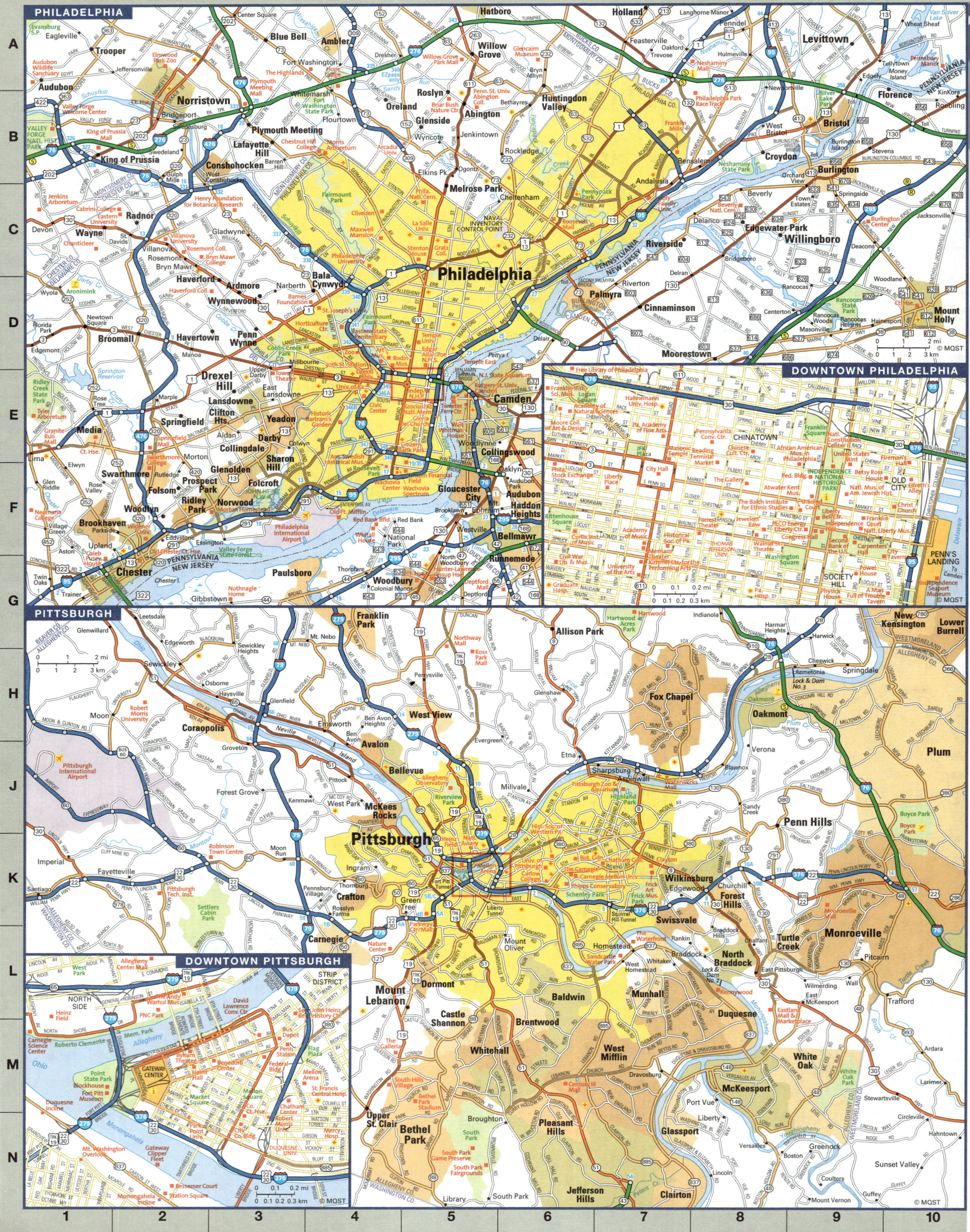

Index
page 140

PHILADELPHIA

Philadelphia, Norristown, King of Prussia, Conshohocken, Plymouth Meeting, Lafayette Hill, Blue Bell, Ambler, Fort Washington, Willow Grove, Hatboro, Roslyn, Oreland, Glenside, Abington, Jenkintown, Huntingdon Valley, Holland, Feasterville, Trevose, Levittown, Florence, Bristol, Croydon, Bensalem, Andalusia, Burlington, Beverly, Edgewater Park, Willingboro, Riverside, Delanco, Palmyra, Riverton, Cinnaminson, Moorestown, Mount Holly, Cheltenham, Melrose Park, Elkins Park, Wyncote, Radnor, Wayne, Devon, Villanova, Rosemont, Bryn Mawr, Haverford, Ardmore, Narberth, Bala-Cynwyd, Wynnewood, Havertown, Penn Wynne, Broomall, Newtown Square, Drexel Hill, Lansdowne, Clifton Hts., Yeadon, Darby, Collingdale, Sharon Hill, Folcroft, Glenolden, Prospect Park, Norwood, Ridley Park, Media, Springfield, Swarthmore, Folsom, Woodlyn, Brookhaven, Upland, Chester, Eddystone, Essington, Paulsboro, Woodbury, Gloucester City, Camden, Collingswood, Audubon, Haddon Heights, Bellmawr, Runnemede, National Park, Westville, Gibbstown, Pennsauken, Merchantville, Delair

DOWNTOWN PHILADELPHIA

City Hall, Chinatown, Independence National Historical Park, Old City, Society Hill, Penn's Landing, Washington Square, Franklin Square, Logan Square, JFK Plaza

PITTSBURGH

Pittsburgh, Coraopolis, Moon, Imperial, Fayetteville, Forest Grove, Robinson Town Centre, Moon Run, Crafton, Carnegie, Ingram, Green Tree, Mount Lebanon, Dormont, Castle Shannon, Upper St. Clair, Bethel Park, Baldwin, Brentwood, Whitehall, Pleasant Hills, West Mifflin, Munhall, Homestead, Duquesne, McKeesport, Glassport, Clairton, Jefferson Hills, Port Vue, Liberty, White Oak, Swissvale, Rankin, Braddock, North Braddock, Wilkinsburg, Edgewood, Forest Hills, Churchill, Turtle Creek, Monroeville, Pitcairn, Trafford, Penn Hills, Plum, Oakmont, Verona, Fox Chapel, Sharpsburg, Aspinwall, Etna, Millvale, Allison Park, West View, Bellevue, Avalon, Emsworth, Ben Avon, McKees Rocks, Sewickley, Edgworth, Glenfield, Franklin Park, New Kensington, Lower Burrell, Springdale

DOWNTOWN PITTSBURGH

North Side, Strip District, Gateway Center, Point State Park, Duquesne Incline, Monongahela Incline, Mt. Washington Overlook, Station Square

© MQST

	BOSTON, MA	BRISTOL	EAST GREENWICH	FALL RIVER, MA	HOPE VALLEY	KINGSTON	NEWPORT	PROVIDENCE	WARWICK	WESTERLY	WICKFORD	WOONSOCKET
NEWPORT	73	14	20	20	28	17		33	27	41	13	46
PROVIDENCE	52	16	12	17	30	29	33		12	46	20	15
WARWICK	63	25	6	26	24	23	27	12		40	14	26
WESTERLY	97	60	41	61	17	26	41	46	40		34	59
WOONSOCKET	52	30	26	31	43	42	46	16	26	59	33	

Index page 140

"While I Breathe, I Hope"

	AUGUSTA, GA	CHARLOTTE, NC	CHARLESTON	COLUMBIA	FLORENCE	GREENVILLE	HILTON HEAD ISLAND	MYRTLE BEACH	ROCK HILL	SAVANNAH, GA	SPARTANBURG	SUMTER
CHARLESTON	142	204		110	127	205	95	92	183	107	200	100
COLUMBIA	70	91	110		80	97	152	146	70	159	92	45
FLORENCE	147	107	127	80		174	170	66	115	176	169	39
GREENVILLE	110	96	205	97	174		248	241	88	255	30	142
MYRTLE BEACH	213	173	92	146	66	241	190		181	197	235	93

DRIVING DISTANCES IN MILES

SEE ALSO MILEAGE AND DRIVING TIME MAP ON PAGE 144

"Under God the People Rule"

Index page 140

	ABERDEEN	BELLE FOURCHE	BROOKINGS	HOT SPRINGS	HURON	MITCHELL	MOBRIDGE	PIERRE	RAPID CITY	SIOUX FALLS	WATERTOWN	YANKTON
ABERDEEN		310	150	412	90	146	99	160	357	204	98	231
PIERRE	160	247	188	247	115	155	107		193	226	189	240
RAPID CITY	357	56	390	56	313	275	243	193		346	436	360
SIOUX FALLS	204	401	57	401	127	73	303	226	346		103	80
WATERTOWN	98	360	49	490	86	162	196	189	436	103		179

DRIVING DISTANCES IN MILES

SEE ALSO MILEAGE AND DRIVING TIME MAP ON PAGE 144

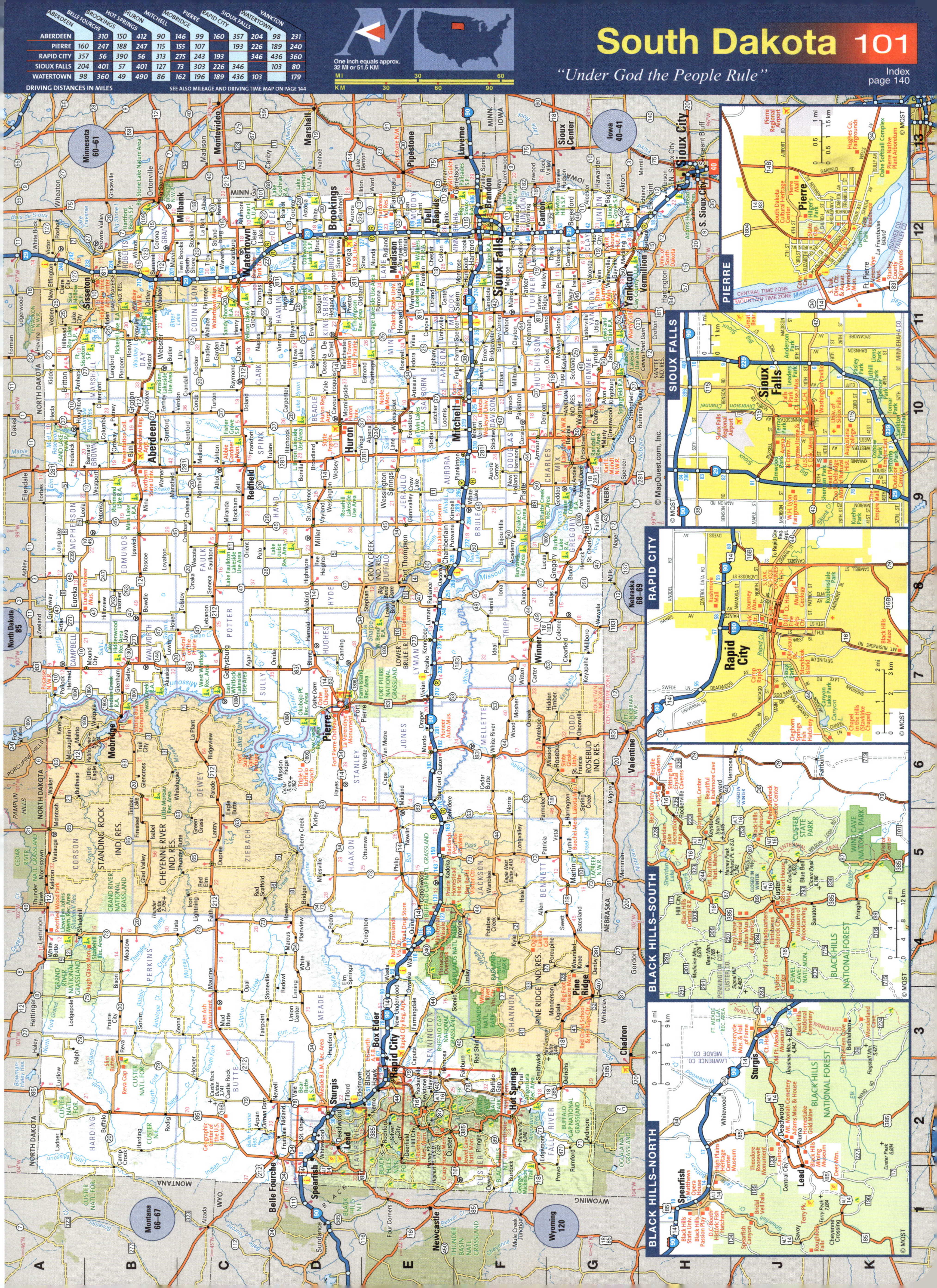

Index page 140

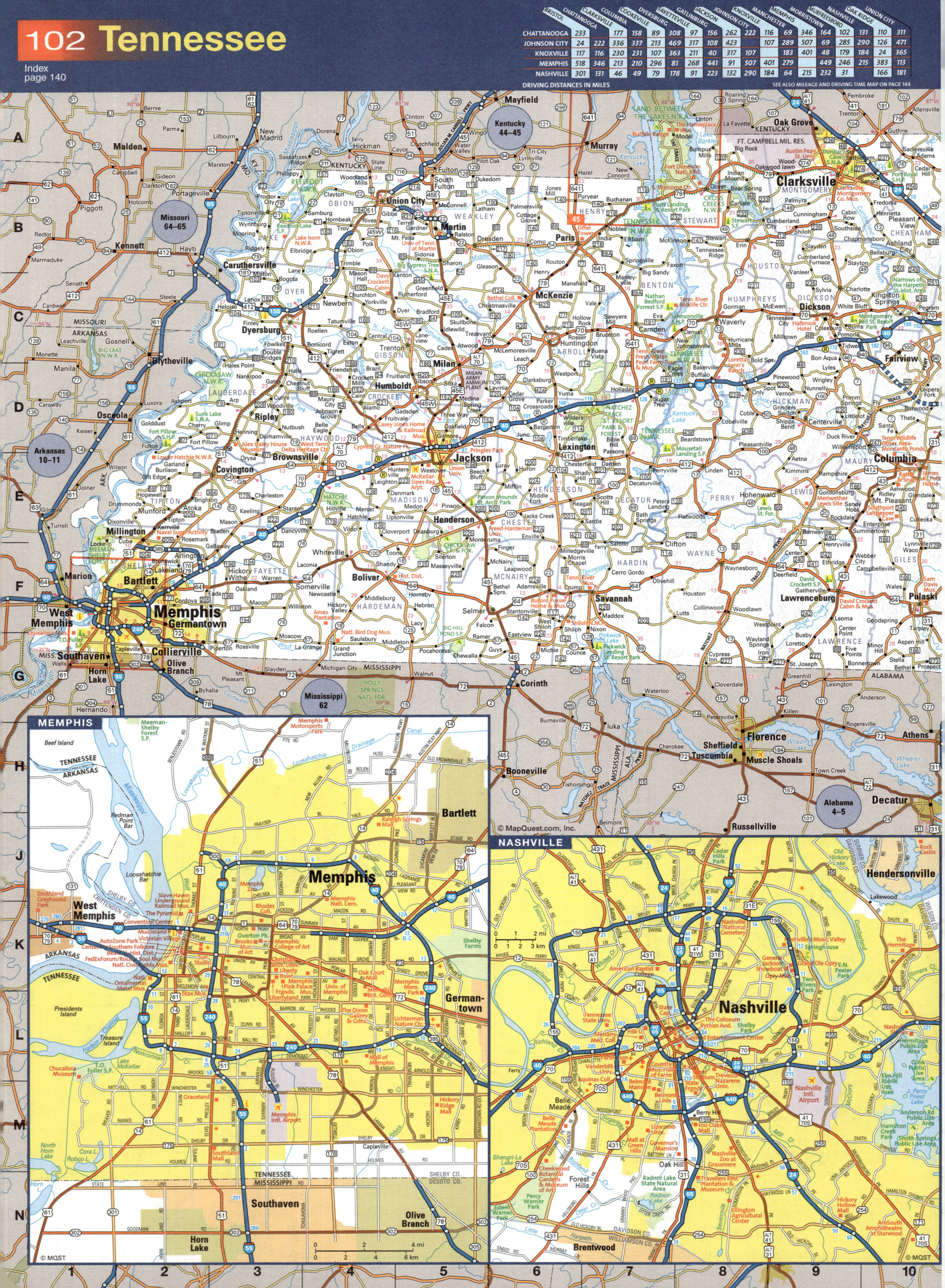

	BRISTOL	CHATTANOOGA	CLARKSVILLE	COLUMBIA	COOKEVILLE	DYERSBURG	FAYETTEVILLE	GATLINBURG	JACKSON	JOHNSON CITY	KNOXVILLE	MANCHESTER	MEMPHIS	MORRISTOWN	MURFREESBORO	NASHVILLE	OAK RIDGE	UNION CITY
CHATTANOOGA	233		177	158	89	308	97	156	262	222	116	69	346	164	102	131	110	311
JOHNSON CITY	24	222	336	337	213	469	317	108	423		107	289	507	69	285	290	126	471
KNOXVILLE	117	116	230	231	107	363	211	40	317	107		183	401	48	179	184	24	365
MEMPHIS	518	346	213	210	296	81	268	441	91	507	401	279		449	246	215	383	113
NASHVILLE	301	131	46	49	79	178	91	223	132	290	184	64	215	232	31		166	181

DRIVING DISTANCES IN MILES

SEE ALSO MILEAGE AND DRIVING TIME MAP ON PAGE 144

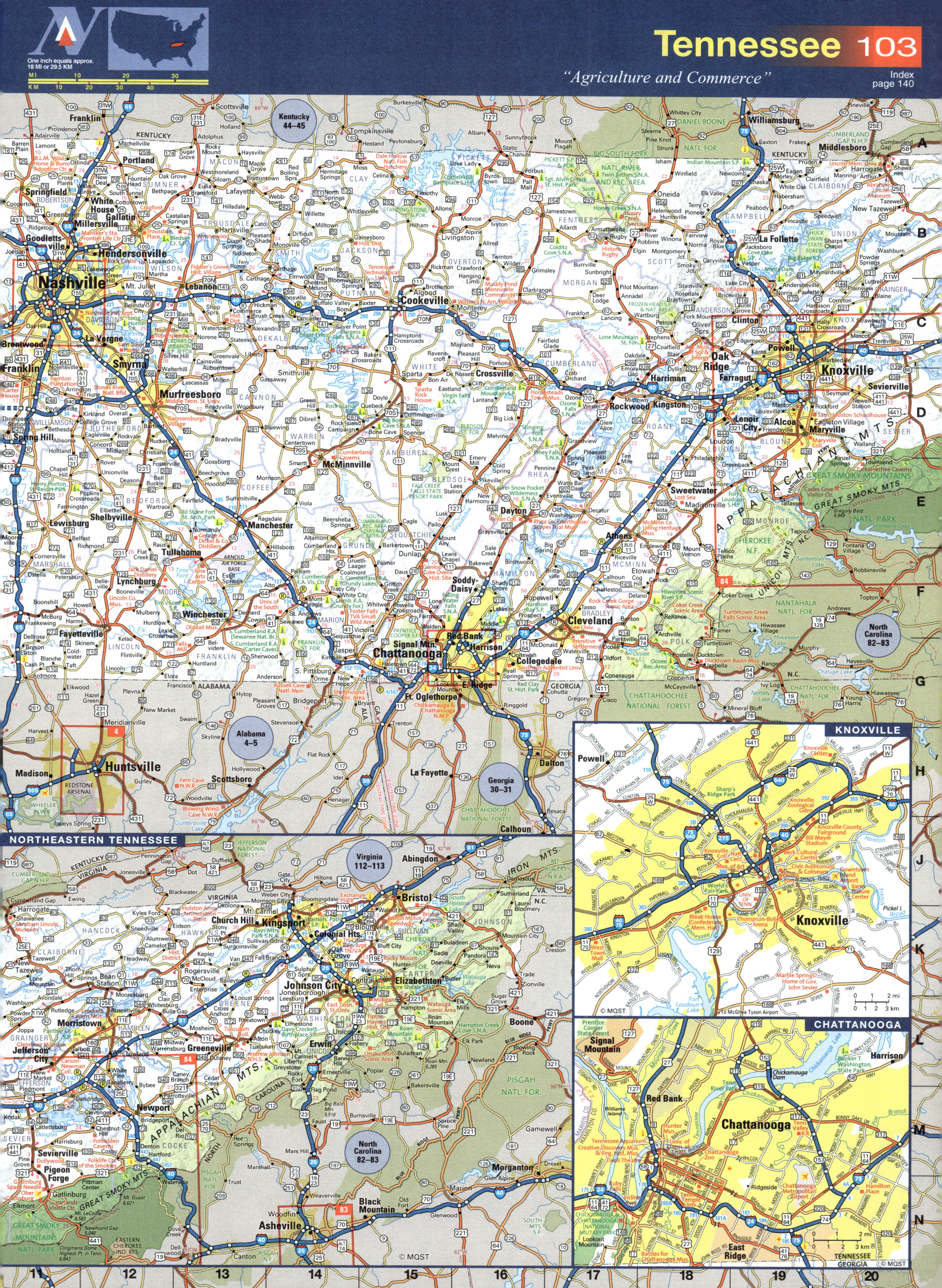

Tennessee
103
"Agriculture and Commerce"
Index page 140
One inch equals approx. 18 MI or 29.5 KM
Kentucky 44–45
Alabama 4–5
Georgia 30–31
North Carolina 82–83
Virginia 112–113
KNOXVILLE
CHATTANOOGA
NORTHEASTERN TENNESSEE
Nashville
Knoxville
Chattanooga
Murfreesboro
Cookeville
Crossville
Hendersonville
Gallatin
Lebanon
Smyrna
Franklin
Spring Hill
Shelbyville
Tullahoma
Manchester
McMinnville
Winchester
Fayetteville
Lewisburg
Lynchburg
Cleveland
Athens
Sweetwater
Maryville
Alcoa
Oak Ridge
Clinton
La Follette
Harriman
Kingston
Rockwood
Dayton
Soddy-Daisy
Signal Mtn.
Red Bank
Collegedale
East Ridge
Sevierville
Pigeon Forge
Gatlinburg
Morristown
Greeneville
Johnson City
Kingsport
Bristol
Elizabethton
Erwin
Newport
Jefferson City
Huntsville
Scottsboro
Dalton
Calhoun
Asheville
Abingdon
Williamsburg
Middlesboro
Harrogate
APPALACHIAN MTS.
GREAT SMOKY MTS.
CHEROKEE N.F.
© MQST

Index page 140

	ABILENE	ALPINE	AMARILLO	BIG BEND N.P.	BIG SPRING	CHILDRESS	DALHART	DALLAS	DEL RIO	EL PASO	FORT STOCKTON	LUBBOCK	ODESSA	PECOS	SAN ANGELO	SAN ANTONIO	VAN HORN	WICHITA FALLS
AMARILLO	290	414		472	230	118	87	470	462	438	349	124	266	340	308	513	427	228
EL PASO	459	232	438	329	347	558	420	647	425		241	341	285	209	416	556	122	596
LUBBOCK	166	291	124	349	106	144	211	354	338	341	226		142	217	185	389	303	207
ODESSA	176	151	266	209	65	276	353	364	246	285	86	142		76	134	342	163	314
SAN ANGELO	91	230	308	287	87	238	395	265	156	416	164	185	134	208		208	295	232

DRIVING DISTANCES IN MILES

SEE ALSO MILEAGE AND DRIVING TIME MAP ON PAGE 144

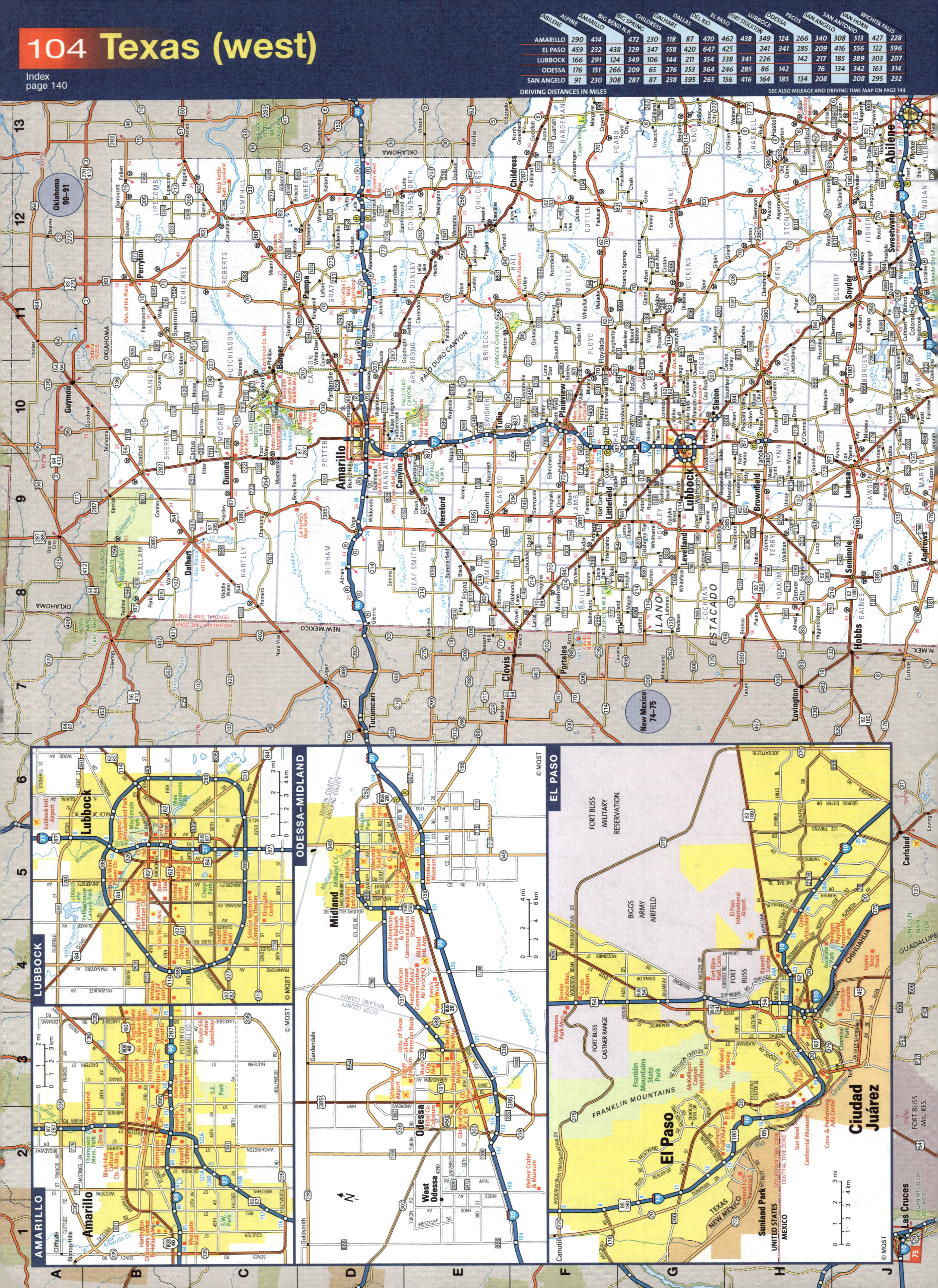

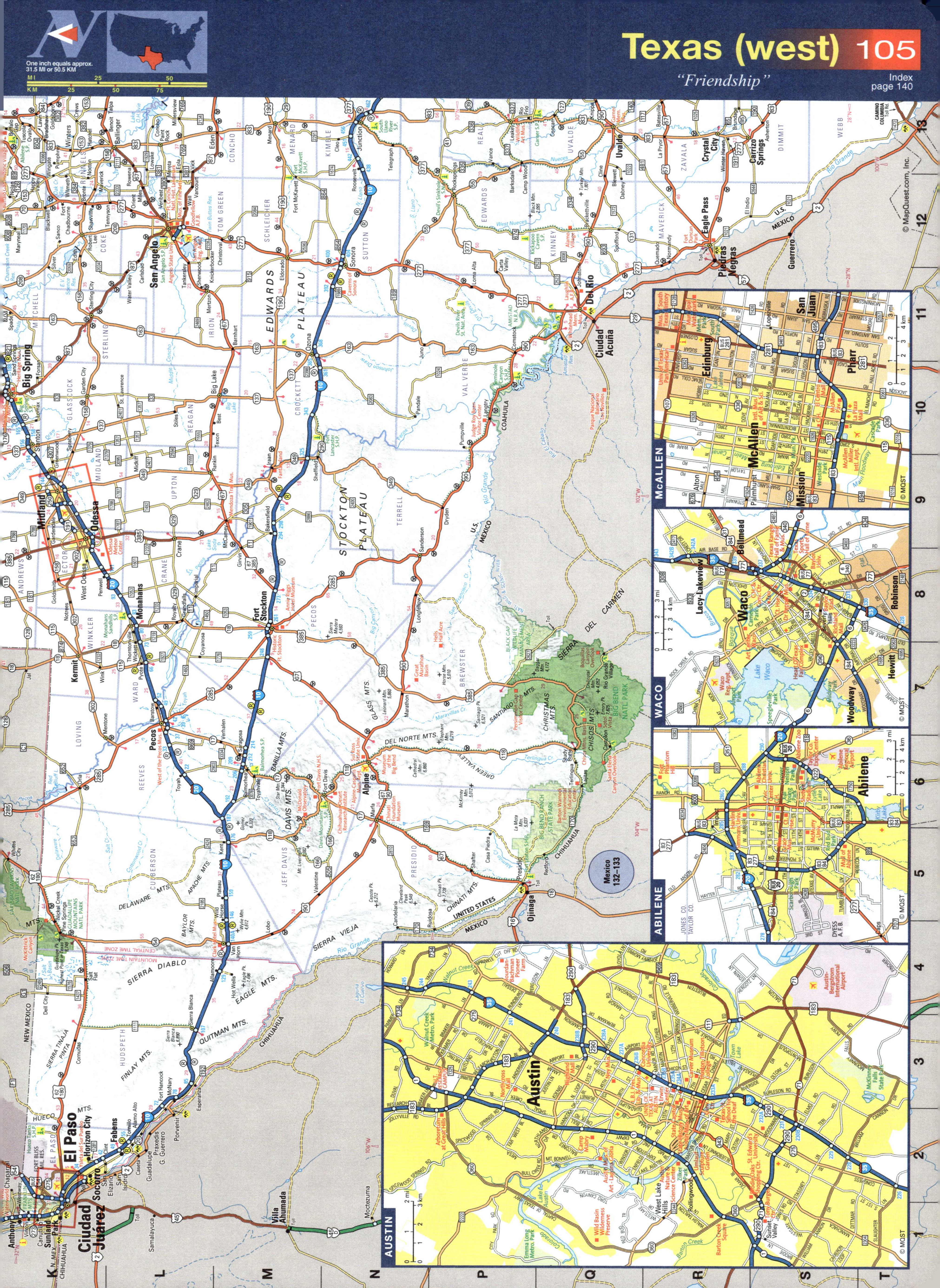
Texas (west)
105
"Friendship"
Index page 140
One inch equals approx. 31.5 MI or 50.5 KM
MI 25 50
KM 25 50 75
Mexico 132-133
McALLEN
WACO
ABILENE
AUSTIN
El Paso
Ciudad Juárez
Midland
Odessa
Big Spring
San Angelo
Fort Stockton
Pecos
Monahans
Alpine
Marfa
Presidio
Ojinaga
Del Rio
Ciudad Acuña
Eagle Pass
Piedras Negras
Sonora
Ozona
Uvalde
EDWARDS PLATEAU
STOCKTON PLATEAU
BIG BEND NAT'L PARK
SIERRA DEL CARMEN
UNITED STATES
MEXICO
COAHUILA
CHIHUAHUA
NEW MEXICO
Rio Grande
Austin
Waco
Abilene
McAllen
Edinburg
Pharr
Mission
San Juan
© MapQuest.com, Inc.
© MOST

Index page 140

	ABILENE	AUSTIN	BEAUMONT	BROWNSVILLE	COLLEGE STATION	CORPUS CHRISTI	DALLAS	DEL RIO	FORT WORTH	HOUSTON	LAREDO	MC ALLEN	SAN ANGELO	SAN ANTONIO	TEXARKANA	TYLER	WACO	WICHITA FALLS
AUSTIN	217		250	350	108	217	195	229	187	166	238	313	207	78	375	229	105	301
CORPUS CHRISTI	411	217	293	157	254		411	272	403	211	141	152	362	147	591	445	321	517
DALLAS	191	195	323	544	184	411		422	32	241	432	507	265	271	179	100	94	141
HOUSTON	425	166	84	351	106	211	241	349	275		355	346	410	200	290	202	203	382
SAN ANTONIO	258	78	284	279	171	147	271	152	264	200	157	243	208		452	306	182	378

DRIVING DISTANCES IN MILES

SEE ALSO MILEAGE AND DRIVING TIME MAP ON PAGE 144

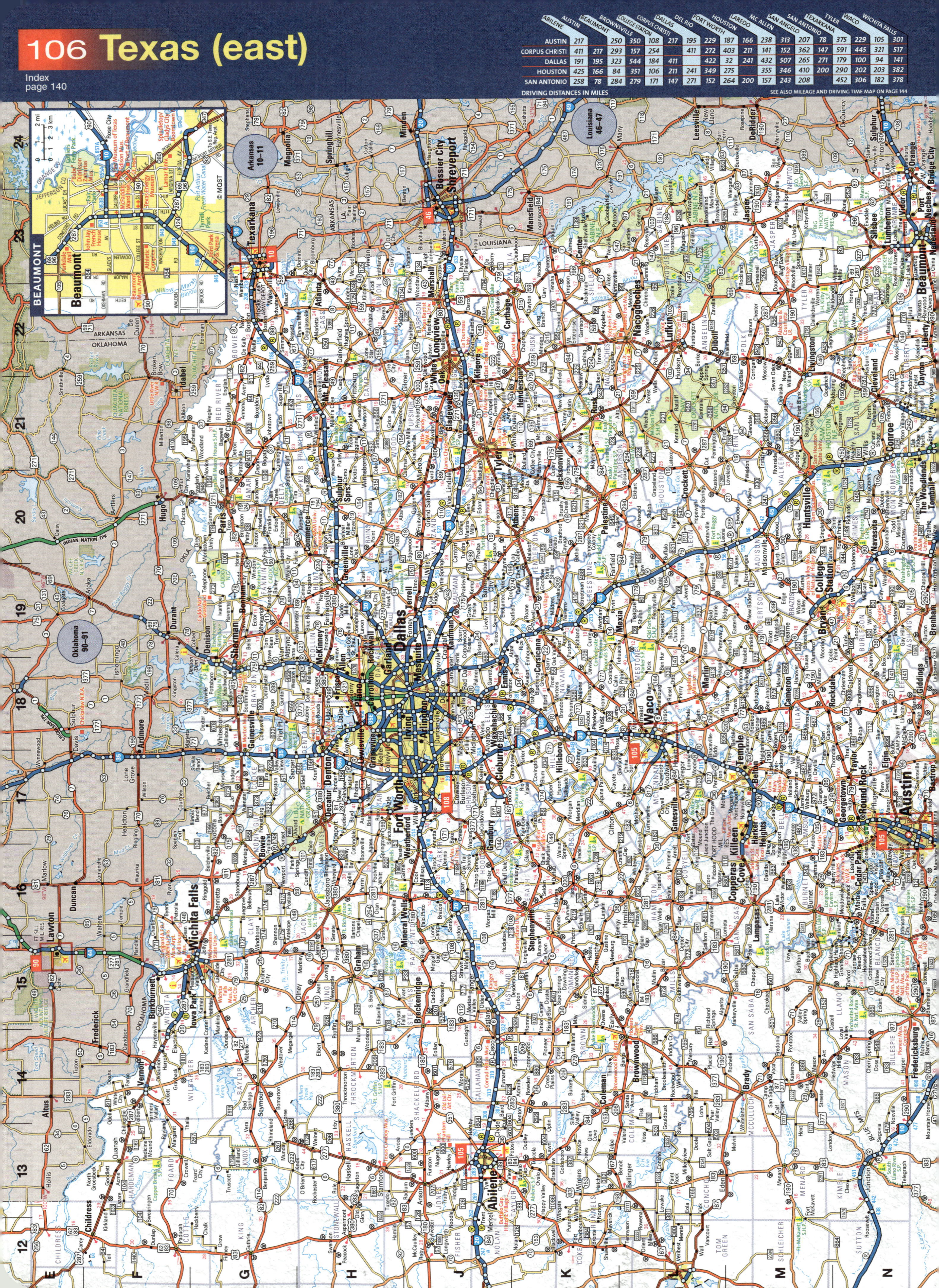

"Friendship"

Index page 140

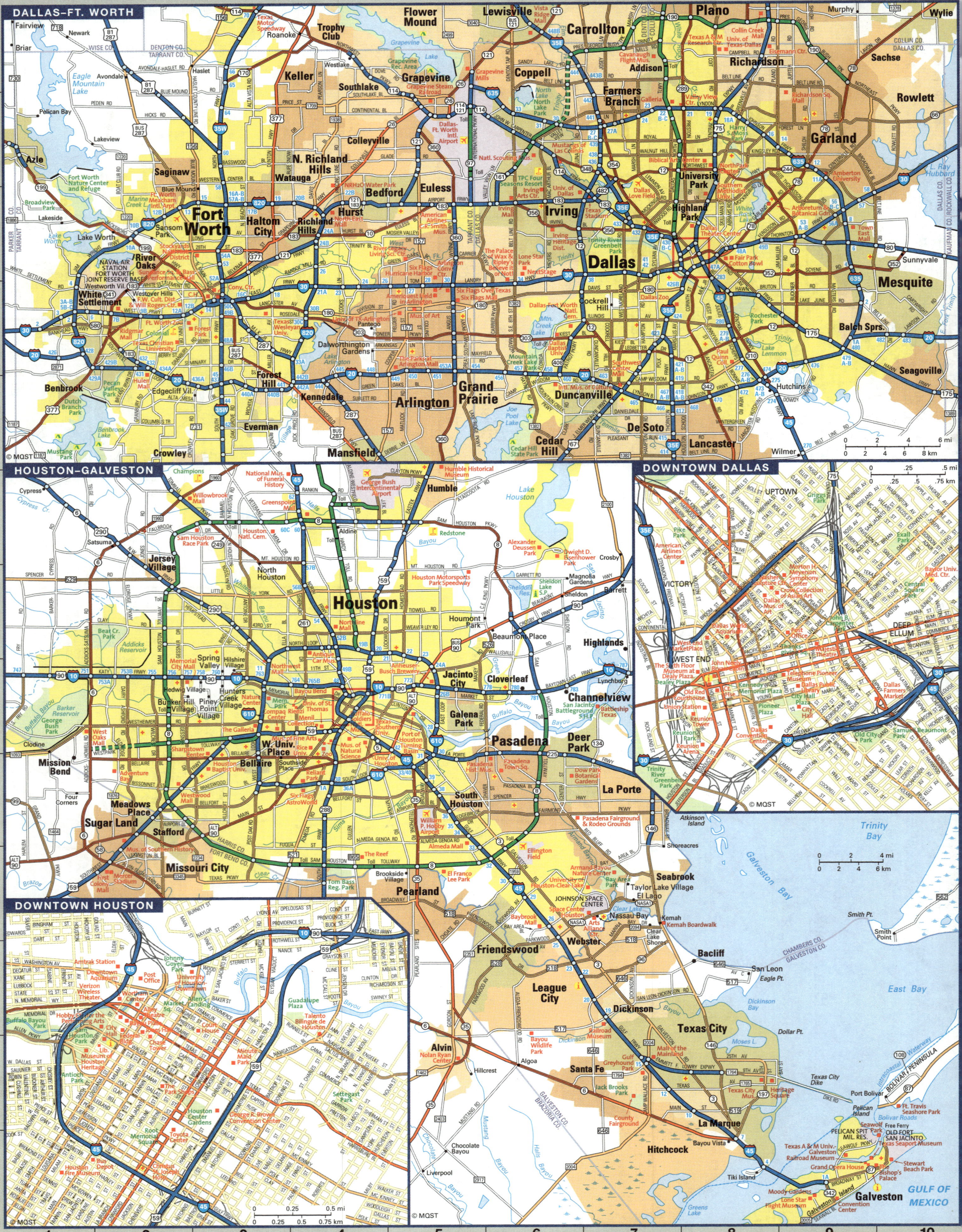

Index page 140

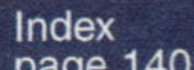

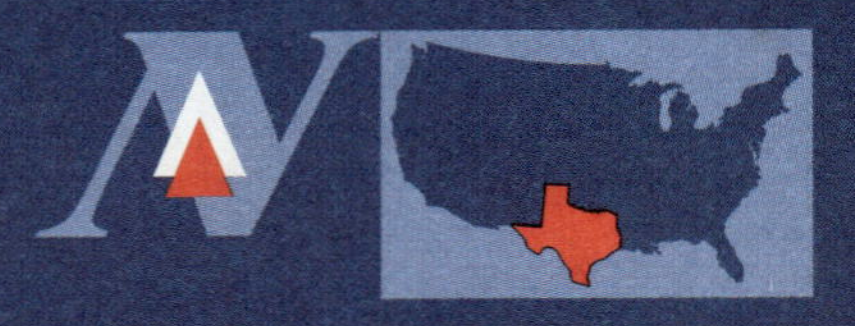

DALLAS–FT. WORTH

HOUSTON–GALVESTON

DOWNTOWN DALLAS

DOWNTOWN HOUSTON

© MQST

	CEDAR CITY	GREEN RIVER	LOGAN	MOAB	OGDEN	PRICE	PROVO	RICHFIELD	ST. GEORGE	SALT LAKE CITY	VERNAL	ZION N.P.
CEDAR CITY		235	325	289	283	234	204	111	53	247	346	66
GREEN RIVER	235		259	54	217	62	137	124	287	180	175	300
LOGAN	325	259		313	46	195	125	233	377	78	252	390
PROVO	204	137	125	192	83	74		111	256	47	155	269
SALT LAKE CITY	247	180	78	235	37	117	47	154	299		173	312

DRIVING DISTANCES IN MILES

SEE ALSO MILEAGE AND DRIVING TIME MAP ON PAGE 144

Index page 141

"Freedom and Unity"

	BENNINGTON	BRATTLEBORO	BURLINGTON	MIDDLEBURY	MONTPELIER	NEWPORT	RUTLAND	ST. ALBANS	ST. JOHNSBURY	SPRINGFIELD	VERGENNES	WHITE RIVER JCT.
BENNINGTON		38	127	91	124	200	58	150	161	63	105	98
BURLINGTON	127	148		36	39	81	69	23	76	120	22	91
MONTPELIER	124	112	39	56		64	66	60	37	84	58	54
RUTLAND	58	72	69	33	66	129		93	107	39	47	44
WHITE RIVER JCT.	98	62	91	66	54	104	44	112	65	34	80	

DRIVING DISTANCES IN MILES

SEE ALSO MILEAGE AND DRIVING TIME MAP ON PAGE 144

One inch equals approx. 13.5 MI or 21.5 KM

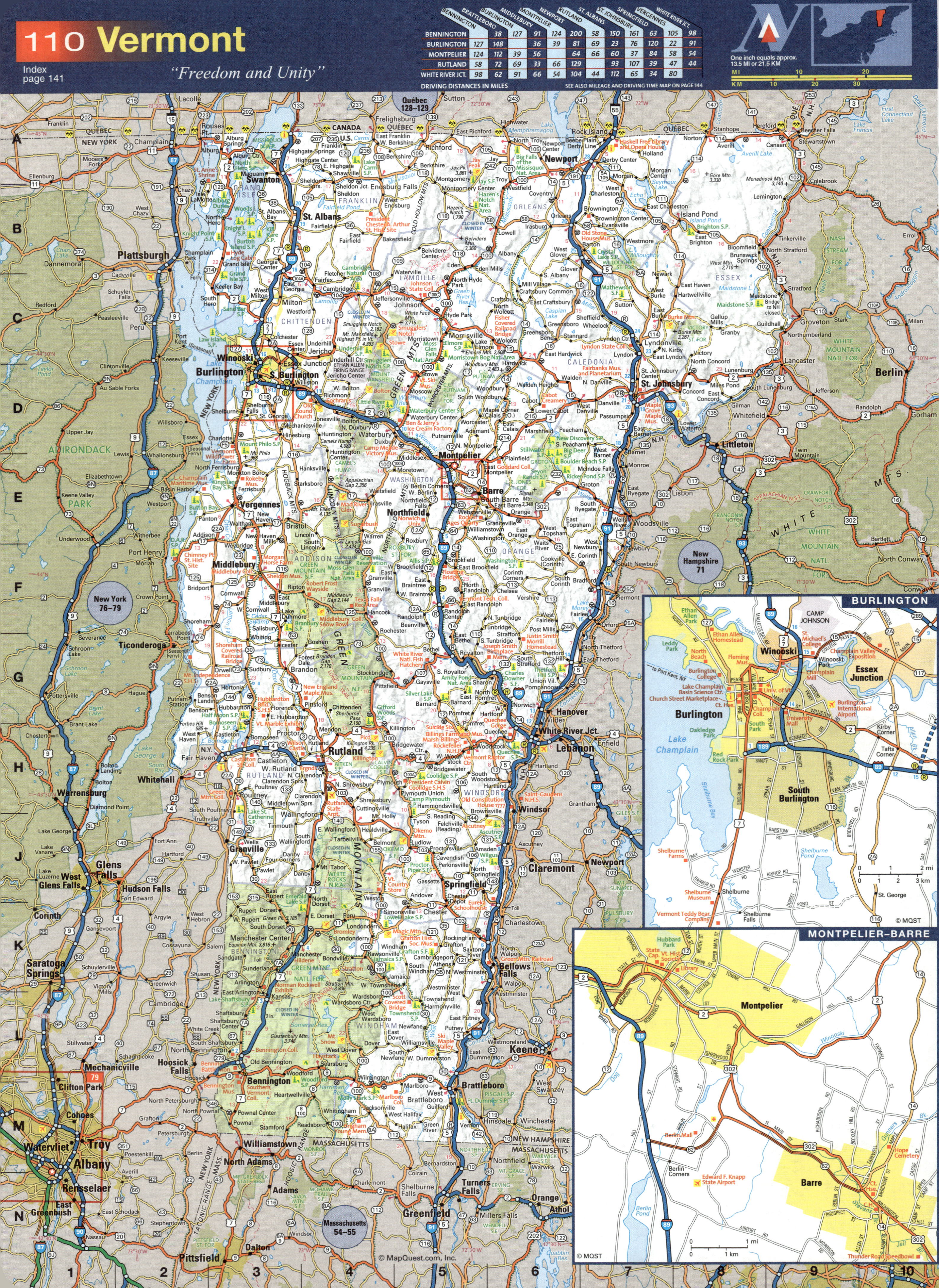

CHARLOTTESVILLE

Charlottesville

© MQST

WASHINGTON, DC AREA

Washington, Arlington, Alexandria, Bethesda, Rockville, Silver Spring, Reston, Herndon, Centreville, Manassas, Fairfax, Vienna, Leesburg

© MQST

PETERSBURG

Petersburg, Colonial Heights, Hopewell, Ettrick

© MQST

NORFOLK-VIRGINIA BEACH-NEWPORT NEWS

Norfolk, Virginia Beach, Newport News, Hampton, Portsmouth, Chesapeake, Suffolk, Poquoson, Smithfield

Chesapeake Bay

ATLANTIC OCEAN

© MQST

COLONIAL NATL. HIST. PARK

Williamsburg, Yorktown, Jamestown Island

© MQST

Index page 141

	BRISTOL	CHARLOTTESVILLE	CHINCOTEAGUE	DANVILLE	EMPORIA	FREDERICKSBURG	HARRISONBURG	LEXINGTON	LYNCHBURG	NORFOLK	PETERSBURG	RICHMOND	ROANOKE	VIRGINIA BEACH	WASHINGTON, DC	WILLIAMSBURG	WINCHESTER	WYTHEVILLE
CHARLOTTESVILLE	258		255	131	140	70	62	69	67	164	95	71	123	180	118	122	100	187
NORFOLK	420	164	101	191	78	145	225	231	203		79	91	285	18	196	43	235	350
RICHMOND	327	71	182	160	69	57	131	138	114	91	24		192	107	108	49	147	256
ROANOKE	149	123	377	83	180	192	117	54	55	285	216	192		301	245	243	184	78
WASHINGTON, DC	380	118	158	268	177	54	131	191	183	196	133	108	245	212		153	92	309

DRIVING DISTANCES IN MILES

SEE ALSO MILEAGE AND DRIVING TIME MAP ON PAGE 144

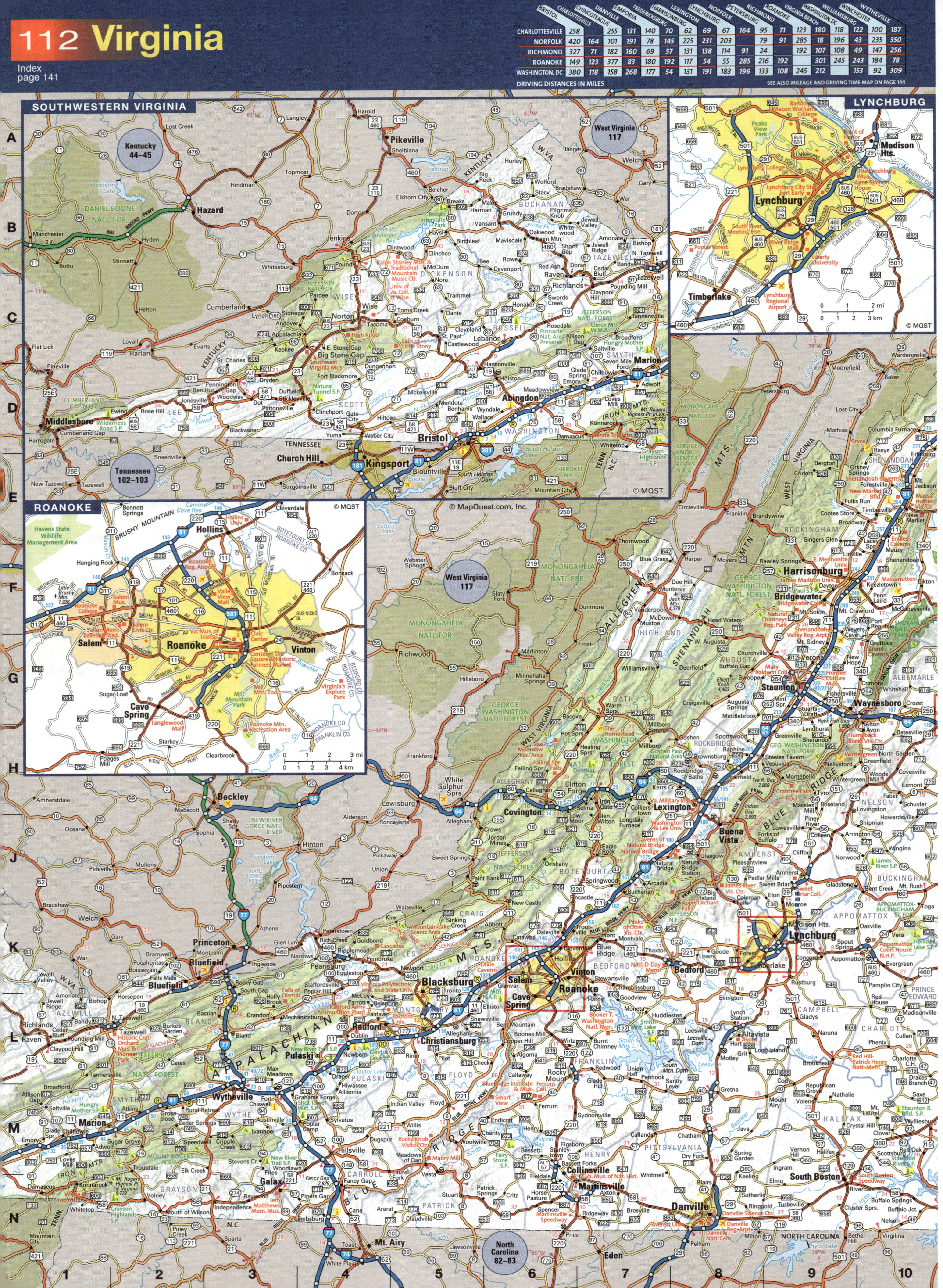

One inch equals approx. 17.5 MI or 28 KM
MI
KM
RICHMOND
Pennsylvania 94–97
West Virginia 117
Maryland 50–51
DC 116
Delaware 24
North Carolina 82–83
PENNSYLVANIA
MARYLAND
Hagerstown
Martinsburg
Frederick
Baltimore
Towson
Dundalk
Columbia
Glen Burnie
Annapolis
Washington
Arlington
Alexandria
Bowie
Rockville
Leesburg
Reston
Manassas
Woodbridge
Dale City
Winchester
Front Royal
Warrenton
Culpeper
Fredericksburg
Charlottesville
Ashland
Richmond
Mechanicsville
Lakeside
Bon Air
Chester
Colonial Hts.
Petersburg
Hopewell
Farmville
Williamsburg
Newport News
Hampton
Poquoson
Norfolk
Portsmouth
Virginia Beach
Chesapeake
Suffolk
Franklin
Emporia
Roanoke Rapids
Salisbury
Cambridge
St. Charles
La Plata
Chesapeake Bay
ATLANTIC OCEAN
Pocomoke Sound
Tangier Sound
CHESAPEAKE BAY BRIDGE-TUNNEL
GREAT DISMAL SWAMP N.W.R.
Shenandoah Natl. Park
Hanover
Gettysburg
Waynesboro
Westminster
Thurmont
Chambersburg
Mt. Airy
Olney
Laurel
Germantown
Gaithersburg
Wheaton
Bethesda
Vienna
Oakton
Fairfax
Springfield
Centreville
Chantilly
Sterling
Herndon
Manassas Park
Mount Vernon
Quantico
Triangle
Dumfries
Stafford
Spotsylvania
Orange
Louisa
Goochland
Powhatan
Amelia
Dinwiddie
Sussex
Southampton
Surry
Isle of Wight
Gloucester
Mathews
Middlesex
Lancaster
Northumberland
Westmoreland
King George
King William
King and Queen
New Kent
Charles City
James City
York
Essex
Richmond
Caroline
Hanover
Cumberland
Prince Edward
Nottoway
Lunenburg
Mecklenburg
Brunswick
Greensville
Prince George
Accomack
Northampton
Chincoteague
Onancock
Cape Charles
Cape Henry
Smithfield
Midlothian
Sandston
Varina
Highland Springs
Tuckahoe
Short Pump
Glen Allen
Laurel
Ashland
Chesterfield
Bensley
Bellwood
Centralia
Rivermont
Wrightsville
Stafford
Kilmarnock
Tappahannock
West Point
Warsaw
Montross
Colonial Beach
Dahlgren
Jarratt
Lawrenceville
South Hill
Blackstone
Crewe
Burkeville
Keysville
Victoria
Kenbridge
Chase City
Boydton
La Crosse
Gasburg
Wakefield
Waverly
Courtland
Ivor
Zuni
Windsor
Carrollton
Smithfield
Tabb
Yorktown
Seaford
Gloucester Point
Hayes
Whaleyville
Moyock
Fruitland
Berlin
Snow Hill
Pocomoke City
Crisfield
Princess Anne
Stockton
Greenbackville
Tangier
Saxis
Parksley
Bloxom
Wachapreague
Exmore
Nassawadox
Eastville
Cheriton
Cape Charles
Fishermans Island N.W.R.
Eastern Shore of Virginia N.W.R.

Index page 141

	ABERDEEN	BELLINGHAM	EVERETT	KENNEWICK	LEWISTON, ID	LONGVIEW	MOUNT RANIER N.P.	OKANOGAN	OLYMPIA	PORT ANGELES	PORTLAND, OR	PULLMAN	SEATTLE	SPOKANE	TACOMA	WALLA WALLA	WENATCHEE	YAKIMA
BELLINGHAM	196		61	307	420	215	186	195	147	127*	261	390	88	360	122	353	185	221
OLYMPIA	49	147	86	275	387	68	73	282		117	114	358	56	327	27	320	196	188
SEATTLE	105	88	28	226	338	124	96	223	56	83*	170	309		278	31	271	148	140
SPOKANE	376	360	299	139	103	395	290	148	327	362*	351	73	278		303	167	171	203
YAKIMA	237	221	161	86	214	170	87	194	188	223*	187	233	140	203	164	132	115	

DRIVING DISTANCES IN MILES

* DISTANCE INCLUDES FERRY TRAVEL

Washington 115
"By and By"
Index page 141
One inch equals approx. 22 MI or 35.5 KM
British Columbia 122
Idaho 33
Oregon 92–93
CANADA
UNITED STATES
BRITISH COLUMBIA
Spokane
Spokane Valley
Country Homes
Wenatchee
East Wenatchee
Ellensburg
Yakima
Union Gap
Selah
Moses Lake
Ephrata
Quincy
Othello
Richland
West Richland
Kennewick
Pasco
Walla Walla
College Place
Pullman
Clarkston
Lewiston
Colville
Cheney
Toppenish
Sunnyside
Grandview
The Dallas
Pendleton
Milton-Freewater
Hermiston
Moscow
Coeur d'Alene
Post Falls
Trail
COLVILLE INDIAN RESERVATION
YAKAMA INDIAN RESERVATION
SPOKANE IND. RES.
U.S. DEPT. OF ENERGY HANFORD SITE
U.S. MIL. RES. YAKIMA TRAINING CENTER
OKANOGAN NATIONAL FOREST
WENATCHEE NATIONAL FOREST
COLVILLE NATL. FOR.
KETTLE RIVER RANGE
SELKIRK MTS.
HORSE HEAVEN HILLS
RATTLESNAKE HILLS
SADDLE MTS.
NORTH CASCADES NATL. PARK
YAKIMA
SPOKANE
© MapQuest.com, Inc.
© MQST

Index page 135

One inch equals approx. 2.5 MI or 4 KM

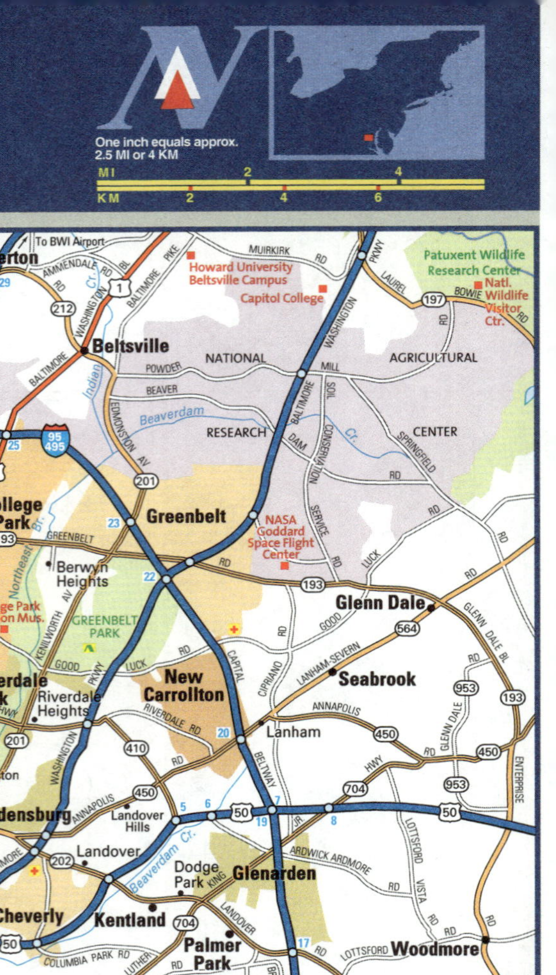

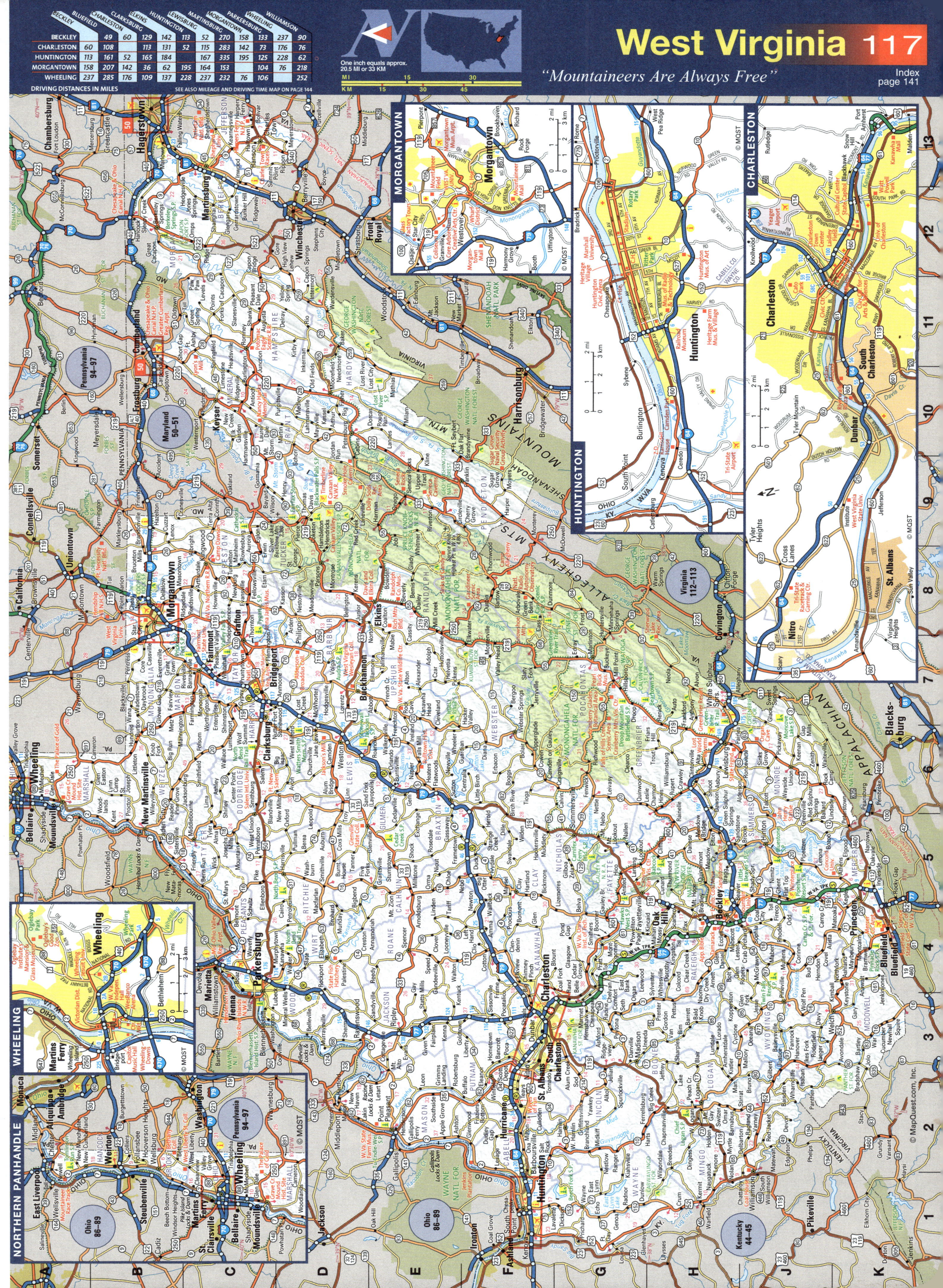

West Virginia 117
"Mountaineers Are Always Free"
Index page 141
One inch equals approx. 20.5 MI or 33 KM
BECKLEY BLUEFIELD CHARLESTON CLARKSBURG ELKINS HUNTINGTON LEWISBURG MARTINSBURG MORGANTOWN PARKERSBURG WHEELING WILLIAMSON
BECKLEY 49 60 129 142 113 52 270 158 133 237 90
CHARLESTON 60 108 113 131 52 115 283 142 73 176 76
HUNTINGTON 113 161 52 165 184 167 335 195 125 228 62
MORGANTOWN 158 207 142 36 62 195 164 153 104 76 218
WHEELING 237 285 176 109 137 228 237 232 76 106 252
DRIVING DISTANCES IN MILES
SEE ALSO MILEAGE AND DRIVING TIME MAP ON PAGE 144
MORGANTOWN
HUNTINGTON
CHARLESTON
WHEELING
NORTHERN PANHANDLE
Pennsylvania 94-97
Maryland 50-51
Virginia 112-113
Ohio 86-89
Kentucky 44-45
SHENANDOAH MOUNTAINS
ALLEGHENY MTS.
APPALACHIAN
MONONGAHELA NATL FOR.
WAYNE NATL FOR.
Charleston
Huntington
Parkersburg
Wheeling
Morgantown
Clarksburg
Beckley
Bluefield
© MapQuest.com, Inc.

Index page 141

	APPLETON	ASHLAND	BELOIT	EAU CLAIRE	GREEN BAY	KENOSHA	LA CROSSE	MADISON	MARINETTE	MILWAUKEE	OSHKOSH	PORTAGE	PRAIRIE DU CHIEN	RHINELANDER	ST. PAUL, MN	SHEBOYGAN	SUPERIOR	WAUSAU
EAU CLAIRE	178	163	225		192	284	81	176	211	246	180	147	151	151	83	227	155	99
GREEN BAY	31	245	189	192		154	205	135	54	115	50	120	234	124	268	61	308	93
MADISON	104	305	56	176	135	116	141		184	78	86	36	102	197	258	132	327	141
MILWAUKEE	105	375	74	246	115	39	211	78	170		87	106	180	239	328	54	397	211
WAUSAU	90	165	190	99	93	249	146	141	112	211	111	105	193	58	174	153	223	

DRIVING DISTANCES IN MILES

SEE ALSO MILEAGE AND DRIVING TIME MAP ON PAGE 144

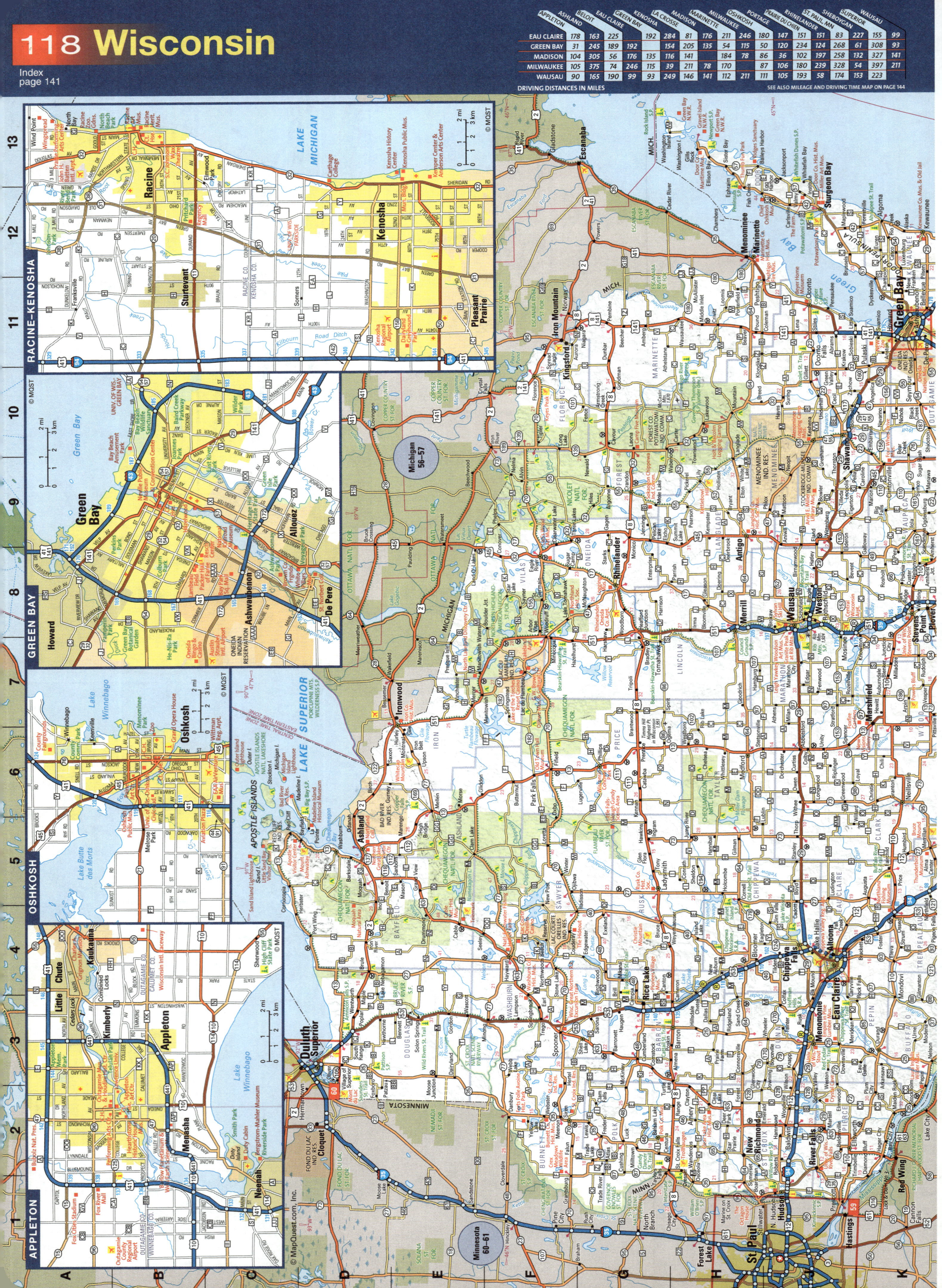

"Forward"
Index page 141
One inch equals approx. 23 MI or 37 KM
LAKE MICHIGAN
Milwaukee
Chicago
Madison
Oshkosh
Appleton
Fond du Lac
Sheboygan
Manitowoc
Racine
Kenosha
Janesville
Rockford
La Crosse
Dubuque
Gary
Joliet
Kankakee
Waukegan
Evanston
Iowa 40-41
Illinois 34-35
Indiana 38-39
Minnesota 60-61
EAU CLAIRE
MADISON
MILWAUKEE
DOWNTOWN MILWAUKEE
CENTRAL TIME ZONE
EASTERN TIME ZONE
© MQST

Index page 142

Wyoming

"Equal Rights"

	Casper	Cheyenne	Cody	Evanston	Gillette	Jackson	Lander	Laramie	Rawlins	Rock Springs	Sheridan	Yellowstone N.P.
CASPER		175	215	308	127	282	144	148	117	214	149	298
CHEYENNE	175		390	353	243	433	276	52	151	260	324	455
JACKSON	282	433	181	195	412		163	383	283	177	376	80
ROCK SPRINGS	214	260	281	97	341	177	118	210	110		363	259
SHERIDAN	149	324	150	457	102	376	238	297	266	363		337

DRIVING DISTANCES IN MILES

SEE ALSO MILEAGE AND DRIVING TIME MAP ON PAGE 144

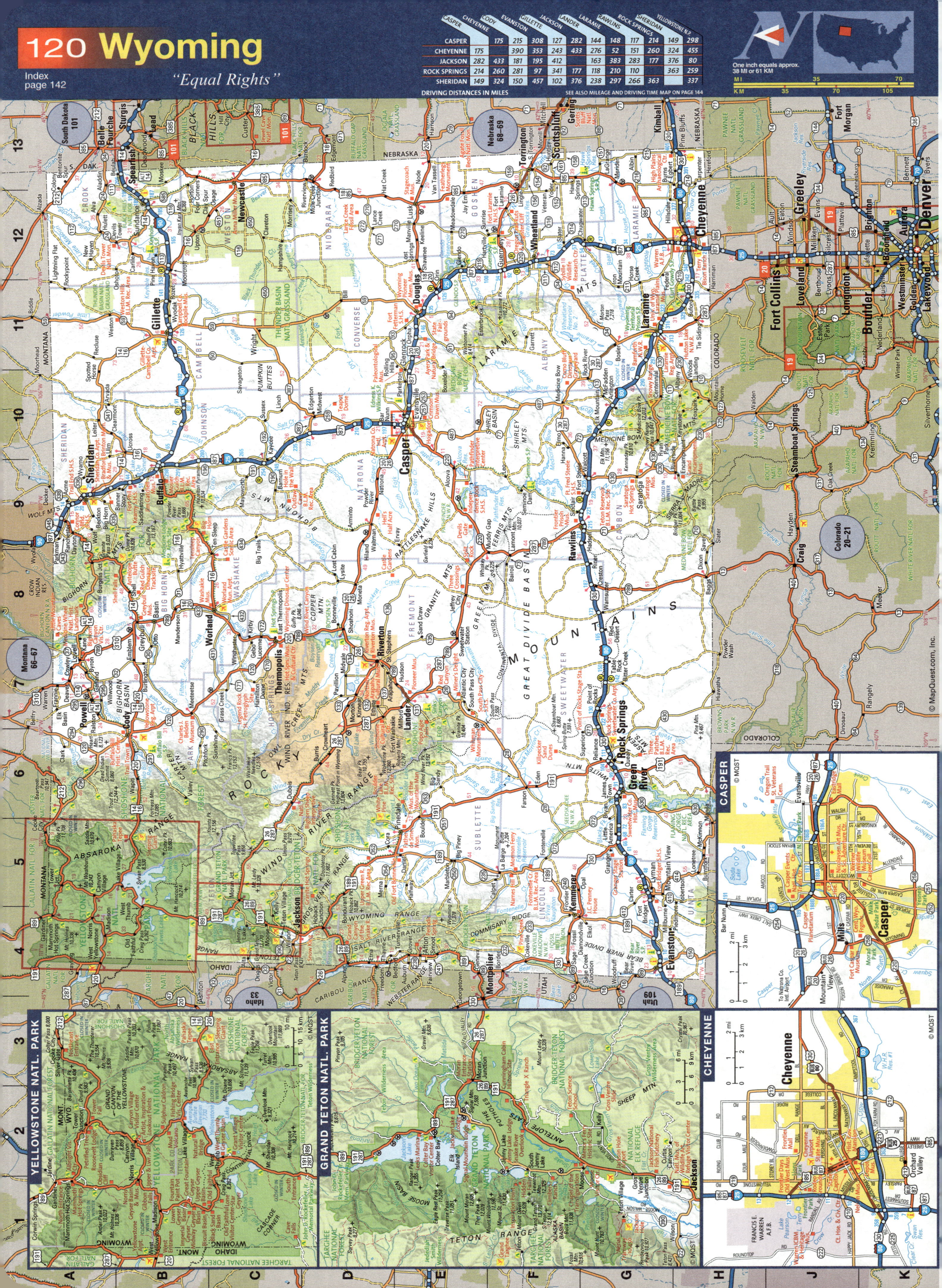

"From Sea to Sea"

Index page 142

One inch equals approx. 259 MI or 417.5 KM

"Splendor Without Diminishment"

	BANFF, AB	CRANBROOK	DAWSON CREEK	JASPER, AB	KAMLOOPS	KELOWNA	NANAIMO	PRINCE GEORGE	PRINCE RUPERT	REVELSTOKE	VANCOUVER	VICTORIA
CRANBROOK	265		985	504	600	513	845*	838	1562	196	765	882*
KAMLOOPS	479	600	931	444		163	359*	525	1249	206	340	396*
KELOWNA	476	513	1094	597	163		383*	688	1409	192	378	420*
PRINCE GEORGE	637	838	406	376	525	688	784*		724	693	778	821*
VANCOUVER	819	765	1184	784	340	378	109*	778	1502	546		93*

DRIVING DISTANCES IN KILOMETERS
* DISTANCE INCLUDES FERRY TRAVEL

"Strong and Free"

Index page 142

	BANFF	CALGARY	CRANBROOK, BC	DAWSON CREEK, BC	EDMONTON	FORT MC MURRAY	GRANDE PRAIRIE	JASPER	LETHBRIDGE	LLOYDMINSTER	MEDICINE HAT	RED DEER
CALGARY	128		383	885	296	726	750	396	216	534	285	145
EDMONTON	412	296	679	597		439	462	367	512	238	579	150
GRANDE PRAIRIE	665	750	861	124	462	756		397	965	700	1033	603
LETHBRIDGE	344	216	296	1101	512	943	965	612		605	164	360
MEDICINE HAT	413	285	460	1168	579	931	1033	681	164	480		430

DRIVING DISTANCES IN KILOMETERS

SEE ALSO MILEAGE AND DRIVING TIME MAP ON PAGE 144

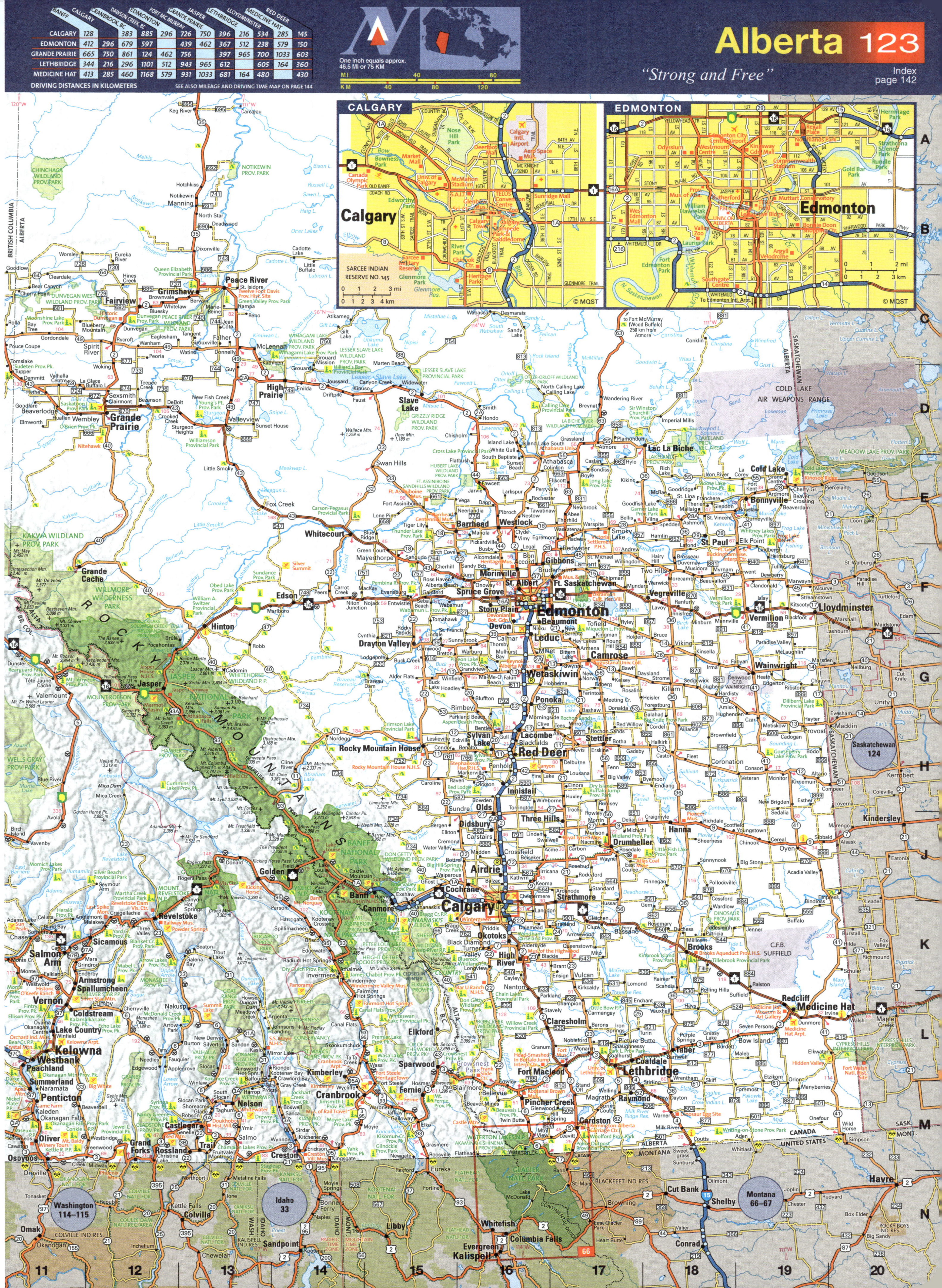

Saskatchewan

Index page 142

"From Many Peoples Strength"

	BRANDON, MB	ESTEVAN	FLIN FLON, MB	LLOYDMINSTER	MEDICINE HAT, AB	MOOSE JAW	NORTH BATTLEFORD	PRINCE ALBERT	REGINA	SASKATOON	SWIFT CURRENT	YORKTON
PRINCE ALBERT	670	570	375	336	618	356	196		374	141	408	391
REGINA	377	196	748	537	455	68	397	374		261	241	195
SASKATOON	639	455	508	275	486	224	137	141	261		267	331
SWIFT CURRENT	598	401	989	441	218	174	301	408	241	267		436
YORKTON	270	289	553	608	650	262	468	391	195	331	436	

DRIVING DISTANCES IN KILOMETERS

SEE ALSO MILEAGE AND DRIVING TIME MAP ON P 144

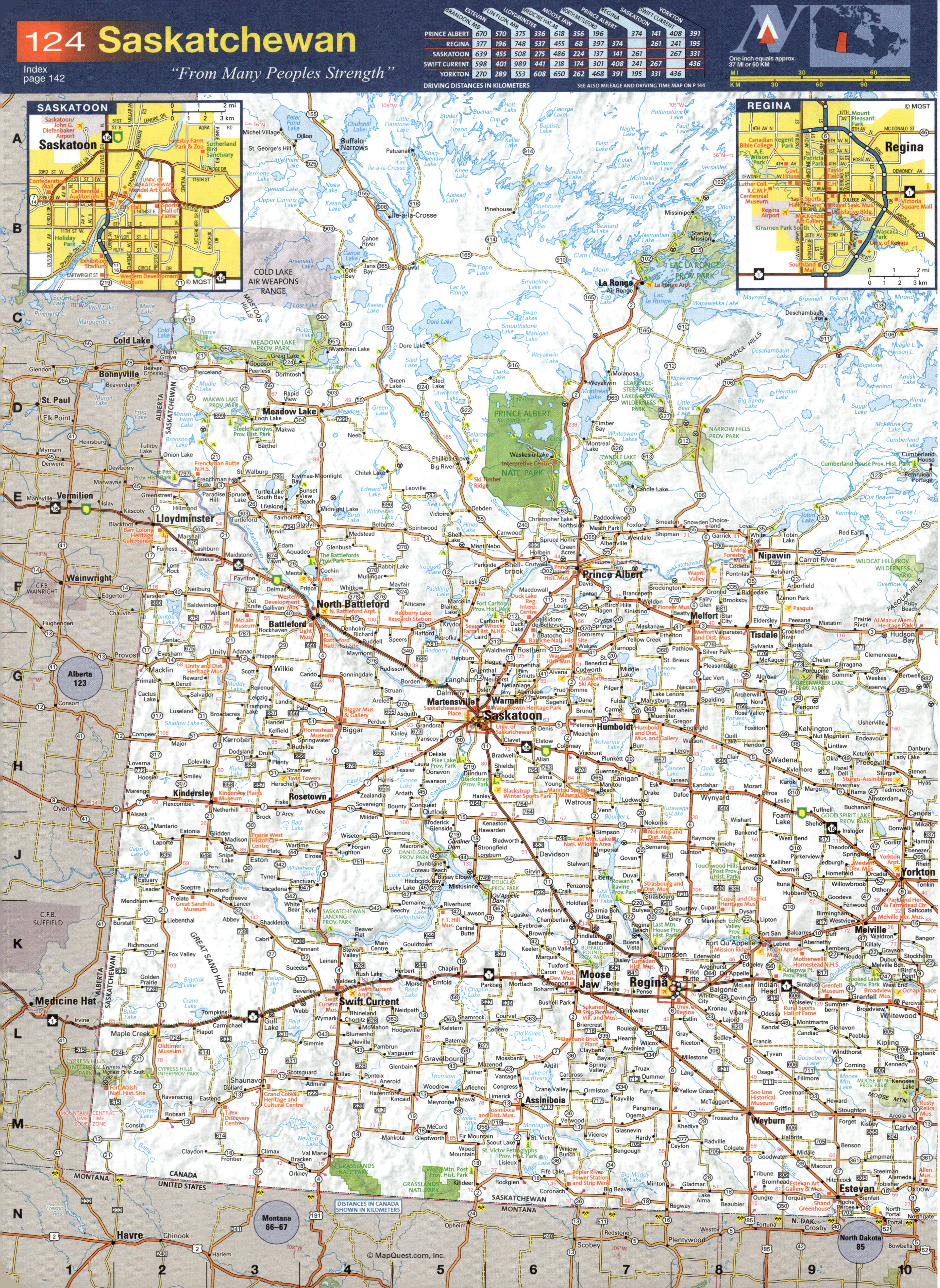

"Glorious and Free"

Index page 142

	BRANDON	DAUPHIN	FLIN FLON	GIMLI	GRAND RAPIDS	KENORA, ON	PORTAGE LA PRAIRIE	SWAN RIVER	THOMPSON	WINKLER	WINNIPEG	YORKTON, SK
BRANDON		166	676	291	525	434	134	333	855	227	216	270
DAUPHIN	166		510	298	403	541	241	167	776	341	322	171
FLIN FLON	676	510		734	389	1051	751	372	380	880	757	553
PORTAGE LA PRAIRIE	134	241	751	164	448	301		407	778	113	82	360
WINNIPEG	216	322	757	88	430	208	82	489	769	118		442

DRIVING DISTANCES IN KILOMETERS

SEE ALSO MILEAGE AND DRIVING TIME MAP ON PAGE 144

One inch equals approx. 37 MI or 60 KM

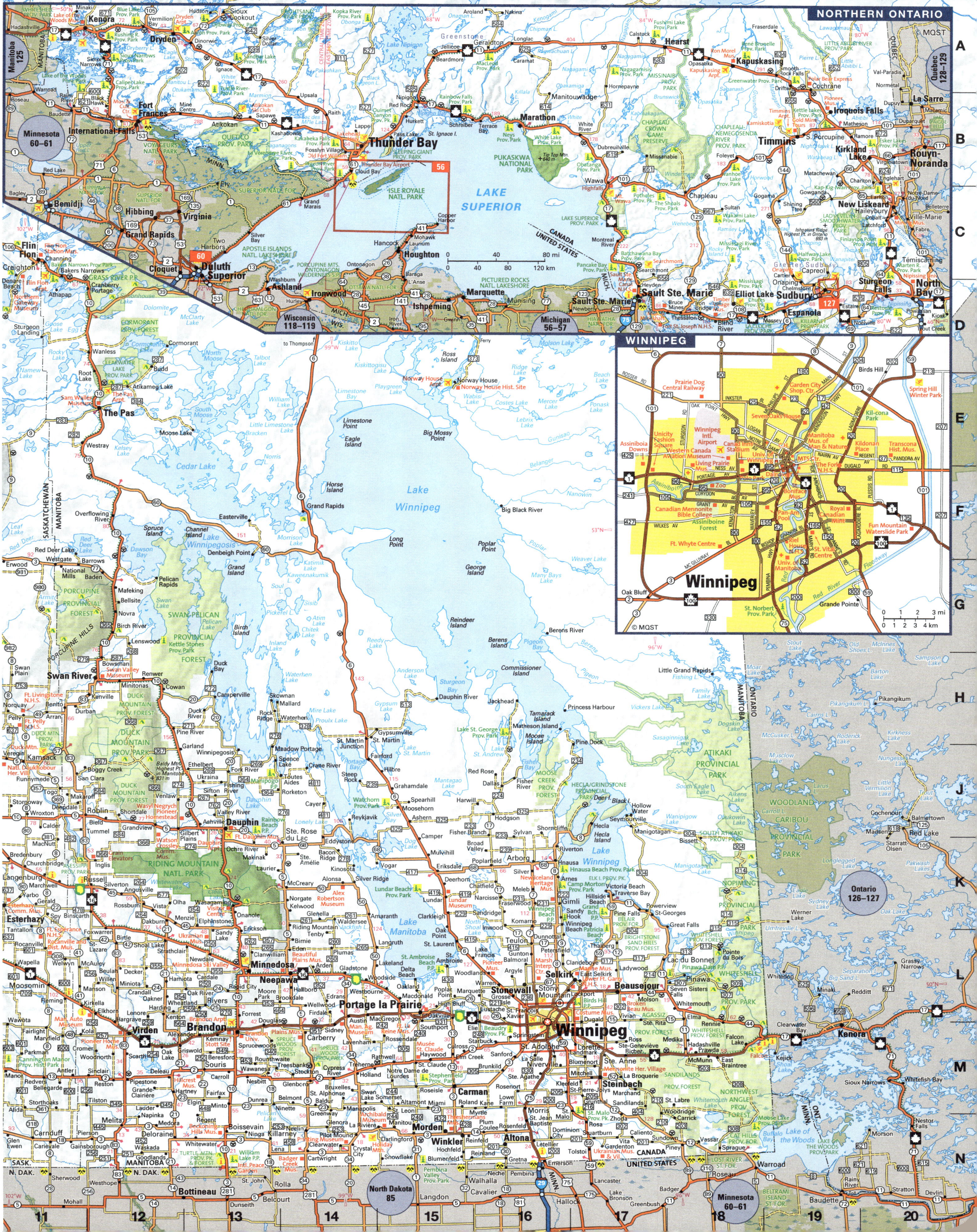

MI 30 60

KM 30 60 90

NORTHERN ONTARIO

WINNIPEG

Winnipeg

Thunder Bay

Lake Superior

Lake Winnipeg

Lake Manitoba

Brandon

Dauphin

Portage la Prairie

Kenora

Dryden

Fort Frances

Timmins

Sault Ste. Marie

Sudbury

North Bay

© MQST

Index page 142

	BARRIE	HAMILTON	KENORA	KINGSTON	KITCHENER	LONDON	NIAGARA FALLS	NORTH BAY	OTTAWA	OWEN SOUND	PETERBOROUGH	SARNIA	SAULT STE. MARIE	SUDBURY	THUNDER BAY	TIMMINS	TORONTO	WINDSOR
LONDON	248	134	1926	434	105		227	499	613	208	309	109	818	570	1467	840	183	195
OTTAWA	442	504	1854	179	496	613	574	364		558	265	714	787	488	1401	705	431	793
SUDBURY	319	462	1407	600	453	570	533	124	488	435	404	673	299		948	290	407	751
THUNDER BAY	1219	1410	459	1548	1401	1467	1481	1072	1401	1335	1371	1621	649	948		735	1355	1699
TORONTO	105	74	1814	251	104	183	145	336	431	183	127	285	674	407	1355	677		364

DRIVING DISTANCES IN KILOMETERS

SEE ALSO MILEAGE AND DRIVING TIME MAP ON PAGE 144

One inch equals approx. 24.5 MI or 39.5 KM
MI 20 40
KM 20 40 60
“Loyal She Began, Loyal She Remains”
SUDBURY
Sudbury
Greater Sudbury
Québec 128–129
North Bay
Pembroke
Petawawa
ALGONQUIN PROV. PARK
Gatineau
Ottawa
Rockland
Hawkesbury
Cornwall
Massena
Huntsville
Bracebridge
Gravenhurst
Orillia
Lindsay
Peterborough
Belleville
Kingston
Napanee
Gananoque
Brockville
Prescott
Ogdensburg
Smiths Falls
Perth
Carleton Place
Arnprior
Renfrew
Arnprior
Trenton
Cobourg
Port Hope
Oshawa
Whitby
Ajax
Pickering
Markham
Newmarket
Uxbridge
Toronto
LAKE ONTARIO
NEW YORK
CANADA
UNITED STATES
Oswego
Fulton
ADIRONDACK PARK
DOWNTOWN TORONTO
Niagara-on-the-Lake
St. Catharines
Niagara Falls
Welland
Port Colborne
Lockport
Buffalo
Rochester
Irondequoit
Batavia
Jamestown
Olean
Salamanca
Bradford
New York 76–79
Pa. 94–97
TORONTO
Vaughan
NORTH YORK
SCARBOROUGH
YORK
EAST YORK
ETOBICOKE
Mississauga
© MQST
11 12 13 14 15 16 17 18 19 20
A B C D E F G H J K L M N

Index page 142

	BAIE-COMEAU	CHICOUTIMI	DRUMMONDVILLE	GASPÉ	MONT-LAURIER	MONTRÉAL	OTTAWA, ON	QUÉBEC	RIMOUSKI	RIVIÈRE-DU-LOUP	ROBERVAL	ROUYN-NORANDA	ST-GEORGES	SEPT-ÎLES	SHERBROOKE	SOREL	TROIS-RIVIÈRES	VICTORIAVILLE
MONTRÉAL	663	461	116	898	230		194	250	535	426	448	616	325	887	143	87	146	164
QUÉBEC	400	211	151	668	439	250	444		305	196	253	879	102	624	233	204	135	114
RIVIÈRE-DU-LOUP	230*	154*	328	472	656	426	620	196	109		249*	1042	272	454*	401	381	333	291
SHERBROOKE	633	444	82	873	373	143	337	233	510	401	417	759	148	857		142	158	97
TROIS-RIVIÈRES	535	346	68	804	376	146	340	135	441	333	296	762	214	759	158	82		65

DRIVING DISTANCES IN KILOMETERS

* DISTANCE INCLUDES FERRY TRAVEL

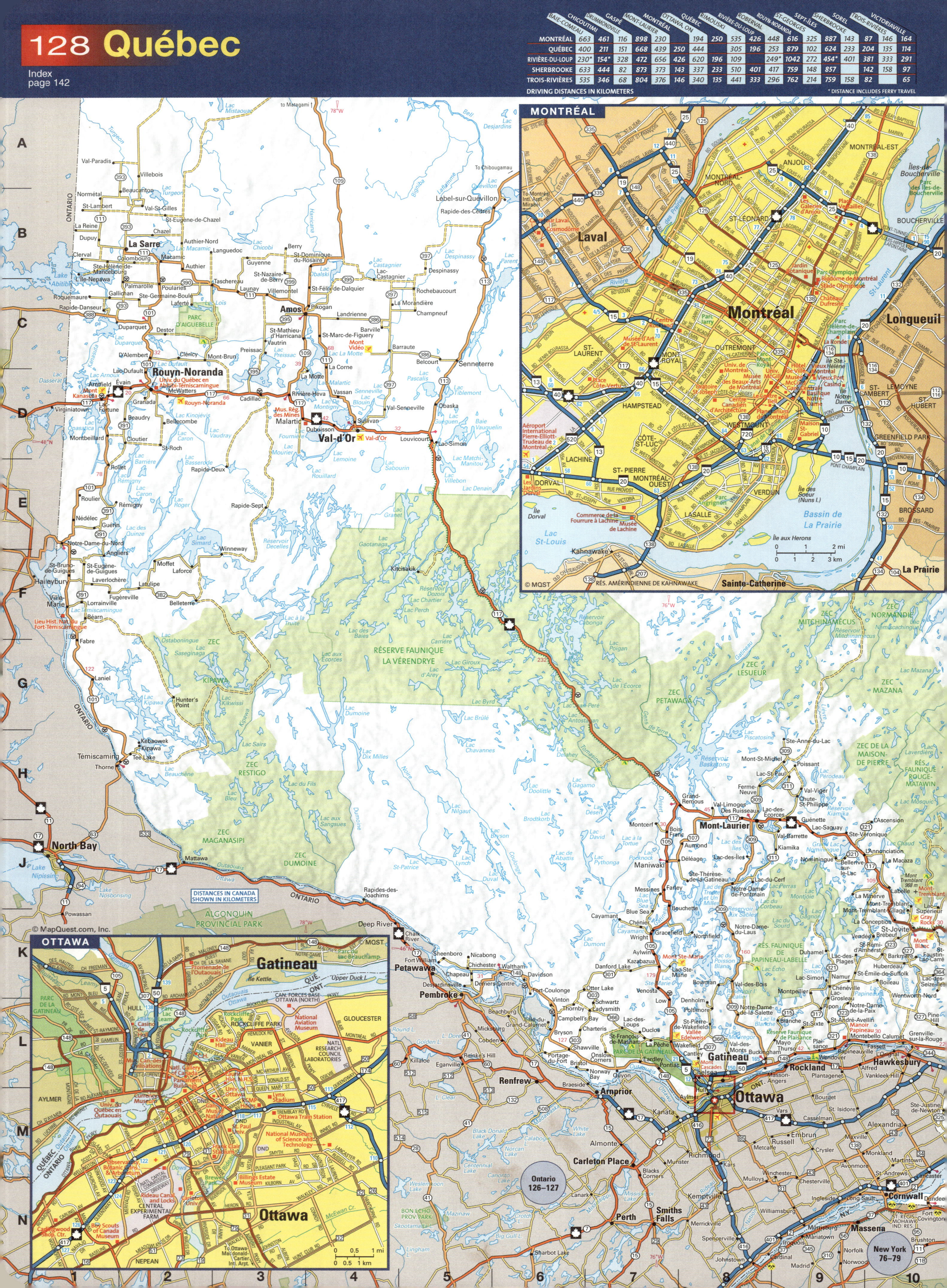

One inch equals approx. 24 MI or 39 KM

"Je Me Souviens (I Remember)"

Index page 142

Atlantic Provinces

Index page 142

NB: *"Hope Restored"*
NS: *"One Defends and the Other Conquers"*

	BATHURST, NB	CAMPBELLTON, NB	CHARLOTTETOWN, PE	DIGBY, NS	EDMUNDSTON, NB	FREDERICTON, NB	GASPÉ, QC	HALIFAX, NS	LUNENBURG, NS	MIRAMICHI, NB	MONCTON, NB	NEW GLASGOW, NS	PORT HAWKESBURY, NS	RIMOUSKI, QC	RIVIÈRE-DU-LOUP, QC	SAINT JOHN, NB	ST. STEPHEN, NB	SYDNEY, NS	TRURO, NS	WOODSTOCK, NB	YARMOUTH, NS
CHARLOTTETOWN, PE	328	434		539	629	354	730	322	419	258	162	110*	224*	620	749	312	417	374*	233	457	616
FREDERICTON, NB	245	351	354	669	275		647	452	549	175	192	425	539	445	395	105	123	689	363	103	746
HALIFAX, NS	452	558	322	217	727	452	854		97	382	260	151	265	744	847	410	515	415	89	555	294
SAINT JOHN, NB	350	456	312	82*	380	105	752	410	258*	280	150	383	497	550	500		105	647	321	208	176*
SYDNEY, NS	689	795	374*	632	964	689	1091	415	512	619	497	264	123	981	1084	647	752		326	792	709

DRIVING DISTANCES IN KILOMETERS

* DISTANCE INCLUDES FERRY TRAVEL

One inch equals approx. 30 MI or 48 KM

	ARGENTIA	BISHOP'S FALLS	BONAVISTA	CHAN.-PT. AUX BASQUES	CORNER BROOK	DEER LAKE	GANDER	GRAND FALLS-WINDSOR	MARYSTOWN	ST. ANTHONY	ST. JOHN'S	STEPHENVILLE
ARGENTIA		363	266	845	643	588	291	381	263	991	134	702
BISHOP'S FALLS	363		307	482	280	225	72	18	384	628	393	339
CHAN.-PT. AUX BASQUES	845	482	789		202	257	554	464	866	660	875	151
CORNER BROOK	643	280	587	202		55	352	262	664	458	673	59
ST. JOHN'S	134	393	296	875	673	618	321	411	293	1021		732

DRIVING DISTANCES IN KILOMETERS
ALL TOWNS ON THIS CHART ARE LOCATED IN NEWFOUNDLAND

Index page 142

One inch equals approx. 94.5 MI or 152 KM

MI 75 150
KM 75 150 225

ARIZONA
NEW MEXICO
SONORA
CHIHUAHUA
COAHUILA
BAJA CALIFORNIA
BAJA CALIFORNIA SUR
SINALOA
DURANGO
ZACATECAS
NAYARIT
JALISCO
COLIMA
MICHOACÁN
AGUASCALIENTES

San Diego
Tijuana
Mexicali
Ensenada
Yuma
San Luis Río Colorado
Tucson
Nogales
Las Cruces
El Paso
Ciudad Juárez
Midland
Hermosillo
Guaymas
Ciudad Obregón
Navojoa
Los Mochis
Chihuahua
Cuauhtémoc
Delicias
Hidalgo del Parral
Culiacán
La Paz
Mazatlán
Durango
Gómez Palacio
Torreón
Fresnillo
Zacatecas
Tepic
Puerto Vallarta
Guadalajara
Zapopan
Colima
Manzanillo
Tecomán
Lázaro Cárdenas

Golfo de California
OCÉANO PACÍFICO / PACIFIC OCEAN
SIERRA MADRE OCCIDENTAL
SIERRA MADRE ORIENTAL

MAZATLÁN

Mazatlán
Railroad Station
Aquarium
Federal Palace
City Hall
Rafael Buelna International Airport
PACIFIC OCEAN
© MQST

MEXICO CITY

México
Nicolás Romero
Cuautitlán Izcalli
Tultitlán
Coacalco
Ciudad López Mateos
Buenavista
Ecatepec de Morelos
Tlalnepantla
Santa Clara
Tepexpan
Tezoyuca
Chiconcuac
San Salvador Atenco
Tulantongo
Texcoco
Naucalpan
San Bernardino
San Miguel Coatlinchan
Santiago Cuautlalpan
Chimalhuacán
Benito Juárez Intl. Airport
Netzahualcóyotl
San Vicente Chicoloapan
Los Reyes
Magdalena Chichicaspa
Cuajimalpa
Ixtapaluca
Ayotla
Tláhuac
Chalco
Xochimilco
San Mateo Huitzilzingo
Milpa Alta
© MQST

ACAPULCO

Acapulco
Fine Arts Regional Center
Convention Center
La Quebrada Diving Gorge
Fort San Diego
Federal Bldg.
Bahía de Acapulco
La Paloma Beach
Submerged Shrine
Bull Ring
Juan N. Álvarez International Airport
PACIFIC OCEAN
© MQST

A B C D E F G H J K L M N

1 2 3 4 5 6 7 8 9 10

Index page 142

	AGUASCALIENTES	CANCÚN	CHIHUAHUA	CIUDAD JUÁREZ	CIUDAD VICTORIA	CULIACÁN	DURANGO	GUADALAJARA	HERMOSILLO	LEÓN	MAZATLÁN	MÉRIDA	MEXICO CITY	MONTERREY	PUEBLA	QUERÉTARO	SAN LUIS POTOSÍ	TAMPICO	TIJUANA	TORREÓN	TUXTLA GUTIÉRREZ	VERACRUZ
ACAPULCO	973	2071	1913	2298	1120	1680	1231	897	2388	866	1450	1777	422	1404	488	611	834	1003	3272	1464	991	830
AGUASCALIENTES		2118	1051	1446	584	940	421	272	1542	126	704	1928	473	579	586	263	168	568	2426	568	1405	838
CANCÚN			3290	3671	2128	3028	2501	2275	3736	2012	2726	321	1736	2416	1603	1958	2161	1754	4620	2679	1080	1395
CHIHUAHUA				385	1086	919	686	1283	579	1209	896	2810	1538	808	1651	1355	1155	1374	1456	449	2417	1817
CIUDAD JUÁREZ					1442	1304	1069	1667	795	1593	1281	3241	1923	1236	1983	1740	1540	1806	1202	834	2847	2247
CIUDAD VICTORIA						1146	912	774	1666	608	1123	1725	682	288	797	636	438	243	2641	637	1331	731
CULIACÁN							235	526	706	737	230	2430	1104	924	1425	921	710	1056	1596	914	2036	1469
DURANGO								599	941	525	319	2182	856	689	1067	673	475	821	1830	266	1788	1221
GUADALAJARA									1233	211	523	1904	578	758	691	394	336	682	2121	958	1510	943
HERMOSILLO										1444	729	3137	1810	1387	2133	1627	1416	1762	884	1028	2742	2176
LEÓN											715	1693	367	679	520	137	171	517	2333	877	1299	732
MAZATLÁN												2408	1081	901	1195	898	687	1033	1822	892	2013	1447
MÉRIDA													1326	2004	1282	1510	1707	1435	4025	2361	786	995
MEXICO CITY														892	133	183	381	473	2700	1089	932	365
MONTERREY															1035	708	509	568	2362	359	1609	1009
PUEBLA																355	496	586	3017	1125	930	346
QUERÉTARO																	198	544	2517	906	1115	549
SAN LUIS POTOSÍ																		346	2305	706	1313	747
TAMPICO																			3005	925	1041	457
TIJUANA																				1905	3631	3064
TORREÓN																					2142	1346
TUXTLA GUTIÉRREZ																						690

	AGUADILLA	ARECIBO	CAGUAS	CAYEY	FAJARDO	GUAYAMA	HUMACAO	MANATÍ	MAYAGÜEZ	PONCE	SAN JUAN	UTUADO
ARECIBO	32		59	70	80	87	74	17	48	52	48	20
CAGUAS	90	59		12	36	28	17	41	97	50	17	76
MAYAGÜEZ	16	48	97	85	129	84	114	64		46	96	48
PONCE	62	52	50	39	85	37	67	52	46		67	32
SAN JUAN	80	48	17	28	34	44	33	31	96	67		67

DRIVING DISTANCES IN MILES

One inch equals approx. 24 MI or 38.5 KM

Alabama–California

Note: Population figures are from the latest census or the most recent available estimates.

ALABAMA
PG. 4-5
CAPITAL: Montgomery
NICKNAME: Heart of Dixie
POPULATION: 4,447,100, rank 23
AREA: 51,705 sq mi, rank 29
STATEHOOD: 1819, rank 22

ALASKA
PG. 6
CAPITAL: Juneau
NICKNAME: Great Land
POPULATION: 626,932, rank 48
AREA: 591,004 sq mi, rank 1
STATEHOOD: 1959, rank 49

ARIZONA
PG. 7–9
CAPITAL: Phoenix
NICKNAME: Grand Canyon State
POPULATION: 5,130,632, rank 20
AREA: 114,000 sq mi, rank 6
STATEHOOD: 1912, rank 48

ARKANSAS
PG. 10–11
CAPITAL: Little Rock
NICKNAME: Natural State
POPULATION: 2,673,400, rank 33
AREA: 53,187 sq mi, rank 27
STATEHOOD: 1836, rank 25

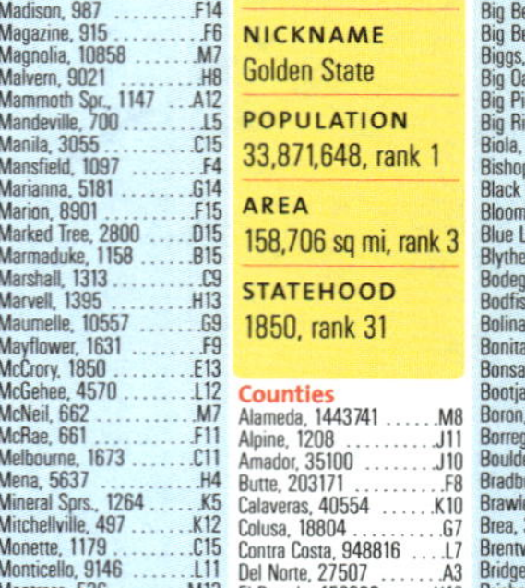
BIXBY BRIDGE, BIG SUR, CALIFORNIA

CALIFORNIA
PG. 12–19
CAPITAL: Sacramento
NICKNAME: Golden State
POPULATION: 33,871,648, rank 1
AREA: 158,706 sq mi, rank 3
STATEHOOD: 1850, rank 31

MOUNT MCKINLEY, DENALI NATIONAL PARK AND PRESERVE, ALASKA

Wofford Hts., 2276 ..... R15
Woodacre, 1393 ..... C1†
Woodcrest, 8342 ..... G16*
Woodlake, 6651 ..... P13
Woodland, 49151 ..... J8
Woodside, 5352 ..... L5†
Woodville, 1678 ..... O13
Wrightwood, 3837 ..... U17
Yermo, 900 ..... T18
Yorba Linda, 58918 ..... G12*
Yountville, 2916 ..... J6
Yreka, 7290 ..... A6
Yuba City, 36758 ..... H8
Yucaipa, 41207 ..... V18
Yucca Valley, 16865 ..... V19

COLORADO

PG. 19–21

CAPITAL Denver

NICKNAME Centennial State

POPULATION 4,301,261, rank 24

AREA 104,091 sq mi, rank 8

STATEHOOD 1876, rank 38

Counties

Adams, 348618 ..... E16
Alamosa, 14966 ..... L12
Arapahoe, 487967 ..... E15
Archuleta, 9898 ..... M9
Baca, 4517 ..... L19
Bent, 5998 ..... K18
Boulder, 269814 ..... D13
Broomfield, 38272 ..... D13
Chaffee, 16242 ..... G11
Cheyenne, 2231 ..... G18
Clear Creek, 9322 ..... E13
Conejos, 8400 ..... M11
Costilla, 3663 ..... M13
Crowley, 5518 ..... J16

Fruita, 6478 ..... F5
Georgetown, 1088 ..... E12
Gilcrest, 1162 ..... C14
Glendale, 4547 ..... L8*
Glenwood Sprs., 7736 ..... E8
Golden, 17159 ..... E13
Granada, 640 ..... J19
Granby, 1525 ..... D12
Grand Jct., 41986 ..... G6
Grand Lake, 447 ..... C12
Grandview, 600 ..... M7
Greeley, 76930 ..... C14
Green Mtn. Falls, 773 ..... D1
Greenwood Vil., 11035 ..... M8*
Gunnison, 5409 ..... H9
Gypsum, 3654 ..... E9
Haxtun, 982 ..... B19
Hayden, 1634 ..... C9
Hermosa, 700 ..... L7
Highlands Ranch, 70931 ..... N7*
Holly, 1048 ..... J20
Holyoke, 2261 ..... C19
Hotchkiss, 968 ..... G8
Hot Sulphur Sprs., 521 ..... D11
Hudson, 1565 ..... D14
Hugo, 885 ..... G17
Idaho Sprs., 1889 ..... L3*
Ignacio, 669 ..... M8
Indian Hills, 1197 ..... M5*
Johnstown, 3827 ..... C14
Julesburg, 1467 ..... A19
Keenesburg, 855 ..... D15
Kersey, 1389 ..... C15
Keystone, 825 ..... E12
Kiowa, 581 ..... F15
Kittredge, 954 ..... M4*
Kremmling, 1578 ..... D11
Lafayette, 23197 ..... D13
La Jara, 877 ..... M12
La Junta, 7568 ..... K17
Lake City, 375 ..... K8
Lakewood, 144126 ..... E13
Lamar, 8869 ..... J19
Laporte, 2691 ..... B13
La Salle, 1849 ..... C14
Las Animas, 2758 ..... K17
La Veta, 924 ..... L14
Leadville, 2821 ..... F11
Limon, 2071 ..... F16
Lincoln Park, 3904 ..... J13
Littleton, 40340 ..... E14
Lochbuie, 2049 ..... H10*
Log Lane Vil., 1006 ..... C16
Lone Tree, 4873 ..... N8*

CONNECTICUT

PG. 22–23

CAPITAL Hartford

NICKNAME Constitution State

POPULATION 3,405,565, rank 29

AREA 5,018 sq mi, rank 48

STATEHOOD 1788, rank 5

Counties

Fairfield, 882567 ..... H6
Hartford, 857183 ..... C9
Litchfield, 182193 ..... D5
Middlesex, 155071 ..... G10
New Haven, 824008 ..... G8
New London, 259088 ..... F13
Tolland, 136364 ..... C12
Windham, 109091 ..... B14

Cities and Towns

Andover, 800 ..... D12
Ansonia, 18554 ..... H7
Attawaugan, 950 ..... C15
Avon, 1500 ..... C8
Ballouville, 950 ..... C15
Baltic, 1500 ..... E14
Bantam, 802 ..... D6
Beacon Falls, 1500 ..... G7
Berkshire, 950 ..... G6
Berlin, 1000 ..... E9
Bethany, 900 ..... G7

Perkins Corner, 1000 ..... D13
Plainfield, 2638 ..... E15
Plainville, 17328 ..... E8
Plantsville, 6400 ..... E8
Pleasure Beach, 1600 ..... H13
Poquetanuck, 1100 ..... F14
Poquonock, 2200 ..... B10
Poquonock Bridge, 1592 ..... H14
Portland, 5534 ..... F10
Prospect, 2200 ..... F7
Putnam, 6746 ..... B15
Quaker Hill, 4200 ..... G14
Quarryville, 2500 ..... D11
Quinebaug, 1122 ..... A15
Redding, 1000 ..... H5
Redding Ridge, 900 ..... H5
Ridgebury, 1200 ..... G4
Ridgefield, 7212 ..... H4
Rockfall, 1500 ..... F9
Rockville, 7708 ..... C11
Rocky Hill, 17966 ..... E10
Salisbury, 700 ..... B4
Saybrook Manor, 1133 ..... H12
Seymour, 15454 ..... G7
Sharon, 800 ..... C4
Shelton, 38101 ..... H7
Sherwood Manor, 5689 ..... A10
Short Beach, 5100 ..... H8
Simsbury, 5603 ..... C9
Somers, 1626 ..... B11
Sound View, 1200 ..... H12
S. Glastonbury, 1900 ..... E10
Southington, 39728 ..... E8
S. Killingly, 750 ..... D16
S. Willington, 1700 ..... C12
S. Windham, 1278 ..... E13
S. Windsor, 700 ..... C11
Southwood Acres, 8067 ..... B10
S. Woodstock, 1211 ..... B15
Stafford, 900 ..... B12
Stafford Sprs., 4100 ..... B12
Stamford, 117083 ..... K3
Sterling, 650 ..... D16
Stevenson, 800 ..... G6

Millville, 259 ..... L5
Milton, 1657 ..... K4
Nassau, 1600 ..... K5
Newark, 28547 ..... C1
New Castle, 4862 ..... C3
Newport, 1122 ..... C2
Oak Orchard, 750 ..... L5
Ocean View, 1006 ..... L5
Odessa, 286 ..... E2
Pinetown, 1100 ..... K5
Plymouth, 350 ..... H3
Reeves Crossing, 450 ..... H3
Rehoboth Beach, 1495 ..... K5
Rising Sun, 2458 ..... G3
Rodney Vil., 1602 ..... M8
Rosedale Beach, 750 ..... L5
Roseville Park, 6200 ..... C2
Roxana, 375 ..... M5
Seaford, 6699 ..... L2
Selbyville, 1645 ..... M5
Slaughter Beach, 198 ..... J4
Smyrna, 5679 ..... F2
S. Bethany, 492 ..... M6
Stanton, 5000 ..... C2
Star Hill, 600 ..... N8
Swann Keys, 700 ..... M5
Talleyville, 6300 ..... B3
Townsend, 346 ..... E2
Williamsville, 350 ..... M5
Wilmington, 72664 ..... B3
Wilmington Manor, 8262 ..... D8
Woodside, 184 ..... H3
Workmans Corners, 400 ..... L4
Wyoming, 1141 ..... G3

DISTRICT OF COLUMBIA

PG. 116

POPULATION 572,059

AREA 69 sq mi

BECAME CAPITAL 1800

Washington, 572059 ..... D-5

FLORIDA

PG. 25–28

CAPITAL Tallahassee

NICKNAME Sunshine State

POPULATION 15,982,378, rank 4

AREA 58,664 sq mi, rank 22

STATEHOOD 1845, rank 27

Counties

Alachua, 217955 ..... G15
Baker, 22259 ..... E15
Bay, 148217 ..... E7
Bradford, 26088 ..... F15
Brevard, 476230 ..... L19
Broward, 1623018 ..... R19
Calhoun, 13017 ..... E7
Charlotte, 141627 ..... P16
Citrus, 118085 ..... J14
Clay, 140814 ..... F16
Collier, 251377 ..... R17
Columbia, 56513 ..... E14
DeSoto, 32209 ..... N16
Dixie, 13827 ..... G13
Duval, 778879 ..... F16
Escambia, 294410 ..... D2
Flagler, 49832 ..... G17
Franklin, 11057 ..... F9
Gadsden, 45087 ..... E9
Gilchrist, 14437 ..... G14
Glades, 10576 ..... P17
Gulf, 13332 ..... F8
Hamilton, 13327 ..... E13
Hardee, 26938 ..... N16
Hendry, 36210 ..... O18
Hernando, 130802 ..... K14
Highlands, 87366 ..... M17
Hillsborough, 998948 ..... M15
Holmes, 18564 ..... D6
Indian River, 112947 ..... M19
Jackson, 46755 ..... D8
Jefferson, 12902 ..... E11
Lafayette, 7022 ..... F13
Lake, 210528 ..... J17
Lee, 440888 ..... O16
Leon, 239452 ..... E10
Levy, 34450 ..... H14
Liberty, 7021 ..... F9
Madison, 18733 ..... E12
Manatee, 264002 ..... N15
Marion, 258916 ..... H15
Martin, 126731 ..... P19
Miami-Dade, 2253362 ..... S19
Monroe, 79589 ..... T18
Nassau, 57663 ..... E16
Okaloosa, 170498 ..... D4
Okeechobee, 35910 ..... N18
Orange, 896344 ..... K18
Osceola, 172493 ..... L18

Cities and Towns

Bellair, 16539 ..... M7
Belleair, 4067 ..... C1*
Belleair Beach, 1751 ..... M14
Belleair Bluffs, 2243 ..... C1*
Belle Glade, 14906 ..... O19
Belle Isle, 5531 ..... J5
Belleview, 3478 ..... J15
Bellview, 21201 ..... B2
Betmar Acres, 4000 ..... L15
Beverly Beach, 547 ..... G18
Beverly Hills, 8317 ..... J14
Big Coppitt Key, 2595 ..... V17
Big Pine Key, 5032 ..... V17
Biscayne Park, 3269 ..... K9*
Bithlo, 4626 ..... K18
Bloomingdale, 19839 ..... C6*
Blountstown, 2444 ..... E8
Boca Grande, 700 ..... O15
Boca Raton, 74764 ..... O21
Bokeelia, 1997 ..... O15
Bonifay, 4078 ..... D7
Bonita Sprs., 32797 ..... R16
Bowling Green, 2892 ..... M16
Boyette, 5895 ..... M15
Boynton Beach, 60389 ..... O21
Bradenton, 49504 ..... N14
Bradenton Beach, 1482 ..... N14
Bradfordville, 1100 ..... E10
Bradley Jct., 850 ..... M16
Brandon, 77895 ..... M15
Branford, 695 ..... F13
Brent, 22257 ..... E3
Bristol, 845 ..... E8
Bronson, 964 ..... H14
Brooksville, 7264 ..... K15
Buckhead Ridge, 1390 ..... N18
Buena Ventura Lakes, 14100 ..... L5
Bunnell, 2122 ..... H17
Bushnell, 2050 ..... K15
Butler Beach, 4436 ..... G17
Callahan, 962 ..... E16
Callaway, 14233 ..... F7
Campbell, 2677 ..... L17
Canal Pt., 525 ..... P19
Cantonment, 2300 ..... D3
Cape Canaveral, 8829 ..... K19
Cape Coral, 102286 ..... O16
Carol City, 59443 ..... R20
Carrabelle, 1303 ..... G9
Carrollwood, 33519 ..... B4*
Casselberry, 22629 ..... K17
Cedar Grove, 5367 ..... F7
Cedar Key, 790 ..... H13
Celebration, 2736 ..... M2
Center Hill, 910 ..... K16
Century, 1714 ..... C3
Charlotte Beach, 1600 ..... P15
Charlotte Harbor, 3647 ..... P15
Chassahowitzka, 700 ..... K14
Chattahoochee, 3287 ..... D9
Chiefland, 1993 ..... H13
Chipley, 3592 ..... D7
Christmas, 1162 ..... K18
Chuluota, 1921 ..... K18
Citra, 800 ..... H15
Citrus Park, 20226 ..... B3*
Citrus Sprs., 4157 ..... J14
Clearwater, 108787 ..... L14
Clermont, 9333 ..... K16
Cleveland, 3268 ..... P16
Clewiston, 6460 ..... P18
Cocoa, 16412 ..... K19
Cocoa Beach, 12482 ..... K19
Cocoa West, 5921 ..... C18
Coconut Creek, 43566 ..... F9*
Coleman, 647 ..... J15
Conway, 14394 ..... J5
Cooper City, 27939 ..... J8*
Coral Gables, 42249 ..... S20
Coral Sprs., 117549 ..... R20
Cortez, 4491 ..... N14
Cottage Hill, 1300 ..... D3
Cottondale, 869 ..... D7
Crawfordville, 750 ..... F10
Crescent Beach, 985 ..... G17
Crescent City, 1776 ..... H17
Crestview, 14766 ..... D5
Crooked Lake Park, 1682 ..... M17
Cross City, 1775 ..... G13
Crystal Beach, 4000 ..... B2*
Crystal River, 3485 ..... J14
Crystal Sprs., 1175 ..... L15

SOUTH BEACH, MIAMI BEACH, FLORIDA

DELAWARE

PG. 24

CAPITAL Dover

NICKNAME First State

POPULATION 783,600, rank 45

AREA 2,044 sq mi, rank 49

STATEHOOD 1787, rank 1

Counties

Kent, 126697 ..... G2
New Castle, 500265 ..... E2
Sussex, 156638 ..... K4

Cities and Towns

Arden, 474 ..... B3
Ardencroft, 267 ..... A10
Ardentown, 300 ..... A10
Argos Corner, 550 ..... J4
Bear, 17593 ..... C2

GEORGIA

PG. 29–31

CAPITAL Atlanta

NICKNAME Empire State of the South

POPULATION 8,186,453, rank 10

AREA 58,910 sq mi, rank 21

STATEHOOD 1788, rank 4

Counties

Appling, 17419 ..... M9
Atkinson, 7609 ..... N7
Bacon, 10103 ..... M9
Baker, 4074 ..... N4
Baldwin, 44700 ..... H6
Banks, 14422 ..... D6
Barrow, 46144 ..... E5
Bartow, 76019 ..... D3
Ben Hill, 17484 ..... M7
Berrien, 16235 ..... N7
Bibb, 153887 ..... H5
Bleckley, 11666 ..... K6
Brantley, 14629 ..... N10
Brooks, 16450 ..... O6
Bryan, 23417 ..... L11
Bulloch, 55983 ..... K10
Burke, 22243 ..... H10
Butts, 19522 ..... G5
Calhoun, 6320 ..... M3

Ashburn, 4419 ..... M6
Athens, 101489 ..... E6
Atlanta, 416474 ..... F4
Auburn, 6904 ..... E5
Augusta, 199775 ..... F10
Austell, 5359 ..... E2*
Avondale Estates, 2609 ..... F8*
Baconton, 804 ..... N4
Bainbridge, 11722 ..... O3
Baldwin, 2425 ..... C6
Ball Ground, 730 ..... D4
Barnesville, 5972 ..... H4
Baxley, 4150 ..... M9
Belvedere, 11100 ..... G8*
Bemiss, 1500 ..... P7
Berkeley Lake, 1695 ..... B9*
Berlin, 595 ..... P6
Bethlehem, 716 ..... E6
Blackshear, 3283 ..... N9
Blackwells, 2200 ..... E4
Blairsville, 659 ..... B5
Blakely, 5696 ..... N2
Bloomingdale, 2665 ..... T9
Blue Ridge, 1210 ..... B4
Blythe, 718 ..... G9
Bogart, 1049 ..... E6
Bonaire, 800 ..... J6
Boston, 1417 ..... O5
Bowdon, 1959 ..... F2
Bowman, 898 ..... D7
Braselton, 1206 ..... E5
Bremen, 4579 ..... F2
Brooklet, 1113 ..... K11
Brooks, 553 ..... G4
Broxton, 1428 ..... M8
Brunswick, 15600 ..... P11
Buchanan, 941 ..... E2
Buena Vista, 1664 ..... K4
Buford, 10668 ..... E5
Butler, 1907 ..... J4
Byron, 2887 ..... J5
Cairo, 9239 ..... O4
Calhoun, 10667 ..... C3
Camilla, 5669 ..... P4
Canon, 755 ..... D7
Canton, 7709 ..... D4
Carnesville, 541 ..... D7

Lumber City, 1247 ..... L8
Lumpkin, 1369 ..... L3
Luthersville, 783 ..... G3
Lyons, 4169 ..... K9
Mableton, 29733 ..... E3
Macon, 97255 ..... H6
Madison, 3636 ..... F6
Manchester, 3988 ..... H3
Marietta, 58748 ..... E3
Marshallville, 1335 ..... K5
Maysville, 1247 ..... D6
McCaysville, 1071 ..... B4
McDonough, 8493 ..... G4
McIntyre, 718 ..... H7
McRae, 2682 ..... L8
Meigs, 1090 ..... P5
Metter, 3879 ..... K10
Midway, 1100 ..... M11
Milan, 1012 ..... L7
Milledgeville, 18757 ..... H7
Millen, 3492 ..... J10
Milner, 522 ..... H4
Monroe, 11407 ..... F6
Montezuma, 3999 ..... K5
Monticello, 2428 ..... G6
Morgan, 1464 ..... N3
Morrow, 4882 ..... F4
Morven, 634 ..... P6
Moultrie, 14387 ..... P5
Mtn. City, 829 ..... B6
Mt. Airy, 604 ..... C6
Mt. Vernon, 2082 ..... L8
Mt. Zion, 1275 ..... F2
Nahunta, 930 ..... P10
Nashville, 4697 ..... P7
Nelson, 626 ..... D4
Newborn, 520 ..... F6
New Hope, 750 ..... E3
Newnan, 16242 ..... G3
Newton, 851 ..... N4
Nicholls, 1008 ..... N8
Nicholson, 1247 ..... E6
Norcross, 8410 ..... E4
Norman Park, 849 ..... N6
N. Atlanta, 38579 ..... D7*
N. Decatur, 15270 ..... F7*
N. Druid Hills, 18852 ..... E7*

HAWAII

PG. 32

CAPITAL Honolulu

NICKNAME Aloha State

POPULATION 1,211,537, rank 42

AREA 6,471 sq mi, rank 47

STATEHOOD 1959, rank 50

Counties

Hawaii, 148677 ..... C9
Honolulu, 876156 ..... A8
Kalawao, 147 ..... A8
Kauai, 58463 ..... A7
Maui, 128094 ..... B9

Cities and Towns

Ahuimanu, 8506 ..... G5
Aiea, 9019 ..... G4
Anahola, 1932 ..... B4
Captain Cook, 3206 ..... L7
Eleele, 2040 ..... C2
Ewa Beach, 14650 ..... H3
Ewa Villages, 4741 ..... H3
Haiku, 6578 ..... D9
Halawa, 13891 ..... C7
Haleiwa, 2225 ..... E2
Haliimaile, 895 ..... D9
Hana, 709 ..... E10
Hanamaulu, 3272 ..... C4
Hanapepe, 2153 ..... C2

Waikoloa Vil., 4806 ..... K7
Wailua, 2083 ..... B4
Wailuku, 12296 ..... D8
Waimalu, 29371 ..... G4
Waimanalo, 3664 ..... G6
Waimanalo Beach, 4271 ..... H6
Waimea, 1787 ..... C2
Waimea (Kamuela), 7028 ..... K8
Waipahu, 33108 ..... G3
Waipio, 11672 ..... G3
Waipio Acres, 5298 ..... F3
Whitmore Vil., 4057 ..... F3

IDAHO

PG. 33

CAPITAL Boise

NICKNAME Gem State

POPULATION 1,293,953, rank 39

AREA 83,564 sq mi, rank 13

STATEHOOD 1890, rank 43

Counties

Ada, 300904 ..... L2
Adams, 3476 ..... H2
Bannock, 75565 ..... M7
Bear Lake, 6411 ..... M8
Benewah, 9171 ..... D2
Bingham, 41735 ..... L7
Blaine, 18991 ..... L5
Boise, 6670 ..... J3
Bonner, 36835 ..... B2
Bonneville, 82522 ..... L8
Boundary, 9871 ..... A2
Butte, 2899 ..... K6
Camas, 991 ..... K4
Canyon, 131441 ..... K2

Kootenai, 108685 ..... C2
Latah, 34935 ..... E2
Lemhi, 7806 ..... H5
Lewis, 3747 ..... E2
Lincoln, 4044 ..... L5
Madison, 27467 ..... K8
Minidoka, 20174 ..... M5
Nez Perce, 37410 ..... F2
Oneida, 4125 ..... M7
Owyhee, 10644 ..... M2
Payette, 20578 ..... J2
Power, 7538 ..... M7
Shoshone, 13771 ..... D3
Teton, 5999 ..... K8
Twin Falls, 64284 ..... M4
Valley, 7651 ..... H3
Washington, 9977 ..... J1

Cities and Towns

Aberdeen, 1840 ..... L6
Ahsahka, 600 ..... E2
Albion, 262 ..... M6
American Falls, 4111 ..... M6
Ammon, 6187 ..... K8
Arco, 1026 ..... K6
Arimo, 348 ..... M7
Ashton, 1129 ..... J8
Athol, 676 ..... C2
Bancroft, 382 ..... M8
Basalt, 419 ..... L7
Bellevue, 1876 ..... K5
Blackfoot, 10419 ..... L7
Bliss, 275 ..... L4
Bloomington, 251 ..... N8
Boise, 185787 ..... K2
Bonners Ferry, 2515 ..... A2
Bovill, 305 ..... D2
Buhl, 3985 ..... M4
Burley, 9316 ..... M5
Caldwell, 25967 ..... K2
Cambridge, 360 ..... H2
Carey, 513 ..... L5
Cascade, 997 ..... J2
Castleford, 277 ..... M4
Challis, 909 ..... J5
Chubbuck, 9700 ..... L7
Clark Fork, 530 ..... B2

Moscow, 21291 ..... E1
Mtn. Home, 11143 ..... L3
Moyie Sprs., 656 ..... A2
Mud Lake, 270 ..... K7
Mullan, 840 ..... C3
Murphy, 40 ..... L2
Nampa, 51867 ..... K2
Newdale, 358 ..... K8
New Meadows, 533 ..... H2
New Plymouth, 1400 ..... K1
Nezperce, 523 ..... F2
Notus, 458 ..... K1
Oakley, 668 ..... N5
Onaway, 230 ..... D2
Orofino, 3247 ..... E2
Osburn, 1545 ..... C3
Paris, 576 ..... N8
Parker, 319 ..... K8
Parma, 1771 ..... K1
Paul, 998 ..... M5
Payette, 7054 ..... J1
Pierce, 617 ..... E3
Pinehurst, 1661 ..... C2
Plummer, 990 ..... D2
Pocatello, 51466 ..... L7
Ponderay, 638 ..... B2
Post Falls, 17247 ..... C1
Potlatch, 791 ..... D1
Preston, 4682 ..... N8
Priest River, 1754 ..... B2
Rathdrum, 4816 ..... C2
Rexburg, 17257 ..... K8
Richfield, 412 ..... L5
Rigby, 2998 ..... K8
Riggins, 410 ..... G2
Ririe, 545 ..... K8
Roberts, 647 ..... K7
Rockland, 316 ..... M6
Rupert, 5645 ..... M5
Sagle, 425 ..... B2
St. Anthony, 3342 ..... J8
St. Maries, 2652 ..... D2
Salmon, 3122 ..... G5
Sandpoint, 6835 ..... B2
Shelley, 3813 ..... L7
Shoshone, 1398 ..... L4
Smelterville, 651 ..... C2
Soda Sprs., 3381 ..... M8
Spirit Lake, 1376 ..... C2
Star, 1795 ..... A6
Stites, 226 ..... F3
Sugar City, 1242 ..... K8
Sun Valley, 1427 ..... K5
Swan Valley, 213 ..... K8
Teton, 569 ..... K8

ILLINOIS

PG. 34–37

CAPITAL Springfield

NICKNAME Land of Lincoln

POPULATION 12,419,293, rank 5

AREA 56,345 sq mi, rank 24

STATEHOOD 1818, rank 21

Counties

Adams, 68277 ..... K3
Alexander, 9590 ..... U7
Bond, 17633 ..... P7
Boone, 41786 ..... A9
Brown, 6950 ..... K4
Bureau, 35503 ..... D7
Calhoun, 5084 ..... M4
Carroll, 16674 ..... B6
Cass, 13695 ..... K5
Champaign, 179669 ..... J10
Christian, 35372 ..... M8
Clark, 17008 ..... M12
Clay, 14560 ..... P10
Clinton, 35535 ..... O7
Coles, 53196 ..... L11
Cook, 5376741 ..... D11
Crawford, 20452 ..... N12
Cumberland, 11253 ..... M10
DeKalb, 88969 ..... J9
De Witt, 16798 ..... C9
Douglas, 19922 ..... L11

Bement, 1784 ..... K10
Benld, 1541 ..... N7
Bensenville, 20703 ..... G5*
Benton, 6880 ..... S9
Berkeley, 5245 ..... H5*
Berwyn, 54016 ..... C12
Bethalto, 9454 ..... P6
Bethany, 1287 ..... L9
Blandinsville, 777 ..... H4
Bloomingdale, 21675 ..... G4*
Bloomington, 64808 ..... H9
Blue Island, 23463 ..... L8*
Blue Mound, 1129 ..... L8
Bluffs, 748 ..... L4
Bluford, 785 ..... R9
Bolingbrook, 56321 ..... D11
Boulder Hill, 8169 ..... K1*
Bourbonnais, 15256 ..... E11
Braceville, 792 ..... E10
Bradford, 787 ..... E7
Bradley, 12784 ..... F11
Braidwood, 5203 ..... E11
Breese, 4048 ..... O7
Bridgeport, 2168 ..... P12
Bridgeview, 15335 ..... K6*
Brighton, 2196 ..... N5
Brimfield, 933 ..... G6
Broadview, 8264 ..... H6*
Brookfield, 19085 ..... J6*
Brooklyn, 676 ..... E17†
Brookport, 1054 ..... V10
Brownstown, 705 ..... N9
Buffalo Grove, 42909 ..... D5*
Bull Valley, 726 ..... A10
Bunker Hill, 1801 ..... N6
Burbank, 27902 ..... K7*
Burnham, 4170 ..... L9*
Burr Ridge, 10408 ..... J5*
Bushnell, 3221 ..... H5
Byron, 2917 ..... B8
Cahokia, 16391 ..... O5
Cairo, 3632 ..... V8
Calumet City, 39071 ..... D12
Calumet Park, 8516 ..... L8*
Cambria, 1330 ..... T8
Cambridge, 2180 ..... E5
Camp Pt., 1244 ..... J3

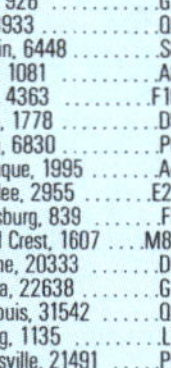

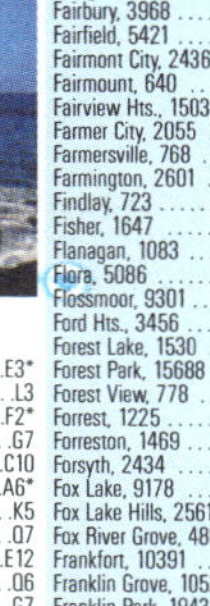

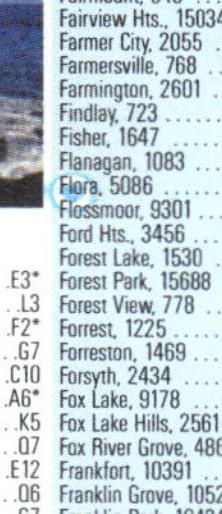

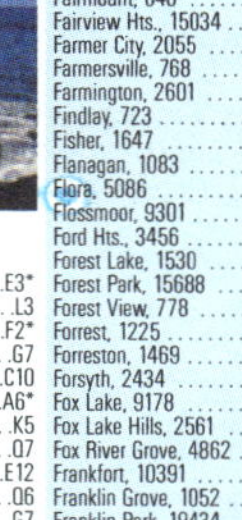

ROCKY COAST NEAR HONOLULU, HAWAII

Wood Dale, 13535 ....F5*
Woodhull, 809 ....E5
Woodlawn, 630 ....R8
Woodridge, 30934 ....J4*
Wood River, 11296 ....P6
Woodstock, 20151 ....A10
Worden, 905 ....P6
Worth, 11047 ....K7*
Wyanet, 1028 ....E7
Wyoming, 1424 ....F6
Yates City, 725 ....G6
Yorkville, 6189 ....D10
Zeigler, 1669 ....S8
Zion, 22866 ....A11

INDIANA
PG. 37–39

CAPITAL
Indianapolis

NICKNAME
Hoosier State

POPULATION
6,080,485, rank 14

AREA
36,185 sq mi, rank 38

STATEHOOD
1816, rank 19

Counties
Adams, 33625 ....F12
Allen, 331849 ....D11
Bartholomew, 71435 ....N9
Benton, 9421 ....F4
Blackford, 14048 ....G11
Boone, 46107 ....J7

Williamsport, 1935 ....H4
Winamac, 2418 ....D7
Winchester, 5037 ....H12
Windfall, 712 ....H9
Winfield, 2298 ....C4
Winona Lake, 3987 ....D9
Winslow, 881 ....S4
Wolcott, 989 ....F5
Wolcottville, 933 ....B11
Woodburn, 1579 ....D13
Worthington, 1481 ....N5
Yorktown, 4785 ....H10
Zanesville, 602 ....E11
Zionsville, 8775 ....J8

IOWA
PG. 40–41

CAPITAL
Des Moines

NICKNAME
Hawkeye State

POPULATION
2,926,324, rank 30

AREA
56,275 sq mi, rank 25

STATEHOOD
1846, rank 29

Counties
Adair, 8243 ....K7
Adams, 4482 ....L6
Allamakee, 14675 ....B16
Appanoose, 13721 ....M12
Audubon, 6830 ....H6

Whittemore, 530 ....C7
Williamsburg, 2622 ....H14
Wilton, 2829 ....J17
Windsor Hts., 4805 ....B18
Winfield, 1131 ....K16
Winterset, 4768 ....K8
Winthrop, 772 ....E15
Woodbine, 1564 ....H4
Woodward, 1200 ....H9
Wyoming, 626 ....G17
Zearing, 617 ....F11

KANSAS
PG. 42–43

CAPITAL
Topeka

NICKNAME
Sunflower State

POPULATION
2,688,418, rank 32

AREA
82,277 sq mi, rank 14

STATEHOOD
1861, rank 34

Counties
Allen, 14385 ....H17
Anderson, 8110 ....F17
Atchison, 16774 ....C17
Barber, 5307 ....J9
Barton, 28205 ....F9
Bourbon, 15379 ....G18
Brown, 10724 ....B16

Wellsville, 1606 ....E17
Westmoreland, 631 ....C14
Westwood, 1533 ....G4*
White City, 518 ....E14
Whitewater, 653 ....G13
Wichita, 344284 ....H12
Wilson, 799 ....E10
Winchester, 579 ....C17
Winfield, 12206 ....J13
Yates Ctr., 1599 ....G16

KENTUCKY
PG. 44–45

CAPITAL
Frankfort

NICKNAME
Bluegrass State

POPULATION
4,041,769, rank 25

AREA
40,409 sq mi, rank 37

STATEHOOD
1792, rank 15

Counties
Adair, 17244 ....L10
Allen, 17800 ....M7
Anderson, 19111 ....G11
Ballard, 8286 ....D3
Barren, 38033 ....M7
Bath, 11085 ....G14
Bell, 30060 ....M15
Boone, 85991 ....D12
Bourbon, 19360 ....F13

SIM SMITH COVERED BRIDGE, PARKE COUNTY, INDIANA

LOUISIANA
PG. 46–47

CAPITAL
Baton Rouge

NICKNAME
Pelican State

POPULATION
4,468,976, rank 22

AREA
47,751 sq mi, rank 31

STATEHOOD
1812, rank 18

Parishes
Acadia, 58861 ....K8
Allen, 25440 ....H7
Ascension, 76627 ....J13
Assumption, 23388 ....L12
Avoyelles, 41481 ....H9
Beauregard, 32986 ....J6
Bienville, 15752 ....C7
Bossier, 98310 ....B5
Caddo, 252161 ....C5
Calcasieu, 183577 ....K5
Caldwell, 10560 ....D9
Cameron, 9991 ....K5
Catahoula, 10920 ....E10
Claiborne, 16851 ....B7
Concordia, 20247 ....F11
De Soto, 25494 ....D5
E. Baton Rouge, 412852 ....H13
E. Carroll, 9421 ....B12

KENTUCKY HORSE FARM

MAINE
PG. 48–49

CAPITAL
Augusta

NICKNAME
Pine Tree State

POPULATION
1,274,923, rank 40

AREA
33,265 sq mi, rank 39

STATEHOOD
1820, rank 23

MARYLAND
PG. 50–52

CAPITAL
Annapolis

NICKNAME
Old Line State

POPULATION
5,296,486, rank 19

AREA
10,460 sq mi, rank 42

STATEHOOD
1788, rank 7

MASSACHUSETTS
PG. 53–55

CAPITAL
Boston

NICKNAME
Bay State

POPULATION
6,349,097, rank 13

AREA
8,284 sq mi, rank 45

STATEHOOD
1788, rank 6

PEMAQUID POINT LIGHTHOUSE, MAINE

MICHIGAN
PG. 56–58

CAPITAL
Lansing

NICKNAME
Great Lakes State

POPULATION
9,938,444, rank 8

AREA
58,527 sq mi, rank 23

STATEHOOD
1837, rank 26

MINNESOTA STATE CAPITOL BUILDING, ST. PAUL, MINNESOTA

MINNESOTA
PG. 59–61

CAPITAL
St. Paul

NICKNAME
Gopher State

POPULATION
4,919,479, rank 21

AREA
84,402 sq mi, rank 12

STATEHOOD
1858, rank 32

MISSISSIPPI
PG. 62

CAPITAL
Jackson

NICKNAME
Magnolia State

POPULATION
2,844,658, rank 31

AREA
47,689 sq mi, rank 32

STATEHOOD
1817, rank 20

MISSOURI
PG. 63–65

CAPITAL Jefferson City

NICKNAME Show Me State

POPULATION 5,595,211, rank 17

AREA 69,697 sq mi, rank 19

STATEHOOD 1821, rank 24

MONTANA
PG. 66–67

CAPITAL Helena

NICKNAME Treasure State

POPULATION 902,195, rank 44

AREA 147,046 sq mi, rank 4

STATEHOOD 1889, rank 41

GLACIER NATIONAL PARK, MONTANA

NEBRASKA
PG. 68–69

CAPITAL Lincoln

NICKNAME Cornhusker State

POPULATION 1,711,263, rank 38

AREA 77,355 sq mi, rank 15

STATEHOOD 1867, rank 37

NEVADA
PG. 70

CAPITAL Carson City

NICKNAME Silver State

POPULATION 1,998,257, rank 35

AREA 110,561 sq mi, rank 7

STATEHOOD 1864, rank 36

NEW HAMPSHIRE
PG. 71

CAPITAL Concord

NICKNAME Granite State

POPULATION 1,235,786, rank 41

AREA 9,279 sq mi, rank 44

STATEHOOD 1788, rank 9

NEW JERSEY
PG. 72–73

CAPITAL Trenton

NICKNAME Garden State

POPULATION 8,414,350, rank 9

AREA 7,787 sq mi, rank 46

STATEHOOD 1787, rank 3

COVERED WAGON IN FRONT OF EAGLE ROCK, NEBRASKA

NEW MEXICO
PG. 74–75

CAPITAL Santa Fe

NICKNAME Land of Enchantment

POPULATION 1,819,046, rank 36

AREA 121,593 sq mi, rank 5

STATEHOOD 1912, rank 47

NEW YORK
PG. 76–81

CAPITAL Albany

NICKNAME Empire State

POPULATION 18,976,457, rank 3

AREA 49,108 sq mi, rank 30

STATEHOOD 1788, rank 11

Place	Grid
Worcester, 900	N19
Wurtsboro, 1234	T20
Wynantskill, 3018	S30
Yaphank, 5025	X26
Yonkers, 196086	W22
Yorkshire, 1403	N5
Yorktown, 14891	U23
Yorktown Hts., 7972	V23
Yorkville, 2675	R25
Youngstown, 1957	K3
Zena, 1119	R22

NORTH CAROLINA
PG. 82–84

CAPITAL
Raleigh

NICKNAME
Tar Heel State

POPULATION
8,049,313, rank 11

AREA
52,669 sq mi, rank 28

STATEHOOD
1789, rank 12

Counties

County	Grid
Alamance, 130800	D9
Alexander, 33603	D4
Alleghany, 10677	B4
Anson, 25275	H6
Ashe, 24384	B3
Avery, 17167	D1
Beaufort, 44958	F16
Bertie, 19773	C16
Bladen, 32278	J11
Brunswick, 73143	K12
Buncombe, 206330	L6
Burke, 89148	D2
Cabarrus, 131063	F5
Caldwell, 77415	C2
Camden, 6885	B18
Carteret, 59383	H17

NORTH DAKOTA
PG. 85

CAPITAL
Bismarck

NICKNAME
Flickertail State

POPULATION
642,200, rank 47

AREA
70,703 sq mi, rank 17

STATEHOOD
1889, rank 39

Counties

County	Grid
Adams, 2593	H3
Barnes, 11775	E11
Benson, 6964	C8
Billings, 888	F2
Bottineau, 7149	B6
Bowman, 3242	H1
Burke, 2242	A4
Burleigh, 69416	E7
Cass, 123138	E12
Cavalier, 4831	A9
Dickey, 5757	G10
Divide, 2283	A2
Dunn, 3600	E3
Eddy, 2757	D9
Emmons, 4331	G7
Foster, 3759	D9
Golden Valley, 1924	E1
Grand Forks, 66109	D11
Grant, 2841	G5
Griggs, 2754	D10
Hettinger, 2715	G3
Kidder, 2753	E8
LaMoure, 4701	G10
Logan, 2308	G8
McHenry, 5987	B6
McIntosh, 3390	H8
McKenzie, 5737	C2
McLean, 9311	D5
Mercer, 8644	E4
Morton, 25303	F5
Mountrail, 6631	C4
Nelson, 3715	C10
Oliver, 2065	E5
Pembina, 8585	B11
Pierce, 4675	C7
Ramsey, 12066	C10
Ransom, 5890	F11

Place	Grid
White Shield, 348	D5
Williston, 12512	C2
Willow City, 221	B7
Wilton, 807	E6
Wimbledon, 237	E10
Wishek, 1122	G8
Wyndmere, 533	G12
Zap, 231	E4

OHIO
PG. 86–89

CAPITAL
Columbus

NICKNAME
Buckeye State

POPULATION
11,353,140, rank 7

AREA
41,330 sq mi, rank 35

STATEHOOD
1803, rank 17

Counties

County	Grid
Adams, 27330	T7
Allen, 108473	H4
Ashland, 52523	H12
Ashtabula, 102728	D18
Athens, 62223	R13
Auglaize, 46611	K4
Belmont, 70226	M17
Brown, 42285	S6
Butler, 332807	Q2
Carroll, 28836	J17
Champaign, 38890	L6
Clark, 144742	N6
Clermont, 177977	R4
Clinton, 40543	Q6
Columbiana, 112075	J18
Coshocton, 36655	K13
Crawford, 46966	H9
Cuyahoga, 1393978	F14
Darke, 53309	L2
Defiance, 39500	F3
Delaware, 109989	K9

Place	Grid
Woodmere, 828	B16
Woodsfield, 2598	N17
Woodville, 1977	E8
Wooster, 24811	H14
Worthington, 14125	M9
Wyoming, 8261	R3
Xenia, 24164	P5
Yellow Sprs., 3761	N6
Yorkville, 1230	M19
Youngstown, 82026	G19
Zanesville, 25586	N13

OKLAHOMA
PG. 90–91

CAPITAL
Oklahoma City

NICKNAME
Sooner State

POPULATION
3,450,654, rank 27

AREA
69,956 sq mi, rank 18

STATEHOOD
1907, rank 46

Counties

County	Grid
Adair, 21038	D19
Alfalfa, 6105	B11
Atoka, 13879	J16
Beaver, 5857	B6
Beckham, 19799	G8
Blaine, 11976	E11
Bryan, 36534	K16
Caddo, 30150	G11
Canadian, 87697	F12
Carter, 45621	J13
Cherokee, 42521	D18
Choctaw, 15342	K17
Cimarron, 3148	B2

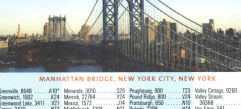

MANHATTAN BRIDGE, NEW YORK CITY, NEW YORK

CAPE HATTERAS BEACH, OUTER BANKS, NORTH CAROLINA

OREGON
PG. 92–93

CAPITAL
Salem

NICKNAME
Beaver State

POPULATION
3,421,399, rank 28

AREA
97,073 sq mi, rank 10

STATEHOOD
1859, rank 33

PENNSYLVANIA
PG. 94–98

CAPITAL
Harrisburg

NICKNAME
Keystone State

POPULATION
12,281,054, rank 6

AREA
45,308 sq mi, rank 33

STATEHOOD
1787, rank 2

OLD BARN, OREGON

RHODE ISLAND
PG. 99

CAPITAL
Providence

NICKNAME
Ocean State

POPULATION
1,048,319, rank 43

AREA
1,212 sq mi, rank 50

STATEHOOD
1790, rank 13

SOUTH CAROLINA
PG. 100

CAPITAL
Columbia

NICKNAME
Palmetto State

POPULATION
4,012,012, rank 26

AREA
31,113 sq mi, rank 40

STATEHOOD
1788, rank 8

SOUTH DAKOTA
PG. 101

CAPITAL
Pierre

NICKNAME
Mount Rushmore State

POPULATION
754,844, rank 46

AREA
77,116 sq mi, rank 16

STATEHOOD
1889, rank 40

NEWPORT BRIDGE, NEWPORT, RHODE ISLAND

TENNESSEE
PG. 102–103

CAPITAL
Nashville

NICKNAME
Volunteer State

POPULATION
5,689,283, rank 16

AREA
42,144 sq mi, rank 34

STATEHOOD
1796, rank 16

TEXAS
PG. 104–108

CAPITAL
Austin

NICKNAME
Lone Star State

POPULATION
20,851,820, rank 2

AREA
266,807 sq mi, rank 2

STATEHOOD
1845, rank 28

Clifton Forge, 4289 . . . . . . H7
Clinchco, 424 . . . . B5
Clintwood, 1549 . . . . B5
Cloverdale, 2986 . . . . K6
Coeburn, 1996 . . . . C5
Collinsville, 7777 . . . . N6
Colonial Beach, 3228 . . . G15
Colonial Hts., 16897# . . . K14
Concord, 800 . . . . K9
Countryside, 8300 . . . . . . B6*
Courtland, 1270 . . . . M15
Covington, 6303# H6
Craigsville, 979 . . . . G8
Crewe, 2378 . . . . L12
Crimora, 1796 . . . . G10
Crozet, 2820 . . . . G10
Culpeper, 9664 . . . . F12
Cumberland, 125 . . . . . . K12
Dahlgren, 997 . . . . F15
Dale City, 55971 . . . . . . E14
Daleville, 1454 . . . . K6
Damascus, 981 . . . . N1
Dante, 650 . . . . C5
Danville, 48411# N8
Dayton, 1344 . . . . F9
Deltaville, 800 . . . . J17
Dillwyn, 447 . . . . J11
Dinwiddie, 350 . . . . L14
Drakes Branch, 504 . . . . L10
Dranesville, 2400 . . . . . . C7*
Dryden, 1253 . . . . D3
Dublin, 2288 . . . . L4
Dumfries, 4937 . . . . E14
Dunn Loring, 7861 . . . . . D8*
Earlysville, 750 . . . . G11
E. Highland Park, 12488 . B19

Powhatan, 550 . . . . J13
Prince George, 750 . . . . K14
Pulaski, 9473 . . . . L4
Purcellville, 3584 . . . . . C13
Quantico, 561 . . . . F14
Radford, 15859# L4
Raven, 2593 . . . . L1
Reedville, 600 . . . . H17
Remington, 624 . . . . F13
Reston, 56407 . . . . D14
Rich Creek, 665 . . . . K4
Richlands, 4144 . . . . L1
Richmond, 197790# J14
Ridgeway, 775 . . . . N7
Roanoke, 94911# K6
Rocky Mount, 4066 . . . . . L6
Rose Hill, 714 . . . . D2
Rose Hill, 15058 . . . . F9*
Round Hill, 500 . . . . C13
Rural Retreat, 1350 . . . . M2
Rushmere, 1083 . . . . L16
Rustburg, 1271 . . . . K9
St. Paul, 1000 . . . . C5
Salem, 24747# K6
Saltville, 2204 . . . . M1
Saluda, 250 . . . . J16
Sandston, 3400 . . . . J14
Scottsville, 555 . . . . H11
Seaford, 2000 . . . . L17
Selma, 485 . . . . H7
Seven Corners, 8701 . . . . D9*
Shawsville, 1029 . . . . L5
Shenandoah, 1878 . . . . . F10
Sherando, 665 . . . . H9
Smithfield, 6324 . . . . . . L16
S. Boston, 8491 . . . . N9

VERMONT
PG. 110

CAPITAL
Montpelier

NICKNAME
Green Mountain State

POPULATION
608,827, rank 49

AREA
9,614 sq mi, rank 43

STATEHOOD
1791, rank 14

Counties
Addison, 35974 . . . . F4
Bennington, 36994 . . . . . K3
Caledonia, 29702 . . . . . . D6
Chittenden, 146571 . . . . C3
Essex, 6459 . . . . C8
Franklin, 45417 . . . . B4
Grand Isle, 6901 . . . . . . B3
Lamoille, 23233 . . . . C5
Orange, 28226 . . . . F6
Orleans, 26277 . . . . B6
Rutland, 63400 . . . . H3
Washington, 58039 . . . . E5
Windham, 44216 . . . . L4
Windsor, 57418 . . . . H5

Cities and Towns
Alburg, 488 . . . . A3
Arlington, 1199 . . . . K3
Ascutney, 450 . . . . J6
Barre, 9291 . . . . E5
Barton, 742 . . . . B7
Bellows Falls, 3165 . . . . K6
Bennington, 9168 . . . . . . L3
Berlin Corners, 300 . . . . E5
Bethel, 800 . . . . G5
Bolton, 300 . . . . D4
Bradford, 815 . . . . F7
Brandon, 1684 . . . . G3
Brattleboro, 8289 . . . . . M5
Bristol, 1800 . . . . E3
Burlington, 38889 . . . . . D3
Canaan, 550 . . . . A9
Castleton, 1500 . . . . . . H3
Center Rutland, 300 . . . H4
Chelsea, 275 . . . . F6
Chester, 999 . . . . K5
Chester Depot, 850 . . . . J5
Chittenden, 400 . . . . . . G4
Colchester, 1000 . . . . . . C3
Danville, 475 . . . . D7
Derby Ctr., 670 . . . . A7
Derby Line, 776 . . . . A7
Dorset, 400 . . . . K3
Duxbury, 325 . . . . D5
E. Arlington, 750 . . . . . . L3
E. Barre, 2136 . . . . E6
E. Hardwick, 300 . . . . . . C6
E. Middlebury, 650 . . . . . F3
E. Montpelier, 450 . . . . . E5
E. Poultney, 400 . . . . . . H3
E. Putney, 350 . . . . L5
Enosburg Falls, 1473 . . . A4
Essex Ctr., 2700 . . . . . . C3
Essex Jct., 8591 . . . . D3
Fairfax, 600 . . . . C4

Hardwick, 1100 . . . . C6
Harmonyville, 325 . . . . . L5
Hartland, 500 . . . . H6
Highgate Ctr., 600 . . . . . A4
Hinesburg, 900 . . . . D3
Hyde Park, 415 . . . . C5
Island Pond, 849 . . . . . . B8
Jeffersonville, 568 . . . . . C4
Jericho, 1457 . . . . C4
Jericho Ctr., 375 . . . . . . D4
Johnson, 1420 . . . . C5
Jonesville, 375 . . . . D4
Londonderry, 300 . . . . . . K4
Ludlow, 958 . . . . J5
Lunenburg, 325 . . . . D8
Lyndon, 375 . . . . C7
Lyndon Ctr., 1200 . . . . . C7
Lyndonville, 1227 . . . . . C7
Manchester, 602 . . . . K3
Manchester Ctr., 2065 . . . K3
Marshfield, 262 . . . . D6
Mechanicsville, 500 . . . . D3
Middlebury, 6252 . . . . . . F3
Middletown Sprs., 300 . . H3
Milton, 1537 . . . . C3
Montpelier, 8035 . . . . . . E5
Morrisville, 2009 . . . . . . C5
Newbury, 396 . . . . F7
Newfane, 116 . . . . L5
Newport, 5005 . . . . A6
Newport Ctr., 300 . . . . . A6
N. Bennington, 1428 . . . . L3
N. Clarendon, 700 . . . . . H4
N. Ferrisburg, 500 . . . . . E3
Northfield, 3208 . . . . E5
Northfield Falls, 650 . . . . E5
N. Hartland, 425 . . . . . . H6
N. Hero, 100 . . . . B3
N. Springfield, 1100 . . . . J5
N. Troy, 593 . . . . A6
N. Westminster, 271 . . . . K6
Norwich, 1200 . . . . G6
Orleans, 826 . . . . B6
Pittsford, 950 . . . . G4
Plainfield, 850 . . . . E6
Poultney, 1575 . . . . H3
Pownal, 700 . . . . M3

VIRGINIA
PG. 111–113

CAPITAL
Richmond

NICKNAME
Old Dominion

POPULATION
7,078,515, rank 12

AREA
40,767 sq mi, rank 36

STATEHOOD
1788, rank 10

Counties
Accomack, 38305 . . . . . H20
Albemarle, 79236 . . . . . G10
Alleghany, 17215 . . . . . . H6
Amelia, 11400 . . . . K12
Amherst, 31894 . . . . J8
Appomattox, 13705 . . . . . K9
Arlington, 189453 . . . . . D15
Augusta, 65615 . . . . G8
Bath, 5048 . . . . G7
Bedford, 60371 . . . . K7

Waples, 800 . . . . J17
Waskom, 2068 . . . . J23
Watauga, 21908 . . . . B3*
Waxahachie, 21426 . . . . J18
Weatherford, 19000 . . . . J16
Webster, 9083 . . . . L6*
Weimar, 1981 . . . . P18
Weir, 591 . . . . M17
Wellington, 2275 . . . . . . E12
Wells, 769 . . . . L21
Weslaco, 26935 . . . . . . W16
West, 2692 . . . . K18
W. Columbia, 4255 . . . . . Q20
Westfield, 1700 . . . . P21
W. Lake Hills, 3116 . . . . N16
W. Odessa, 17799 . . . . . . K8
Weston, 635 . . . . H18
W. Orange, 4111 . . . . . . N24
Westover Hills, 658 . . . . . D2*
W. Tawakoni, 1462 . . . . . H19
W. University Place, 14211 . . H3*
Westway, 3829 . . . . K1
Westworth Vil., 2124 . . . . D2*
Wharton, 9237 . . . . Q20
Wheeler, 1378 . . . . D12
White Deer, 1060 . . . . . . D11
Whitehouse, 5346 . . . . . . K21
White Oak, 5624 . . . . J21
Whitesboro, 3760 . . . . . . G18
White Settlement, 14831 . . D1*
Whitewright, 1740 . . . . . G19
Whitney, 1833 . . . . K17
Wichita Falls, 104197 . . . G15
Willis, 3985 . . . . N21
Willow Park, 2849 . . . . . . J17
Wills Pt., 3496 . . . . J19
Wilmer, 3393 . . . . E9*
Wimberley, 2685 . . . . P16
Windcrest, 5105 . . . . Q16
Wink, 919 . . . . K7
Winnie, 2914 . . . . P23
Winnsboro, 3584 . . . . . . H21
Winters, 2880 . . . . K13
Wolfe City, 1566 . . . . . . G19
Wolfforth, 2554 . . . . G9
Woodbranch, 1305 . . . . . N21
Woodcreek, 1274 . . . . . . P16
Woodsboro, 1685 . . . . . . S17
Woodville, 2415 . . . . . . M22
Woodway, 8733 . . . . L17
Wortham, 1082 . . . . K19
Wylie, 15132 . . . . H19
Yoakum, 5731 . . . . Q18
Yorktown, 2271 . . . . R17
Zapata, 4856 . . . . U14
Zavalla, 647 . . . . L22

DELICATE ARCH, ARCHES NATIONAL PARK, UTAH

UTAH
PG. 109

CAPITAL
Salt Lake City

NICKNAME
Beehive State

POPULATION
2,233,169, rank 34

AREA
84,899 sq mi, rank 11

STATEHOOD
1896, rank 45

Counties
Beaver, 6005 . . . . L2
Box Elder, 42745 . . . . . . D3
Cache, 91391 . . . . D5
Carbon, 20422 . . . . H6
Daggett, 921 . . . . F8
Davis, 238994 . . . . F4
Duchesne, 14371 . . . . . . G6
Emery, 10860 . . . . J6
Garfield, 4735 . . . . L5
Grand, 8485 . . . . J8
Iron, 33779 . . . . M2
Juab, 8238 . . . . H3

Levan, 688 . . . . H5
Lewiston, 1877 . . . . D5
Lindon, 8363 . . . . A3
Loa, 525 . . . . L5
Logan, 42670 . . . . D5
Maeser, 2855 . . . . F8
Magna, 22770 . . . . C7
Manila, 308 . . . . E8
Manti, 3040 . . . . J5
Mantua, 791 . . . . D4
Mapleton, 5809 . . . . G5
Marriott-Slaterville, 1425 . . A5
Marysvale, 381 . . . . K4
Mayfield, 420 . . . . J5
Midvale, 27029 . . . . D8
Midway, 2121 . . . . F5
Milford, 1451 . . . . L3
Minersville, 817 . . . . L3
Moab, 4779 . . . . K8
Mona, 850 . . . . H4
Monroe, 1845 . . . . K4
Montezuma Creek, 507 . . . N8
Monticello, 1958 . . . . . . M8
Morgan, 2635 . . . . E5
Moroni, 1280 . . . . H5
Mt. Pleasant, 2707 . . . . . H5
Murray, 34024 . . . . F4
Myton, 539 . . . . G7
Naples, 1300 . . . . G8
Neola, 533 . . . . G7
Nephi, 4733 . . . . H5
Newton, 699 . . . . D4
N. Ogden, 15026 . . . . . . E4
N. Salt Lake, 8749 . . . . . F4
Oak City, 650 . . . . J4
Oakley, 948 . . . . F5
Ogden, 77226 . . . . E4
Orangeville, 1398 . . . . . . J6
Orderville, 596 . . . . N3
Orem, 84324 . . . . G5
Panguitch, 1623 . . . . . . M4
Paradise, 759 . . . . D5
Paragonah, 470 . . . . M3
Park City, 7371 . . . . F5
Parowan, 2565 . . . . M3
Payson, 12716 . . . . G5

WASHINGTON
PG. 114–115

CAPITAL
Olympia

NICKNAME
Evergreen State

POPULATION
5,894,121, rank 15

AREA
68,138 sq mi, rank 20

STATEHOOD
1889, rank 42

Counties
Adams, 16428 . . . . G17
Asotin, 20551 . . . . K19
Benton, 142475 . . . . K15
Chelan, 66616 . . . . E12
Clallam, 64525 . . . . D6
Clark, 345238 . . . . L8
Columbia, 4064 . . . . J18
Cowlitz, 92948 . . . . K8
Douglas, 32603 . . . . E14
Ferry, 7260 . . . . C17
Franklin, 49347 . . . . J16
Garfield, 2397 . . . . J19
Grant, 74698 . . . . G15
Grays Harbor, 67194 . . . . G6
Island, 71558 . . . . C8
Jefferson, 25953 . . . . E6
King, 1737034 . . . . F10
Kitsap, 231969 . . . . F7
Kittitas, 33362 . . . . G13
Klickitat, 19161 . . . . L12
Lewis, 68600 . . . . H8
Lincoln, 10184 . . . . E17
Mason, 49405 . . . . F7
Okanogan, 39564 . . . . . . B14
Pacific, 20984 . . . . J6
Pend Oreille, 11732 . . . . C19

Camas, 12534
Carbonado, 621
Carlsborg, 855
Carnation, 1893
Carson, 1200
Cashmere, 2965
Castle Rock, 2130
Cathcart, 3015
Cathlamet, 565
Centralia, 14742
Chehalis, 7057
Chelan, 3522
Cheney, 8832
Chewelah, 2186
Chinook, 457
Clallam Bay, 850
Clarkston, 7337
Clear Lake, 942
Cle Elum, 1755
Clinton, 868
Clyde Hill, 2890
Colfax, 2844
Colville, 4988
Concrete, 790
Connell, 2956
Cosmopolis, 1595
Coulee City, 600
Coupeville, 1723
Covington, 13783
Darrington, 1136
Davenport, 1730

Lake Stevens, 6361 . . . . . D9
Lakewood, 58211 . . . . . . G8
Langley, 959 . . . . D8
Leavenworth, 2074 . . . . . F12
Liberty Lake, 3076 . . . . . E20
Lind, 582 . . . . G17
Long Beach, 1283 . . . . . . J5
Longview, 34660 . . . . K7
Lyle, 530 . . . . L11
Lynden, 9020 . . . . B8
Lynnwood, 33847 . . . . . . E9
Mabton, 1891 . . . . K14
Maltby, 8267 . . . . H4
Manchester, 4958 . . . . . . K1
Manson, 900 . . . . E13
Maple Valley, 14209 . . . . F9
Marietta, 3594 . . . . B8
Martha Lake, 12633 . . . . H3
Marysville, 25315 . . . . . . D9
Mattawa, 2609 . . . . H14
McCleary, 1454 . . . . G7
McKenna, 800 . . . . H8
Mead, 2100 . . . . E19
Medical Lake, 3758 . . . . F18
Medina, 3011 . . . . K3
Mercer Island, 22036 . . . K3
Midland, 7414 . . . . N2
Mill Creek, 11525 . . . . . . E9
Millwood, 1649 . . . . E19
Milton, 5795 . . . . N3
Moclips, 615 . . . . G5
Monroe, 13795 . . . . E9
Montesano, 3312 . . . . . . G6
Morton, 1045 . . . . J9
Moses Lake, 14953 . . . . G15
Mossyrock, 486 . . . . J8
Mountlake Terrace, 20362 . . H3
Mt. Vernon, 26232 . . . . . C9
Moxee, 821 . . . . J13
Mukilteo, 18019 . . . . E9
Naches, 643 . . . . H12
Napavine, 1361 . . . . J7
Neah Bay, 794 . . . . C4
Newcastle, 7737 . . . . K3
Newport, 1921 . . . . D20
Nooksack, 851 . . . . B9
Normandy Park, 6392 . . . L2
N. Bend, 4746 . . . . F10
N. Bonneville, 593 . . . . . L9
Oak Harbor, 19795 . . . . . C8

WEST VIRGINIA
PG. 117

CAPITAL
Charleston

NICKNAME
Mountain State

POPULATION
1,808,344, rank 37

AREA
24,231 sq mi, rank 41

STATEHOOD
1863, rank 35

Counties
Barbour, 15557 . . . . D7
Berkeley, 75905 . . . . . . C12
Boone, 25535 . . . . G3
Braxton, 14702 . . . . E5
Brooke, 25447 . . . . B2
Cabell, 96784 . . . . F2
Calhoun, 7582 . . . . E5
Clay, 10330 . . . . F5
Doddridge, 7403 . . . . . . C6
Fayette, 47579 . . . . G5
Gilmer, 7160 . . . . E5
Grant, 11299 . . . . D10
Greenbrier, 34453 . . . . . H6
Hampshire, 20203 . . . . . D11
Hancock, 32667 . . . . A2
Hardy, 12669 . . . . D10
Harrison, 68652 . . . . C7
Jackson, 28000 . . . . E3
Jefferson, 42190 . . . . . . C13
Kanawha, 200073 . . . . . . F4
Lewis, 16919 . . . . D6
Lincoln, 22108 . . . . G2
Logan, 37710 . . . . H3
Marion, 56598 . . . . B7
Marshall, 35519 . . . . B6
Mason, 25957 . . . . E2
McDowell, 27329 . . . . . . K3
Mercer, 62980 . . . . J5
Mineral, 27078 . . . . C10
Mingo, 28253 . . . . H2
Monongalia, 81866 . . . . . B7
Monroe, 14583 . . . . J6
Morgan, 14943 . . . . B12
Nicholas, 26562 . . . . G5
Ohio, 47427 . . . . A6
Pendleton, 8196 . . . . F9

Logan, 1630 . . . . H2
Lost Creek, 467 . . . . D7
Lubeck, 1303 . . . . C3
Lumberport, 937 . . . . C7
Mabscott, 1403 . . . . H4
Madison, 2677 . . . . G3
Malden, 750 . . . . K13
Mallory, 1143 . . . . J3
Man, 770 . . . . H3
Mannington, 2124 . . . . . C7
Marlinton, 1204 . . . . G7
Marlowe, 1300 . . . . B13
Marmet, 1693 . . . . G3
Martinsburg, 14972 . . . . C13
Mason, 1064 . . . . D2
Masontown, 647 . . . . B8
Matewan, 498 . . . . J2
Maybeury, 550 . . . . K4
McMechen, 1937 . . . . . . A6
Middlebourne, 870 . . . . . C5
Mill Creek, 662 . . . . E8
Milton, 2206 . . . . F2
Mineral Wells, 1860 . . . . D4
Monongah, 939 . . . . C7
Montcalm, 885 . . . . K4
Montgomery, 1942 . . . . . G4
Moorefield, 2375 . . . . . D10
Morgantown, 26809 . . . . B8
Moundsville, 9998 . . . . . A6
Mt. Gay, 2623 . . . . H2
Mt. Hope, 1487 . . . . H4
Mullens, 1769 . . . . J4
New Cumberland, 1099 . . A2
Newell, 1602 . . . . A1
New Haven, 1559 . . . . . . D2
New Martinsville, 5984 . . B5
Nitro, 6824 . . . . F3
Northfork, 519 . . . . K4
Nutter Fort, 1686 . . . . . . C7
Oak Hill, 7589 . . . . H4
Oceana, 1550 . . . . J3
Paden City, 2860 . . . . . . B5
Parkersburg, 33099 . . . . C4
Parsons, 1463 . . . . D8
Paw Paw, 524 . . . . C11
Pennsboro, 1199 . . . . . . C5
Petersburg, 2423 . . . . . D10
Peterstown, 499 . . . . K5
Philippi, 2870 . . . . D7
Piedmont, 1014 . . . . C10
Pinch, 2811 . . . . F4

W. Milford, 651 . . . . D6
Weston, 4317 . . . . D6
Westover, 3941 . . . . E12
W. Pea Ridge, 6363 . . . . G13
W. Union, 806 . . . . C5
Wheeling, 31419 . . . . A6
Whitehall, 595 . . . . C7
White Sulphur Sprs., 2315 . . H7
Whitesville, 520 . . . . H3
Wiley Ford, 1095 . . . . . . G4*
Williamson, 3414 . . . . . . J2
Williamstown, 2996 . . . . C4
Windsor Hts., 431 . . . . . . B1
Winfield, 1858 . . . . F3

WISCONSIN
PG. 118–119

CAPITAL
Madison

NICKNAME
Badger State

POPULATION
5,363,675, rank 18

AREA
56,153 sq mi, rank 26

STATEHOOD
1848, rank 30

Counties
Adams, 18643 . . . . M7
Ashland, 16866 . . . . E5
Barron, 44963 . . . . G3
Bayfield, 15013 . . . . E4
Brown, 226778 . . . . L11
Buffalo, 13804 . . . . K3
Burnett, 15674 . . . . F2
Calumet, 40631 . . . . . . M10
Chippewa, 55195 . . . . . . H5
Clark, 33557 . . . . K5
Columbia, 52468 . . . . . . P8

MOUNT RAINIER NATIONAL PARK, WASHINGTON

Wyoming

PG. 120

CAPITAL
Cheyenne

NICKNAME
Equality State

POPULATION
493,782, rank 50

AREA
97,809 sq mi, rank 9

STATEHOOD
1890, rank 44

Cities and Towns

Counties

Canada

Alberta

PG. 123

CAPITAL
Edmonton

POPULATION
2,974,807, rank 4

AREA
255,541 sq mi, rank 6

ENTERED CANADA
1905

Cities and Towns

British Columbia

PG. 122–123

CAPITAL
Victoria

POPULATION
3,907,738, rank 3

AREA
364,764 sq mi, rank 5

ENTERED CANADA
1871

Cities and Towns

Manitoba

PG. 125

CAPITAL
Winnipeg

POPULATION
1,119,583, rank 5

AREA
250,116 sq mi, rank 8

ENTERED CANADA
1870

Cities and Towns

New Brunswick

PG. 130

CAPITAL
Fredericton

POPULATION
729,498, rank 8

AREA
28,150 sq mi, rank 11

ENTERED CANADA
1867

Cities and Towns

Newfoundland and Labrador

PG. 131

CAPITAL
St. John's

POPULATION
512,930, rank 9

AREA
156,453 sq mi, rank 10

ENTERED CANADA
1949

Cities and Towns

Northwest Territories

PG. 121

CAPITAL
Yellowknife

POPULATION
37,360, rank 11

AREA
519,734 sq mi (est.), rank 3

ENTERED CANADA
1870

Cities and Towns

Nova Scotia

PG. 130–131

CAPITAL
Halifax

POPULATION
908,007, rank 7

AREA
21,345 sq mi, rank 12

ENTERED CANADA
1867

Cities and Towns

Nunavut

PG. 121

CAPITAL
Iqaluit

POPULATION
26,745, rank 13

AREA
808,185 sq mi (est.), rank 1

ENTERED CANADA
1999

Cities and Towns

Ontario

PG. 125–127

CAPITAL
Toronto

POPULATION
11,410,046, rank 1

AREA
415,598 sq mi, rank 4

ENTERED CANADA
1867

Cities and Towns

Prince Edward Island

PG. 130–131

CAPITAL
Charlottetown

POPULATION
135,294, rank 10

AREA
2,185 sq mi, rank 13

ENTERED CANADA
1873

Cities and Towns

Québec

PG. 128–130

CAPITAL
Québec

POPULATION
7,237,479, rank 2

AREA
595,391 sq mi, rank 2

ENTERED CANADA
1867

Cities and Towns

Saskatchewan

PG. 124–125

CAPITAL
Regina

POPULATION
978,933, rank 6

AREA
251,366 sq mi, rank 7

ENTERED CANADA
1905

Cities and Towns

Yukon Territory

PG. 121

CAPITAL
Whitehorse

POPULATION
28,674, rank 12

AREA
186,272 sq mi, rank 9

ENTERED CANADA
1898

Cities and Towns

Mexico

Mexico

PG. 132–133

CAPITAL
Mexico City

POPULATION
95,772,462

AREA
756,066 sq mi

Cities and Towns

Puerto Rico

Puerto Rico

PG. 134

CAPITAL
San Juan

POPULATION
3,808,610

AREA
3,435 sq mi

Cities and Towns

Distances in chart are in miles. To convert miles to kilometers, multiply the distance in miles by 1.609

Example:
New York, NY to Boston, MA = 215 miles or 346 kilometers (215 x 1.609)

	ALBANY, NY	ALBUQUERQUE, NM	AMARILLO, TX	ATLANTA, GA	BALTIMORE, MD	BILLINGS, MT	BIRMINGHAM, AL	BISMARCK, ND	BOISE, ID	BOSTON, MA	BUFFALO, NY	BURLINGTON, VT	CHARLESTON, SC	CHARLESTON, WV	CHARLOTTE, NC	CHEYENNE, WY	CHICAGO, IL	CINCINNATI, OH	CLEVELAND, OH	COLUMBUS, OH	DALLAS, TX	DENVER, CO	DES MOINES, IA	DETROIT, MI	EL PASO, TX	HARTFORD, CT	HOUSTON, TX	INDIANAPOLIS, IN	JACKSON, MS	JACKSONVILLE, FL	KANSAS CITY, MO	LAS VEGAS, NV	LITTLE ROCK, AR	LOS ANGELES, CA
ALBANY, NY		2095	1811	1010	333	2083	1093	1675	2526	172	292	147	913	634	771	1789	832	730	484	621	1680	1833	1155	571	2326	111	1768	795	1331	1094	1282	2586	1354	2859
ALBUQUERQUE, NM	2095		286	1490	1902	991	1274	1333	966	2240	1808	2178	1793	1568	1649	538	1352	1409	1619	1476	754	438	1091	1608	263	2139	994	1298	1157	1837	894	578	900	806
AMARILLO, TX	1811	286		1206	1618	988	991	1398	1266	1957	1524	1894	1510	1285	1365	534	1069	1126	1335	1192	470	434	808	1324	438	1855	711	1014	874	1517	610	864	617	1092
ATLANTA, GA	1010	1490	1206		679	1889	150	1559	2218	1100	910	1158	317	503	238	1482	717	476	726	577	792	1403	967	735	1437	998	800	531	386	344	801	2067	528	2237
BALTIMORE, MD	333	1902	1618	679		1959	795	1551	2401	422	370	481	583	352	441	1665	708	521	377	420	1399	1690	1031	532	2045	321	1470	600	1032	763	1087	2445	1072	2705
BILLINGS, MT	2083	991	988	1889	1959		1839	413	626	2254	1796	2181	2157	1755	2012	455	1246	1552	1597	1608	1433	554	1007	1534	1255	2153	1673	1432	1836	2237	1088	965	1530	1239
BIRMINGHAM, AL	1093	1274	991	150	795	1839		1509	2170	1215	909	1241	466	578	389	1434	667	475	725	576	647	1356	919	734	1292	1114	678	481	241	494	753	1852	381	2092
BISMARCK, ND	1675	1333	1398	1559	1551	413	1509		1039	1846	1388	1773	1749	1347	1604	594	838	1144	1189	1200	1342	693	675	1126	1597	1745	1582	1024	1548	1906	801	1378	1183	1702
BOISE, ID	2526	966	1266	2218	2401	626	2170	1039		2697	2239	2624	2520	2182	2375	737	1708	1969	2040	2036	1711	833	1369	1977	1206	2595	1952	1852	2115	2566	1376	760	1808	1033
BOSTON, MA	172	2240	1957	1100	422	2254	1215	1846	2697		462	214	1003	741	861	1961	1003	862	654	760	1819	2004	1326	741	2465	102	1890	940	1453	1184	1427	2757	1493	3046
BUFFALO, NY	292	1808	1524	910	370	1796	909	1388	2239	462		375	899	431	695	1502	545	442	197	333	1393	1546	868	277	2039	401	1513	508	1134	1080	995	2299	1066	2572
BURLINGTON, VT	147	2178	1894	1158	481	2181	1241	1773	2624	214	375		1061	782	919	1887	930	817	567	704	1763	1931	1253	652	2409	231	1916	878	1479	1242	1366	2684	1437	2957
CHARLESTON, SC	913	1793	1510	317	583	2157	466	1749	2520	1003	899	1061		468	204	1783	907	622	724	637	1109	1705	1204	879	1754	901	1110	721	703	238	1102	2371	900	2554
CHARLESTON, WV	634	1568	1285	503	352	1755	578	1347	2182	741	431	782	468		265	1445	506	209	255	168	1072	1367	802	410	1718	639	1192	320	816	649	764	2122	745	2374
CHARLOTTE, NC	771	1649	1365	238	441	2012	389	1604	2375	861	695	919	204	265		1637	761	476	520	433	1031	1559	1057	675	1677	760	1041	575	625	385	956	2225	754	2453
CHEYENNE, WY	1789	538	534	1482	1665	455	1434	594	737	1961	1502	1887	1783	1445	1637		972	1233	1304	1300	979	100	633	1241	801	1859	1220	1115	1382	1829	640	843	1076	1116
CHICAGO, IL	832	1352	1069	717	708	1246	667	838	1708	1003	545	930	907	506	761	972		302	346	359	936	1015	337	283	1543	901	1108	184	750	1065	532	1768	662	2042
CINCINNATI, OH	730	1409	1126	476	521	1552	475	1144	1969	862	442	817	622	209	476	1233	302		253	105	958	1200	599	261	1605	760	1079	116	700	803	597	1955	632	2215
CLEVELAND, OH	484	1619	1335	726	377	1597	725	1189	2040	654	197	567	724	255	520	1304	346	253		144	1208	1347	669	171	1854	570	1328	319	950	904	806	2100	882	2374
COLUMBUS, OH	621	1476	1192	577	420	1608	576	1200	2036	760	333	704	637	168	433	1300	359	105	144		1059	1266	665	192	1706	659	1179	176	801	818	663	2021	733	2281
DALLAS, TX	1680	754	470	792	1399	1433	647	1342	1711	1819	1393	1763	1109	1072	1031	979	936	958	1208	1059		887	752	1218	647	1717	241	913	406	1049	554	1331	327	1446
DENVER, CO	1833	438	434	1403	1690	554	1356	693	833	2004	1546	1931	1705	1367	1559	100	1015	1200	1347	1266	887		676	1284	701	1903	1127	1088	1290	1751	603	756	984	1029
DES MOINES, IA	1155	1091	808	967	1031	1007	919	675	1369	1326	868	1253	1204	802	1057	633	337	599	669	665	752	676		606	1283	1225	992	481	931	1315	194	1429	567	1703
DETROIT, MI	571	1608	1324	735	532	1534	734	1126	1977	741	277	652	879	410	675	1241	283	261	171	192	1218	1284	606		1799	679	1338	318	960	1060	795	2037	891	2310
EL PASO, TX	2326	263	438	1437	2045	1255	1292	1597	1206	2465	2039	2409	1754	1718	1677	801	1543	1605	1854	1706	647	701	1283	1799		2364	758	1489	1051	1642	1085	717	974	801
HARTFORD, CT	111	2139	1855	998	321	2153	1114	1745	2595	102	401	231	901	639	760	1859	901	760	570	659	1717	1903	1225	679	2364		1788	839	1351	1082	1326	2655	1391	2944
HOUSTON, TX	1768	994	711	800	1470	1673	678	1582	1952	1890	1513	1916	1110	1192	1041	1220	1108	1079	1328	1179	241	1127	992	1338	758	1788		1033	445	884	795	1474	447	1558
INDIANAPOLIS, IN	795	1298	1014	531	600	1432	481	1024	1852	940	508	878	721	320	575	1115	184	116	319	176	913	1088	481	318	1489	839	1033		675	879	485	1843	587	2104
JACKSON, MS	1331	1157	874	386	1032	1836	241	1548	2115	1453	1134	1479	703	816	625	1382	750	700	950	801	406	1290	931	960	1051	1351	445	675		598	747	1735	269	1851
JACKSONVILLE, FL	1094	1837	1517	344	763	2237	494	1906	2566	1184	1080	1242	238	649	385	1829	1065	803	904	818	1049	1751	1315	1060	1642	1082	884	879	598		1148	2415	873	2441
KANSAS CITY, MO	1282	894	610	801	1087	1088	753	801	1376	1427	995	1366	1102	764	956	640	532	597	806	663	554	603	194	795	1085	1326	795	485	747	1148		1358	382	1632
LAS VEGAS, NV	2586	578	864	2067	2445	965	1852	1378	760	2757	2299	2684	2371	2122	2225	843	1768	1955	2100	2021	1331	756	1429	2037	717	2655	1474	1843	1735	2415	1358		1478	274
LITTLE ROCK, AR	1354	900	617	528	1072	1530	381	1183	1808	1493	1066	1437	900	745	754	1076	662	632	882	733	327	984	567	891	974	1391	447	587	269	873	382	1478		1706
LOS ANGELES, CA	2859	806	1092	2237	2705	1239	2092	1702	1033	3046	2572	2957	2554	2374	2453	1116	2042	2215	2374	2281	1446	1029	1703	2310	801	2944	1558	2104	1851	2441	1632	274	1706	
LOUISVILLE, KY	832	1320	1036	419	602	1547	369	1139	1933	964	545	915	610	251	464	1197	299	106	356	207	852	1118	595	366	1499	862	972	112	594	766	516	1874	526	2126
MEMPHIS, TN	1214	1033	750	389	933	1625	241	1337	1954	1353	927	1297	760	606	614	1217	539	493	742	594	466	1116	720	752	1112	1251	586	464	211	733	536	1611	140	1839
MIAMI, FL	1439	2155	1834	661	1109	2554	812	2224	2883	1529	1425	1587	583	994	730	2147	1382	1141	1250	1163	1367	2069	1632	1401	1959	1427	1201	1196	915	345	1466	2733	1190	2759
MILWAUKEE, WI	929	1426	1142	813	805	1175	763	767	1748	1100	642	1027	1003	601	857	1012	89	398	443	454	1010	1055	378	380	1617	999	1193	279	835	1160	573	1808	747	2082
MINNEAPOLIS, MN	1245	1339	1055	1129	1121	839	1079	431	1465	1417	958	1343	1319	918	1173	881	409	714	760	771	999	924	246	697	1530	1315	1240	596	1151	1477	441	1677	814	1951
MOBILE, AL	1344	1344	1106	332	1013	2019	258	1765	2302	1433	1165	1492	642	837	572	1570	923	731	981	832	639	1478	1115	991	1231	1332	473	737	187	410	930	1922	457	2031
MONTRÉAL, QC	230	2172	1888	1241	564	2093	1289	1685	2535	313	397	92	1145	822	1003	1799	841	815	588	725	1772	1843	1165	564	2363	338	1892	872	1514	1325	1359	2596	1446	2869
NASHVILLE, TN	1003	1248	965	242	716	1648	194	1315	1976	1136	716	1086	543	395	397	1240	474	281	531	382	681	1162	725	541	1328	1034	801	287	423	589	559	1826	355	2054
NEW ORLEANS, LA	1440	1276	993	473	1142	1955	351	1734	2234	1563	1254	1588	783	926	713	1502	935	820	1070	921	525	1409	1117	1079	1118	1461	360	826	185	556	932	1854	455	1917
NEW YORK, NY	151	2015	1731	869	192	2049	985	1641	2491	215	400	299	773	515	631	1755	797	636	466	535	1589	1799	1121	622	2235	115	1660	715	1223	953	1202	2552	1262	2820
NORFOLK, VA	570	1970	1686	558	239	2141	708	1733	2584	660	573	718	437	415	319	1847	890	624	559	604	1350	1782	1213	714	1996	558	1360	735	944	617	1179	2537	1076	2776
OKLAHOMA CITY, OK	1549	546	262	944	1354	1227	729	1136	1506	1694	1262	1632	1248	1022	1102	773	807	863	1073	930	209	681	546	1062	737	1593	449	752	612	1291	348	1124	355	1352
OMAHA, NE	1292	973	726	989	1168	904	941	616	1234	1463	1005	1390	1290	952	1144	497	474	736	806	802	669	541	136	743	1236	1362	910	618	935	1336	188	1294	570	1567
ORLANDO, FL	1235	1934	1613	440	904	2333	591	2003	2662	1324	1221	1383	379	790	525	1926	1161	920	1045	958	1146	1847	1411	1180	1738	1223	980	975	694	141	1245	2512	969	2538
PHILADELPHIA, PA	223	1954	1671	782	104	2019	897	1611	2462	321	414	371	685	454	543	1725	768	576	437	474	1501	1744	1091	592	2147	219	1572	655	1135	866	1141	2500	1175	2760
PHOENIX, AZ	2561	466	753	1868	2366	1199	1723	1662	993	2706	2274	2644	2184	2035	2107	1004	1819	1876	2085	1942	1077	904	1558	2074	432	2605	1188	1764	1482	2072	1360	285	1367	369
PITTSBURGH, PA	485	1670	1386	676	246	1719	763	1311	2161	592	217	587	642	217	438	1425	467	292	136	190	1246	1460	791	292	1893	491	1366	370	988	822	857	2215	920	2476
PORTLAND, ME	270	2338	2054	1197	520	2352	1313	1944	2795	107	560	233	1101	839	959	2059	1101	960	751	858	1917	2102	1424	838	2563	199	1988	1038	1550	1281	1525	2855	1590	3144
PORTLAND, OR	2954	1395	1695	2647	2830	889	2599	1301	432	3126	2667	3052	2948	2610	2802	1166	2137	2398	2469	2464	2140	1261	1798	2405	1767	3024	2381	2280	2544	2994	1805	1188	2237	971
RALEIGH, NC	639	1782	1499	396	309	2110	547	1702	2495	729	642	787	279	313	158	1758	861	522	568	482	1189	1680	1157	724	1834	627	1198	639	783	460	1077	2360	889	2588
RAPID CITY, SD	1750	841	837	1511	1626	379	1463	320	930	1921	1463	1848	1824	1422	1678	305	913	1219	1264	1275	1077	404	629	1201	1105	1820	1318	1101	1458	1859	710	1035	1093	1309
RENO, NV	2747	1020	1306	2440	2623	960	2392	1372	430	2919	2460	2845	2741	2403	2595	959	1930	2191	2262	2257	1933	1054	1591	2198	1315	2817	2072	2073	2337	2787	1598	442	2030	519
RICHMOND, VA	482	1876	1593	527	152	2053	678	1645	2496	572	485	630	428	322	289	1760	802	530	471	517	1309	1688	1126	627	1955	471	1330	641	914	609	1085	2444	983	2682
ST. LOUIS, MO	1036	1051	767	549	841	1341	501	1053	1628	1181	749	1119	850	512	704	892	294	350	560	417	635	855	350	549	1242	1080	863	239	505	896	252	1610	416	1856
SALT LAKE CITY, UT	2224	624	964	1916	2100	548	1868	960	342	2395	1936	2322	2218	1880	2072	436	1406	1667	1738	1734	1410	531	1067	1675	864	2293	1650	1549	1813	2264	1074	417	1507	691
SAN ANTONIO, TX	1953	818	513	1000	1671	1500	878	1599	1761	2092	1665	2036	1310	1344	1241	1046	1270	1231	1481	1332	271	946	1009	1490	556	1990	200	1186	644	1084	812	1272	600	1356
SAN DIEGO, CA	2919	825	1111	2166	2724	1302	2021	1765	1096	3065	2632	3020	2483	2393	2405	1179	2105	2234	2437	2300	1375	1092	1766	2373	730	2963	1487	2122	1780	2370	1695	337	1703	124
SAN FRANCISCO, CA	2964	1111	1397	2618	2840	1176	2472	1749	646	3135	2677	3062	2934	2620	2759	1176	2146	2407	2478	2474	1827	1271	1807	2415	1181	3034	1938	2290	2232	2822	1814	575	2012	385
SEATTLE, WA	2899	1463	1763	2705	2775	816	2657	1229	500	3070	2612	2997	2973	2571	2827	1234	2062	2368	2413	2424	2208	1329	1822	2350	1944	2969	2449	2249	2612	3052	1872	1256	2305	1148
TAMPA, FL	1290	1949	1628	455	960	2348	606	2018	2677	1380	1276	1438	434	845	581	1941	1176	935	1101	1036	1161	1862	1426	1194	1753	1278	995	990	709	196	1259	2526	984	2553
TORONTO, ON	400	1841	1557	958	565	1762	958	1354	2204	570	106	419	1006	537	802	1468	510	484	303	440	1441	1512	834	233	2032	509	1561	541	1183	1187	1028	2265	1115	2538
VANCOUVER, BC	3032	1597	1897	2838	2908	949	2791	1362	633	3204	2745	3130	3106	2705	2960	1368	2196	2501	2547	2558	2342	1463	1956	2483	2087	3102	2583	2383	2746	3186	2007	1390	2439	1291
WASHINGTON, DC	369	1896	1612	636	38	1953	758	1545	2395	458	384	517	539	346	397	1659	701	517	370	416	1362	1686	1025	526	2008	357	1433	596	996	720	1083	2441	1036	2702
WICHITA, KS	1471	707	423	989	1276	1067	838	934	1346	1616	1184	1554	1291	953	1145	613	728	785	995	852	367	521	390	984	898	1515	608	674	771	1337	192	1276	464	1513

	LOUISVILLE, KY	MEMPHIS, TN	MIAMI, FL	MILWAUKEE, WI	MINNEAPOLIS, MN	MOBILE, AL	MONTRÉAL, QC	NASHVILLE, TN	NEW ORLEANS, LA	NEW YORK, NY	NORFOLK, VA	OKLAHOMA CITY, OK	OMAHA, NE	ORLANDO, FL	PHILADELPHIA, PA	PHOENIX, AZ	PITTSBURGH, PA	PORTLAND, ME	PORTLAND, OR	RALEIGH, NC	RAPID CITY, SD	RENO, NV	RICHMOND, VA	ST. LOUIS, MO	SALT LAKE CITY, UT	SAN ANTONIO, TX	SAN DIEGO, CA	SAN FRANCISCO, CA	SEATTLE, WA	TAMPA, FL	TORONTO, ON	VANCOUVER, BC	WASHINGTON, DC	WICHITA, KS
ALBANY, NY	832	1214	1439	929	1245	1344	230	1003	1440	151	570	1549	1292	1235	223	2561	485	270	2954	639	1750	2747	482	1036	2224	1953	2919	2964	2899	1290	400	3032	369	1471
ALBUQUERQUE, NM	1320	1033	2155	1426	1339	1344	2172	1248	1276	2015	1970	546	973	1934	1954	466	1670	2338	1395	1782	841	1020	1876	1051	624	818	825	1111	1463	1949	1841	1597	1896	707
AMARILLO, TX	1036	750	1834	1142	1055	1106	1888	965	993	1731	1686	262	726	1613	1671	753	1386	2054	1695	1499	837	1306	1593	767	964	513	1111	1397	1763	1628	1557	1897	1612	423
ATLANTA, GA	419	389	661	813	1129	332	1241	242	473	869	558	944	989	440	782	1868	676	1197	2647	396	1511	2440	527	549	1916	1000	2166	2618	2705	455	958	2838	636	989
BALTIMORE, MD	602	933	1109	805	1121	1013	564	716	1142	192	239	1354	1168	904	104	2366	246	520	2830	309	1626	2623	152	841	2100	1671	2724	2840	2775	960	565	2908	38	1276
BILLINGS, MT	1547	1625	2554	1175	839	2019	2093	1648	1955	2049	2141	1227	904	2333	2019	1199	1719	2352	889	2110	379	960	2053	1341	548	1500	1302	1176	816	2348	1762	949	1953	1067
BIRMINGHAM, AL	369	241	812	763	1079	258	1289	194	351	985	708	729	941	591	897	1723	763	1313	2599	547	1463	2392	678	501	1868	878	2021	2472	2657	606	958	2791	758	838
BISMARCK, ND	1139	1337	2224	767	431	1765	1685	1315	1734	1641	1733	1136	616	2003	1611	1662	1311	1944	1301	1702	320	1372	1645	1053	960	1599	1765	1749	1229	2018	1354	1362	1545	934
BOISE, ID	1933	1954	2883	1748	1465	2302	2535	1976	2234	2491	2584	1506	1234	2662	2462	993	2161	2795	432	2495	930	430	2496	1628	342	1761	1096	646	500	2677	2204	633	2395	1346
BOSTON, MA	964	1353	1529	1100	1417	1433	313	1136	1563	215	660	1694	1463	1324	321	2706	592	107	3126	729	1921	2919	572	1181	2395	2092	3065	3135	3070	1380	570	3204	458	1616
BUFFALO, NY	545	927	1425	642	958	1165	397	716	1254	400	573	1262	1005	1221	414	2274	217	560	2667	642	1463	2460	485	749	1936	1665	2632	2677	2612	1276	106	2745	384	1184
BURLINGTON, VT	915	1297	1587	1027	1343	1492	92	1086	1588	299	718	1632	1390	1383	371	2644	587	233	3052	787	1848	2845	630	1119	2322	2036	3020	3062	2997	1438	419	3130	517	1554
CHARLESTON, SC	610	760	583	1003	1319	642	1145	543	783	773	437	1248	1290	379	685	2184	642	1101	2948	279	1824	2741	428	850	2218	1310	2483	2934	2973	434	1006	3106	539	1291
CHARLESTON, WV	251	606	994	601	918	837	822	395	926	515	415	1022	952	790	454	2035	217	839	2610	313	1422	2403	322	512	1880	1344	2393	2620	2571	845	537	2705	346	953
CHARLOTTE, NC	464	614	730	857	1173	572	1003	397	713	631	319	1102	1144	525	543	2107	438	959	2802	158	1678	2595	289	704	2072	1241	2405	2759	2827	581	802	2960	397	1145
CHEYENNE, WY	1197	1217	2147	1012	881	1570	1799	1240	1502	1755	1847	773	497	1926	1725	1004	1425	2059	1166	1758	305	959	1760	892	436	1046	1179	1176	1234	1941	1468	1368	1659	613
CHICAGO, IL	299	539	1382	89	409	923	841	474	935	797	890	807	474	1161	768	1819	467	1101	2137	861	913	1930	802	294	1406	1270	2105	2146	2062	1176	510	2196	701	728
CINCINNATI, OH	106	493	1141	398	714	731	815	281	820	636	624	863	736	920	576	1876	292	960	2398	522	1219	2191	530	350	1667	1231	2234	2407	2368	935	484	2501	517	785
CLEVELAND, OH	356	742	1250	443	760	981	588	531	1070	466	559	1073	806	1045	437	2085	136	751	2469	568	1264	2262	471	560	1738	1481	2437	2478	2413	1101	303	2547	370	995
COLUMBUS, OH	207	594	1163	454	771	832	725	382	921	535	604	930	802	958	474	1942	190	858	2464	482	1275	2257	517	417	1734	1332	2300	2474	2424	1036	440	2558	416	852
DALLAS, TX	852	466	1367	1010	999	639	1772	681	525	1589	1350	209	669	1146	1501	1077	1246	1917	2140	1189	1077	1933	1309	635	1410	271	1375	1827	2208	1161	1441	2342	1362	367
DENVER, CO	1118	1116	2069	1055	924	1478	1843	1162	1409	1799	1782	681	541	1847	1744	904	1460	2102	1261	1680	404	1054	1688	855	531	946	1092	1271	1329	1862	1512	1463	1686	521
DES MOINES, IA	595	720	1632	378	246	1115	1165	725	1117	1121	1213	546	136	1411	1091	1558	791	1424	1798	1157	629	1591	1126	350	1067	1009	1766	1807	1822	1426	834	1956	1025	390
DETROIT, MI	366	752	1401	380	697	991	564	541	1079	622	714	1062	743	1180	592	2074	292	838	2405	724	1201	2198	627	549	1675	1490	2373	2415	2350	1194	233	2483	526	984
EL PASO, TX	1499	1112	1959	1617	1530	1231	2363	1328	1118	2235	1996	737	1236	1738	2147	432	1893	2563	1767	1834	1105	1315	1955	1242	864	556	730	1181	1944	1753	2032	2087	2008	898
HARTFORD, CT	862	1251	1427	999	1315	1332	338	1034	1461	115	558	1593	1362	1223	219	2605	491	199	3024	627	1820	2817	471	1080	2293	1990	2963	3034	2969	1278	509	3102	357	1515
HOUSTON, TX	972	586	1201	1193	1240	473	1892	801	360	1660	1360	449	910	980	1572	1188	1366	1988	2381	1198	1318	2072	1330	863	1650	200	1487	1938	2449	995	1561	2583	1433	608
INDIANAPOLIS, IN	112	464	1196	279	596	737	872	287	826	715	735	752	618	975	655	1764	370	1038	2280	639	1101	2073	641	239	1549	1186	2122	2290	2249	990	541	2383	596	674
JACKSON, MS	594	211	915	835	1151	187	1514	423	185	1223	944	612	935	694	1135	1482	988	1550	2544	783	1458	2337	914	505	1813	644	1780	2232	2612	709	1183	2746	996	771
JACKSONVILLE, FL	766	733	345	1160	1477	410	1325	589	556	953	617	1291	1336	141	866	2072	822	1281	2994	460	1859	2787	609	896	2264	1084	2370	2822	3052	196	1187	3186	720	1337
KANSAS CITY, MO	516	536	1466	573	441	930	1359	559	932	1202	1179	348	188	1245	1141	1360	857	1525	1805	1077	710	1598	1085	252	1074	812	1695	1814	1872	1259	1028	2007	1083	192
LAS VEGAS, NV	1874	1611	2733	1808	1677	1922	2596	1826	1854	2552	2537	1124	1294	2512	2500	285	2215	2855	1188	2360	1035	442	2444	1610	417	1272	337	575	1256	2526	2265	1390	2441	1276
LITTLE ROCK, AR	526	140	1190	747	814	457	1446	355	455	1262	1076	355	570	969	1175	1367	920	1590	2237	889	1093	2030	983	416	1507	600	1703	2012	2305	984	1115	2439	1036	464
LOS ANGELES, CA	2126	1839	2759	2082	1951	2031	2869	2054	1917	2820	2776	1352	1567	2538	2760	369	2476	3144	971	2588	1309	519	2682	1856	691	1356	124	385	1148	2553	2538	1291	2702	1513
LOUISVILLE, KY		386	1084	394	711	625	920	175	714	739	666	774	704	863	678	1786	394	1062	2362	564	1215	2155	572	264	1631	1125	2144	2372	2364	878	589	2497	596	705
MEMPHIS, TN	386		1051	624	940	395	1306	215	396	1123	937	487	724	830	1035	1500	780	1451	2382	749	1247	2175	843	294	1652	739	1841	2144	2440	845	975	2574	896	597
MIAMI, FL	1084	1051		1478	1794	727	1671	907	874	1299	962	1609	1654	232	1211	2390	1167	1627	3312	805	2176	3105	954	1214	2581	1401	2688	3140	3370	274	1532	3504	1065	1655
MILWAUKEE, WI	394	624	1478		337	1019	939	569	1020	894	987	880	514	1257	865	1892	564	1198	2063	956	842	1970	899	367	1446	1343	2145	2186	1991	1272	607	2124	799	769
MINNEAPOLIS, MN	711	940	1794	337		1335	1255	886	1337	1211	1303	793	383	1573	1181	1805	881	1515	1727	1273	606	1839	1216	621	1315	1257	2014	2055	1654	1588	924	1788	1115	637
MOBILE, AL	625	395	727	1019	1335		1575	450	146	1203	891	799	1119	506	1115	1662	1019	1531	2731	730	1641	2545	861	688	2000	673	1960	2411	2799	521	1214	2933	970	958
MONTRÉAL, QC	920	1306	1671	939	1255	1575		1094	1632	383	801	1625	1300	1466	454	2637	607	282	2963	871	1758	2756	714	1112	2232	2043	2931	2972	2907	1522	330	3041	600	1547
NASHVILLE, TN	175	215	907	569	886	450	1094		539	906	720	703	747	686	818	1715	569	1234	2405	532	1269	2198	626	307	1675	954	2056	2360	2463	701	764	2597	679	748
NEW ORLEANS, LA	714	396	874	1020	1337	146	1632	539		1332	1032	731	1121	653	1245	1548	1108	1660	2663	871	1643	2431	1002	690	1932	560	1846	2298	2731	668	1302	2865	1106	890
NEW YORK, NY	739	1123	1299	894	1211	1203	383	906	1332		430	1469	1258	1094	91	2481	367	313	2920	499	1716	2713	342	956	2189	1861	2839	2929	2864	1150	507	2998	228	1391
NORFOLK, VA	666	937	962	987	1303	891	801	720	1032	430		1424	1350	758	342	2436	428	757	3012	179	1808	2805	91	927	2282	1560	2725	3022	2957	814	747	3090	196	1368
OKLAHOMA CITY, OK	774	487	1609	880	793	799	1625	703	731	1469	1424		463	1388	1408	1012	1124	1792	1934	1237	871	1727	1331	505	1204	466	1370	1657	2002	1403	1295	2136	1350	161
OMAHA, NE	704	724	1654	514	383	1119	1300	747	1121	1258	1350	463		1433	1228	1440	928	1561	1662	1265	525	1455	1263	440	932	927	1630	1672	1719	1448	971	1853	1162	307
ORLANDO, FL	863	830	232	1257	1573	506	1466	686	653	1094	758	1388	1433		1006	2169	963	1422	3091	601	1955	2884	750	993	2360	1180	2467	2918	3149	82	1327	3283	860	1434
PHILADELPHIA, PA	678	1035	1211	865	1181	1115	454	818	1245	91	342	1408	1228	1006		2420	306	419	2890	411	1686	2683	254	895	2160	1774	2779	2900	2835	1062	522	2968	140	1330
PHOENIX, AZ	1786	1500	2390	1892	1805	1662	2637	1715	1548	2481	2436	1012	1440	2169	2420		2136	2804	1335	2249	1308	883	2343	1517	651	987	358	750	1513	2184	2307	1655	2362	1173
PITTSBURGH, PA	394	780	1167	564	881	1019	607	569	1108	367	428	1124	928	963	306	2136		690	2590	497	1386	2383	341	611	1859	1519	2494	2599	2534	1019	321	2668	240	1046
PORTLAND, ME	1062	1451	1627	1198	1515	1531	282	1234	1660	313	757	1792	1561	1422	419	2804	690		3223	827	2019	3016	670	1279	2493	2189	3162	3233	3168	1478	668	3301	556	1714
PORTLAND, OR	2362	2382	3312	2063	1727	2731	2963	2405	2663	2920	3012	1934	1662	3091	2890	1335	2590	3223		2923	1268	578	2925	2057	771	2322	1093	638	170	3106	2633	313	2824	1775
RALEIGH, NC	564	749	805	956	1273	730	871	532	871	499	179	1237	1265	601	411	2249	497	827	2923		1777	2716	157	825	2193	1398	2563	2894	2926	656	820	3060	265	1266
RAPID CITY, SD	1215	1247	2176	842	606	1641	1758	1269	1643	1716	1808	871	525	1955	1686	1308	1386	2019	1268	1777		1151	1720	963	628	1335	1372	1368	1195	1970	1429	1328	1620	712
RENO, NV	2155	2175	3105	1970	1839	2545	2756	2198	2431	2713	2805	1727	1455	2884	2683	883	2383	3016	578	2716	1151		2718	1850	524	1870	642	217	755	2899	2426	898	2617	1568
RICHMOND, VA	572	843	954	899	1216	861	714	626	1002	342	91	1331	1263	750	254	2343	341	670	2925	157	1720	2718		834	2194	1530	2684	2934	2869	805	660	3003	108	1274
ST. LOUIS, MO	264	294	1214	367	621	688	1112	307	690	956	927	505	440	993	895	1517	611	1279	2057	825	963	1850	834		1326	968	1875	2066	2125	1008	782	2259	837	441
SALT LAKE CITY, UT	1631	1652	2581	1446	1315	2000	2232	1675	1932	2189	2282	1204	932	2360	2160	651	1859	2493	771	2193	628	524	2194	1326		1419	754	740	839	2375	1902	973	2094	1044
SAN ANTONIO, TX	1125	739	1401	1343	1257	673	2043	954	560	1861	1560	466	927	1180	1774	987	1519	2189	2322	1398	1335	1870	1530	968	1419		1285	1737	2275	1195	1714	2410	1635	624
SAN DIEGO, CA	2144	1841	2688	2145	2014	1960	2931	2056	1846	2839	2725	1370	1630	2467	2779	358	2494	3162	1093	2563	1372	642	2684	1875	754	1285		508	1271	2481	2601	1414	2720	1531
SAN FRANCISCO, CA	2372	2144	3140	2186	2055	2411	2972	2360	2298	2929	3022	1657	1672	2918	2900	750	2599	3233	638	2894	1368	217	2934	2066	740	1737	508		816	2933	2643	958	2834	1784
SEATTLE, WA	2364	2440	3370	1991	1654	2799	2907	2463	2731	2864	2957	2002	1719	3149	2835	1513	2534	3168	170	2926	1195	755	2869	2125	839	2275	1271	816		3164	2577	140	2769	1843
TAMPA, FL	878	845	274	1272	1588	521	1522	701	668	1150	814	1403	1448	82	1062	2184	1019	1478	3106	656	1970	2899	805	1008	2375	1195	2481	2933	3164		1383	3297	916	1448
TORONTO, ON	589	975	1532	607	924	1214	330	764	1302	507	747	1295	971	1327	522	2307	321	668	2633	820	1429	2426	660	782	1902	1714	2601	2643	2577	1383		2711	563	1217
VANCOUVER, BC	2497	2574	3504	2124	1788	2933	3041	2597	2865	2998	3090	2136	1853	3283	2968	1655	2668	3301	313	3060	1328	898	3003	2259	973	2410	1414	958	140	3297	2711		2902	1977
WASHINGTON, DC	596	896	1065	799	1115	970	600	679	1106	228	196	1350	1162	860	140	2362	240	556	2824	265	1620	2617	108	837	2094	1635	2720	2834	2769	916	563	2902		1272
WICHITA, KS	705	597	1655	769	637	958	1547	748	890	1391	1368	161	307	1434	1330	1173	1046	1714	1775	1266	712	1568	1274	441	1044	624	1531	1784	1843	1448	1217	1977	1272	

Mileage and Driving Times Map

TEMPERATURE CONVERSIONS

°F	°C	°C	°F
100	37.8	35	95
90	32.2	30	86
80	26.7	25	77
70	21.1	20	68
60	15.6	15	59
50	10.0	10	50
40	4.4	5	41
32	0	0	32
30	-1.1	-5	23
20	-6.7	-10	14
10	-12.2	-15	5
0	-17.8	-20	-4
-10	-23.3	-25	-13
-20	-28.9	-30	-22
-30	-34.4	-35	-31
-40	-40.0	-40	-40
-50	-45.6	-45	-49

VOLUME CONVERSIONS

GALLONS	LITERS	LITERS	GALLONS
1	3.8	1	0.26
2	7.6	2	0.5
3	11.4	3	0.8
4	15.1	4	1.1
5	18.9	5	1.3
10	37.9	10	2.6
15	56.8	20	5.3
20	75.7	30	7.9
25	94.6	40	10.6
30	113.6	50	13.2
40	151.4	75	19.8
50	189.3	100	26.4

DISTANCE CONVERSIONS

MILES	KM	KM	MILES
1	1.6	1	0.6
5	8.0	2	1.2
10	16.1	5	3.1
15	24.1	10	6.2
20	32.2	15	9.3
25	40.2	20	12.4
30	48.3	25	15.5
35	56.3	30	18.6
40	64.4	40	24.9
45	72.4	50	31.1
50	80.5	60	37.3
55	88.5	70	43.5
60	96.6	80	49.7
65	104.6	90	55.9
70	112.7	100	62.1
75	120.7	110	68.4
80	128.7	120	74.6
85	136.8	130	80.8
90	144.8	140	87.0
95	152.9	150	93.2
100	160.9	160	99.4